State Crime

Alan Doig

WILLAN
PUBLISHING

Published by

Willan Publishing
2 Park Square
Milton Park
Abingdon
Oxon
OX14 4RN

Published simultaneously in the USA and Canada by

Willan Publishing
270 Madison Avenue
New York
NY 10016

First published 2011

ISBN   978-1-84392-306-0 paperback
       978-1-84392-307-7 hardback

British Library Cataloguing-in-Publication Data

A catalogue record for this book is available from the British Library

Project managed by Deer Park Productions, Tavistock, Devon
Typeset by GCS, Leighton Buzzard, Bedfordshire
Printed and bound by CPI Antony Rowe, Chippenham, Wiltshire

For Ann

Contents

Abbreviations and acronyms

ATP	Aid and Trade Provision
BAE	British Aerospace
BPL	Blood Products Laboratory
CAAT	Campaign Against Arms Trade
CAG	Comptroller and Auditor General
CIA	Central Intelligence Agency
CID	Criminal Investigation Department
CPS	Crown Prosecution Service
DESO	Defence Exports Services Organisation
DESS	Defence Exports Sales Secretariat
DGSE	General Directorate for External Security
DPP	Director of Public Prosecutions
DTI	Department of Trade and Industry
EC	European Commission
ECGD	Export Credits Guarantee Department
ECHR	European Court of Human Rights
EU	European Union
FAC	Foreign Affairs Committee
FBI	Federal Bureau of Investigation
FCO	Foreign and Commonwealth Office
FRU	Force Research Unit
GCHQ	Government Communications Headquarters
GMC	General Medical Council
HCME	Her Majesty's Customs and Excise
HMIC	Her Majesty's Inspector of Constabulary
HSE	Health and Safety Executive
IAEA	International Atomic Energy Agency
IC	Information Commission

ICC	International Criminal Court
ILC	International Law Commission
IMF	International Monetary Fund
IPCC	Independent Police Complaints Commission
IRA	Irish Republican Army
JIC	Joint Intelligence Committee
MDP	Ministry of Defence Police
MOD	Ministry of Defence
MP	Member of Parliament
MPS	Metropolitan Police Service
MTTA	Machine Tools Trade Association
NAO	National Audit Office
NATO	North Atlantic Treaty Organisation
NDPB	Non-departmental public body
NGO	Non-governmental organisation
NHS	National Health Service
NSA	National Security Agency
NSC	National Security Council
NSPCC	National Society for the Prevention of Cruelty to Children
ODA	Overseas Development Agency
OECD	Organisation for Economic Cooperation and Development
OFT	Office of Fair Trading
PAC	Public Accounts Committee
PCT	Primary Care Trust
PIRA	Provisional Irish Republican Army
PMC	Private Military Company
RCGP	Royal College of General Practitioners
RCMP	Royal Canadian Mounted Police
ROE	Rules of Engagement
RUC	Royal Ulster Constabulary
SAS	Special Air Service
SB	Special Branch
SFO	Serious Fraud Office
SIS	Secret Intelligence Service
SRC	Space Research Corporation
TSO	The Stationery Office
UDI	Unilateral declaration of independence
UNMOVIC	United Nations Monitoring, Verification and Inspection Commission
UNSCOM	United Nations Special Commission
WMD	Weapons of mass destruction

Chapter I

The issue of British state crime: introduction

Inquiries and crime

On 12 January 2010 the Conclusions of the Committee of Inquiry on Iraq were summarised as follows:

the policy was worked out at the start of August 2002 in discussions between the new Minister of Foreign Affairs and a small group of civil servants. This policy subordinated the question of legitimacy under international law to the policy principles defined by the Ministry of Foreign Affairs. Insufficient importance was attached to the information provided by the intelligence services (whose assessments of the threat posed by Iraq's WMD programme were much more equivocal than government ministers were in their communications with Parliament) and the weapons inspection reports. Ministers and departments extracted those statements from the intelligence services' reports that were consistent with the stance already adopted.

The government did not disclose to Parliament the full content of the request that the US made, concerning cooperation with planning for the mobilization of a military force to compel Iraq to comply with Security Council Resolution 1441. Despite the existence of certain ambiguities, the wording of Resolution 1441 could not reasonably be interpreted (as the government did) as authorizing individual Member States to use military force to compel Iraq to comply with the Security Council's resolutions, without authorization from the Security Council.

While much of this may sound familiar, the conclusion is not, however, from the Chilcot Inquiry into the circumstances of the UK's invasion of Iraq. It comes from the inquiry into the Dutch government's involvement in the invasion of Iraq, which concluded that 'the military action had no sound mandate under international law' (*Commissie van onderzoek besluitvorming Irak*, The Hague, p. 531). In other words, the Dutch government stood accused of breaching international law – or put more simply, of committing a state crime.

In December 2009, the *Daily Telegraph* carried an article that asked (rhetorically), 'Is Tony Blair a War Criminal?' – just before the start of the work of the Chilcot Inquiry into the same use of officially sanctioned military force. Comprising of Privy Counsellors and chaired by Sir John Chilcot, a former senior civil servant, with no powers but with a promise from the Prime Minister that it would have access to any British document[1] or witness, the inquiry was to review 'the UK's involvement in Iraq, including the way decisions were made and actions taken, to establish, as accurately as possible, what happened and to identify the lessons that can be learned'.[2]

One of the questions it answered in advance was:

What will the Inquiry do if it receives evidence or information about criminal offences?

If the Inquiry receives credible evidence that criminal offences have been committed that has not previously been referred to the investigating authorities, it would be obliged to refer that evidence to the appropriate investigating authority. (www. iraqinquiry.co.uk/FAQ)

The Chilcot Inquiry's membership, powers and terms of reference were in contrast to another inquiry set up over a decade earlier, in 1998, into the shooting by British soldiers of British citizens in Northern Ireland. This inquiry had High Court status, with consequential powers and personnel; its terms of reference were to review 'the events of Sunday, 30th January 1972 which led to loss of life in connection with the procession in Londonderry on that day, taking account of any new information relevant to events on that day'. It too responded to a similar question:

Have any witnesses been granted immunity from prosecution?

No. However, the Attorney-General has stipulated that any written material or oral evidence provided by a witness cannot be used to incriminate that witness in any later criminal proceedings ... This does not rule out the possibility of future criminal proceedings against an individual, only that their own evidence to the Bloody Sunday Inquiry cannot be used against them. (www.bloody-sunday-inquiry.org/questions-and-answers)

Both UK inquiries involved, and involve, elected politicians and a range of public officials (or, in the case of the armed forces, agents of the state). Both involve official state activities which may or may not be considered to be unlawful or criminal. Both inquiries could thus fall within the academic concept of state crime.

Two contemporary inquiries: from Northern Ireland to Iraq

The Saville Inquiry

The 1972 shootings of protest marchers by 1st Battalion, the Parachute Regiment (1 Para) soldiers in Derry, Northern Ireland raised a number of questions. Were the shootings lawful killings, or did a government, or members of a government, instigate, endorse or approve potentially unlawful actions? What would be their motivation, what controls would be in place to judge their conduct, what institutional structure allows such conduct to take place? The shootings had long been the subject of dispute and debate, not least because of the unique circumstances of soldiers in what was considered to be a western liberal democratic state opening fire on its own citizens exercising their right to peaceful protest against the policies of the region's government.

It is not disputed that there were some armed men and sounds of shooting in the vicinity. It is also not in dispute that none of those shot by the soldiers were involved in the shooting, or carrying weapons, or engaged in any behaviour that could lead to them being suspected of either. What is in dispute is whether the soldiers came under fire and, in responding, inflicted collateral civilian casualties among the innocent protesters, whether they returned fire into that area of the protest march from which they thought the shooting had come, or whether they unilaterally opened fire without justification.

3

There had been an official inquiry in 1972, the Widgery Inquiry. This was also a full-blown statutory tribunal of inquiry, with the powers of a High Court under the 1921 Tribunal of Inquiries Act (see p. 227 below). It was generally assumed to be a pro-government whitewash: the inquiry chair, Lord Widgery, the Lord Chief Justice, argued that the intention of the senior army officers to use the Parachute Battalion as an arrest force, and not for other offensive purposes, was sincere. Allegations to the contrary were dismissed as unsupported by any 'shred of evidence … there is no reason to suppose that the soldiers engaged in the arrest operation would have opened fire if they had not been fired upon first'.[3]

The pressure on the incoming Labour government in 1997 for a new inquiry was one of several demands from Provisional Sinn Fein. This would secure redress of a continuing grievance (over both the shootings and the findings of the Widgery Inquiry) but which could also populate its past with explanations for what it did and what it had to do in terms of violent armed activity. One of these was that the British state had unilaterally initiated officially sanctioned and potentially illegal violence against its citizens. This could more than explain the necessary armed role on the part of what was at the time a small and unorganised Provisional IRA (PIRA). PIRA had been set up by members of a dormant Official IRA in response to the latter's own lack of action to protect Catholics from official state harassment and violence.

This role could be validated, in Republican eyes at least, if it could be shown that it was the British state that had taken the war to the nationalist movement, then involved in peaceful protest, by opening fire without warning on what was to become known as 'Bloody Sunday'. That soldiers may have been ordered to open fire by senior officers – whatever the circumstances on the day – was one issue. Other, more important, issues were whether there was evidence to show that the orders came from the British state, and whether the state fixed the Widgery Inquiry to protect those acting on its behalf.

State crime has as much of a ring about it as the *British state*. To the Republican movement and others, the British state has long been seen as a monolithic structure, dominated by a ruling elite and fronted by a government whose *raison d'être* was representing the interests of that elite, both in Westminster and in Stormont. While the army leadership would clearly be part of that elite and thus culpable if it could be shown that they ordered the shooting without warning or justification, a major goal behind pressure for a new inquiry would be uncovering the authority of the state in ordering the shootings. In other words, 'the use of unlawful lethal force' against its own citizens *and* the subsequent David and Goliath contest facing the embryonic protest movement would show to the world the ruthlessness of the response to any challenge to the state by some of its disenfranchised citizens.

No one would argue too much that the state in Northern Ireland was antagonistic to Roman Catholics. Successive Protestant-dominated governments ensured their political primacy through electoral gerrymandering,[4] openly exercised discrimination in terms of housing, education and employment policy in the public sector, and refused to engage in any dialogue with any group whose loyalties appeared to be openly directed towards becoming part of another sovereign state.[5] There was no doubt that the Northern Ireland politicians would, and often did, increasingly tolerate the use of disproportionate force against the emerging protest movement, also doing so in the full knowledge that their ideological and political stance was shared by the Northern Ireland public sector, law enforcement and criminal justice system in general. Further, their opponents believed that the Northern Ireland government did nothing that did not have the acceptance of the mainland government.

The New Labour government elected in 1997 was keen to deliver what became known as the Good Friday Agreement and demonstrate a major breakthrough in the future of that part of the United Kingdom. At the same time, the government had to take cognisance of the fact that the year was also the 25th anniversary of the shootings and that the Irish government had also issued its view of events, claiming that new material:

> provided fresh grounds for the belief that members of 1 Para wilfully shot and killed unarmed civilians. It suggested that the approach and conduct of the Widgery Inquiry was informed by ulterior political motivation from its inception ... As is evident from the foregoing assessment, it can be concluded that the Widgery Report was fundamentally flawed. It was incomplete in terms of its description of the events on the day and in terms of how those events were apparently shaped by the prior intentions and decisions of the authorities. It was a startlingly inaccurate and partisan version of events ... contrary to the weight of evidence and even its own findings, it exculpated the individual soldiers who used lethal force and thereby exonerated those who were responsible for their deployment and actions. (Department of the Taoiseach 1997)

One of the Labour government's major concessions to facilitate the peace process was the creation in 1998 of the Saville Inquiry, another Tribunal of Inquiry, to establish exactly what happened in 1972.

Evidence produced for the Tribunal provided a somewhat uneven paper trail over military discussions about the use of force, including the shooting of 'selected ringleaders'. When the Saville Inquiry called the then Prime Minister Edward Heath, it met with denials over seeing intelligence briefings, including the 'selected ringleaders' briefing, or putting pressure on the original Tribunal chair on how the findings may be interpreted (Heath warned Lord Widgery before the inquiry started that Britain was locked into a propaganda war, as well as a military war).

Heath, who had lived long enough to be treated as a 'grand old man' of British politics, was not likely to give anything away. He had been Government Chief Whip during the Suez Crisis and knew all about the public and pragmatic sides to politics. When he was asked about the use of force, he brushed aside any suggestion that his government decided to alter its approach to dealing with the disturbances or that it supported an army suggestion to shoot to kill. In that, of course, he was supported by Cabinet minutes and other official documents. But then British Prime Ministers are not likely to put their names to what effectively could have been warrants of execution against British citizens.[6]

Indeed, in the end, the Saville Inquiry quickly dismissed any suggestion that this could have or had happened. It did manage to identify wrongful acts and decisions on the day of the shootings but stopped short of identifying any which could be described as unlawful or so negligent or reckless as to lead to unlawful acts. Overall, its main finding in its June 2010 report was that 'the immediate responsibility for the deaths and injuries on Bloody Sunday lies with those members of Support Company whose unjustifiable firing was the cause of those deaths and injuries' (Bloody Sunday Inquiry 2010, Vol. I, Ch. 4, para 4.1).

This stopped short of the use of the term 'unlawful', as opposed to unjustifiable, because the report believed that indiscriminate and sustained shootings followed mistakes on the day by officers. 1 Para was ordered to undertake arrests when both officers and soldiers were unfamiliar with the location and unclear as to who was to be arrested. 1 Para was also alerted to the possibility of being fired upon.

The evidence for this was a consequence of the report drilling down over a decade into endless detail of which soldier was where on the particular day, and the detail of events as they unfolded to suggest a series of erroneous actions and mistakes which, when combined together, led to the 'serious and widespread loss of fire discipline among the soldiers' (Bloody Sunday Inquiry 2010, Vol. I, Ch. 5, para 5.4).

Even at that level, the report avoided looking to see if there was a prior culture of the unjustified shootings by soldiers who may have thought that they could be immune from sanction. It also dismissed any argument that the army used 1 Para as an arrest force recklessly despite its reputation (in the sense of anticipating if the soldiers were likely to resort to shooting during the arrest process), and nor that it intended to use 1 Para to provoke a confrontation.

The report's attention to the political context was much less detailed. As to the briefing discussing shooting selected ringleaders, the report was 'sure' that this was not adopted or used. In response to the allegations that politicians in both the United Kingdom and Northern Ireland governments, as well as the military authorities, intended to use 1 Para for 'the purpose of carrying out some action, which they knew would involve the deliberate use of unwarranted lethal force or which they sanctioned with reckless disregard as to whether such force was used', the report dismissed this perspective (Bloody Sunday Inquiry 2010, Vol. I, Ch. 4, para 4.2).

It argued that there was no prior plan to use, tolerate or encourage the use of unlawful force, and no one could have anticipated how the day would have unfolded, the officers' decisions to initiate the arrests, and the soldiers' responses to events on the ground. Indeed, the report suggested that the reverse of government intent to cause harm was true. It stated that the UK government was making 'genuine and serious attempts' 'to work towards a peaceful political settlement' and that 'any action involving the use or likely use of unwarranted lethal force' would have been 'entirely counterproductive'. It did not inquire in any depth into the work of the Widgery Inquiry.

The Saville Inquiry has taken over a decade and spent nearly £200 million (half on lawyers' fees) to demonstrate just how complex could be the answer to the simple question as to whether the *British state* committed a *state crime*. Further, part of the complexity arises not just from the reasons or motives for the acts themselves but also from assumptions about the State, and especially a belief in a unitary and monolithic 'British state'. Here various institutions and groups are assumed to work together towards a common interest with a single, auditable chain of command that runs (or ran) all the way to whoever had the authority to represent the British state and authorise whomsoever to commission a state crime. There was, as far as the Saville Inquiry was concerned, a clear firebreak between those on the ground and those in senior military positions and in the government in terms of responsibility, and thus no evidence of any crime instigated or authorised by the state.

The Chilcot Inquiry

Iraq's invasion of Kuwait in 1990 (triggered by Iraq's resentments over Kuwaiti oil production and pricing, as well as its failure to offer any financial support for Iraq's war with Iran) resulted in unequivocal condemnation by the UN and military action led by the US government. The action, authorised by the UN, was intended only to eject Iraq from Kuwait. At that time there was no mention of any overthrow of the regime. On the other hand, Saddam Hussein did not take defeat quietly and a US-inspired internal revolt was ruthlessly crushed. There were concerns in the US and the UK (amplified by some of Iraq's neighbours) about the potential destabilising impact of a humiliated regime with an aggressive leadership (and an equally unpleasant set of heirs-apparent), and allegedly in possession of a range of weapons of mass destruction (nuclear, chemical and biological WMD).

A 1991 UN Resolution (678) imposed a requirement that Iraq destroy its WMD programmes and admit UN inspection teams to oversee this.[7] Post-war sanctions were imposed, primarily focused on the import of weapons, and the production and stockpiling of WMD. A United Nations Special Commission (UNSCOM) was set up to work alongside the International Atomic Energy Agency (IAEA) to inspect Iraqi facilities and destroy WMD and ballistic missiles. During the 1990s the work of the inspectors was criticised by the US and the UK. The US made it plain that the sanctions would continue for the foreseeable future, not least because of the campaign of belligerence, prevarication and obstruction pursued by the regime in relation to the inspections.

At the same time, however, the inconclusive nature of the Kuwait war left the US with a wish to 'create the conditions for the removal of Saddam Hussein from power' (allegedly asked of the CIA by the first President Bush; see Cockburn and Cockburn 2002: 31). This became part of continuing US intelligence imperative, all the more so because of a belief that Hussein's insistence, by mid-1997, that he had fulfilled all the disarmament requirements in fact concealed the opposite of what he was claiming.

Indeed, the regime's continued exploitation of the differences in the inspection methodology and within the UN, pushed the Clinton administration to launch Operation Desert Fox[8] in 1998, after the regime refused any further cooperation with UNSCOM. In that year Congress also approved the Iraq Liberation Act, which stated that 'it should be the policy of the United States to support efforts to remove the regime headed by Saddam Hussein from power in Iraq and to promote the emergence of a democratic government to replace that regime'. It was the intention of the next Republican President, George W. Bush, and in particular his neo-conservative Vice President Dick Cheney, that this should and would be achieved by a military invasion (see, for example, Isikoff and Corn 2007: 29).

Continuing suspicions that Saddam Hussein might be re-establishing his WMD capability, supported by defectors' claims, led to a new inspection body – the United Nations Monitoring, Verification and Inspection Commission (UNMOVIC, led by Hans Blix) – being set up in 1999. Inspections resumed in 2002, following a UN Security Council vote (Resolution 1441) which afforded Iraq 'a final opportunity to comply with its disarmament obligations' and concluded by stating that Iraq faced serious consequences as a result of its 'continued violations of its obligations' unless it accepted the unconditional return of weapons inspectors and had destroyed any WMD.

Using aerial surveillance and no-notice inspections, as well as extensive documentation produced by the regime, UNMOVIC reported in March 2003 that it could find no evidence of underground or mobile manufacturing facilities, and had destroyed the limited amount of weaponry it had found. There was little evidence of any significant production or stockpiles of chemical and biological weapons.

While it acknowledged the continuing failure of the regime to cooperate, as well as the continuing concerns from western intelligence sources, UNMOVIC argued that it was working towards a resolution of whether or not it could state that Iraq was complying with UN Resolutions. The cautiously optimistic reports (which never unequivocally stated the absence of WMD – see Blix 2004; Iraq: UN Documents of early March 2003), were too late; on 20 March, a US- and UK-led military invasion was preceded by extensive air strikes. On 9 April, the armed forces entered Baghdad.

After the terrorist attacks on the World Trade Center in 2001, the Blair government was continuously involved in discussions with the US government on the necessary responses. Initially these included the joint invasion of Afghanistan on the grounds that the Taliban regime, which controlled much of the country following the expulsion of the Russian army, was harbouring and supporting those involved in the attacks. The Blair government knew in 2001 that Iraq was also on the US agenda, primarily as an alleged sponsor of international terrorism and a producer of WMD.

The Prime Minister was also aware that regime change was proposed as an alternative to the existing policy of containment through the use of economic sanctions and the presence of the inspection teams. He became persuaded of three things: 'that America had to be supported more than ever before in its time of need; that it saw the world in a different light; and that the world would face a threat of an altogether different scale if Saddam made his chemical and biological weapons available to terrorist groups. The first was a value judgement. The second was fact. The third was a hypothesis based on an assumption' (Kampfner 2004: 157).

Nevertheless, the official view appeared to be that, to persuade the UN to provide a new Resolution that confirmed a breach of 687, there would need to be 'incontrovertible' evidence of 'large-scale activity' (Butler 2004: 66). There was also the issue of whether it was necessary to secure UN approval for an invasion. Apart from the Desert Fox line of reasoning, which elicited a very mixed response from Security Council members and others, it would normally be expected that it is for the Security Council to decide when the conditions of any Resolution have not been met. The Security Council 'can delegate enforcement to member states, but not the determination of whether enforcement should take place' (Verdirame 2004: 95).[9]

In March 2002 UK public officials were warning that the US was moving towards war, but that the proposed grounds (the threat of WMD, and supporting terrorism) were no further forward in terms of evidence or intelligence. It was at this juncture that one of the Prime Minister's advisers went to Washington and reported to the Bush administration that Blair supported regime change but had to 'manage a press, a Parliament and a public opinion'. At the same time the Bush government policy was for the removal of Saddam Hussein, to be 'justified by the conjunction of terrorism and WMD ... the intelligence and facts were being fixed around the policy' (quoted in Risen 2007: 113).

Blair was aware that the neo-conservatives around Bush were intending to invade with or without UK involvement. Keen to be seen as the equal of the US President in robustly pursuing an international security agenda (Blair's foreign policy adviser described his approach at the Chilcot Inquiry as 'muscular on such occasions'), Blair's advisers and officials worked towards the UK's case for war.

This was publicly presented through two reports and the Attorney-General's legal opinion to provide the only official justification for invasion; the Prime Minister disengaged himself from the normal government decision-making processes once the decision to join with the US had been made. March 2002 was the last time the Cabinet met to discuss a possible invasion. The Foreign Secretary, Robin Cook, noted that the Prime Minister 'does not regard the Cabinet as a place for discussions' (Cook 2004: 115). There 'were frequent informal discussions at Cabinet after the summer of 2002 but there were never any papers or proper analysis of the underlying dangers and the political, diplomatic and military options' (Short 2004: 147). Clare Short, then a cabinet minister, also alleged papers and other strategy material were withheld from the Cabinet. The Cabinet Committee – the Defence and Overseas Policy Committee (DOP) – 'never met … the whole crisis was handled by Tony Blair and his entourage with considerable informality' (Short 2004: 147).

Thereafter, decisions were taken involving a handful of chosen ministers, personal advisers and public officials where 'the government's enthusiasm for action carried over to civil servants and intelligence officials eager to please their masters who provided the type of information they thought was wanted' (O'Malley 2007: 12). The Butler Report later noted:

> … over the period from April 2002 to the start of military action, some 25 meetings attended by the small number of key Ministers, officials and military officers most closely involved provided the framework of discussion and decision-making within Government.
>
> One inescapable consequence of this was to limit wider collective discussion and consideration by the Cabinet to the frequent but unscripted occasions when the Prime Minister, Foreign Secretary and Defence Secretary briefed the Cabinet orally. Excellent quality papers were written by officials, but these were not discussed in Cabinet or in Cabinet Committee. Without papers circulated in advance, it remains possible but is obviously much more difficult for members of the Cabinet outside the small circle directly involved to bring their political judgement and experience to bear on the major decisions for which the Cabinet as a whole must carry responsibility. (Butler 2004: paras 609–10)

To appear to have to initiate military invasion for what was in practice a pre-determined US course of action, the government issued two reports designed to support the government's intentions and sway public and media opinion. The first was issued in September 2002 and the second in February 2003 (another, on human rights abuses, was issued in December 2002).[10] After the publication of the second of the dossiers, the Prime Minister told the House of Commons: 'We issued further intelligence over the weekend about the infrastructure of concealment. It is obviously difficult when we publish intelligence reports, but I hope that people have some sense of the integrity of our security services ... It is clear that a vast amount of concealment and deception is going on' (HC Deb, Vol 399, 3 Feb 2003, col 25).

The material was apparently not cleared either by the relevant intelligence or foreign affairs departments and nor was any minister apparently consulted about it, until it was released to the media. It also included information taken without attribution – and changed – from an article written by an Iraqi PhD student based in the US.

While some ministers later acknowledged that the February dossier should never have been published, the principal figures involved did not unequivocally disassociate themselves from it and apologies were only belatedly offered to the plagiarised author of the article. The parliamentary Foreign Affairs Committee in its July 2003 report summarised its views of this second dossier:

> we conclude that the effect of the February dossier was almost wholly counter-productive. By producing such a document the Government undermined the credibility of their case for war and of the other documents which were part of it ... We further conclude that by referring to the document on the floor of the House as 'further intelligence' the Prime Minister – who had not been informed of its provenance, doubts about which only came to light several days later – misrepresented its status and thus inadvertently made a bad situation worse ... We conclude that it is wholly unacceptable for the Government to plagiarize work without attribution and to amend it without either highlighting the amendments or gaining the assent of the original author. We further conclude that it was fundamentally wrong to allow such a document to be presented to Parliament and made widely available without ministerial oversight. (2003, paras 136–8)

Entitled *Iraq's Weapons of Mass Destruction*, the earlier dossier (September 2002) was a much more important document because it was the key government briefing report, adapted from information provided by the intelligence services and approved for publication by a government committee – the Joint Intelligence Committee (JIC) – on which the services sat with other government departments. This dossier made a number of claims, including Iraq's ability to assemble nuclear weapons within months if fissile material was obtained from abroad (the dossier also mentioned that Iraq had tried to get material from Africa); its capability to manufacture WMD and to launch them by various means and over various distances (including UK bases in Cyprus, Israel and NATO members Greece and Turkey); and to do so quickly (within 45 minutes of the order being given).

The sources for the dossier were claimed to be intelligence briefings, surveillance, UN documents, covert sources, defectors and public domain information. How that material was edited, amended and synthesised was alleged to have been driven by political requirements. The argument for this came from the Hutton Inquiry into the death of David Kelly, a government scientist who spoke off the record to a BBC journalist about the credibility of the dossier (see p. 28; see also Jones 2010).

The inquiry appendices reflected the dossier's drafting process but were ignored by Hutton who was much more concerned about the BBC's handling of the subsequent broadcast, which stated that the dossier was 'sexed up' to suit government purposes (Kelly had used the term 'wordsmith'). This broadcast provoked violent criticism from the government (which Hutton entirely endorsed), leading to the confirmation of Kelly as the source by a government spokesman. Hutton made no comment on the email traffic during the drafting of the dossier, which included phrases such as: 'much of the evidence we have is largely circumstantial ...'; 'crucially, though, it's intell-lite ...'; 'This draft already plays up the nature of intelligence sourcing. I think we could play this up more. The more we advertise that unsupported assertions (e.g. Saddam attaches great inportance (sic) to the possession of WMD) come from intelligence the better ...'; 'we do not differentiate enough between capacity and intent... can we show why we think he intends to use them aggressively, rather than in self-defence ...'; 'Foreword ... needs a killer para ...'; 'we need to do more to back up the assertions ...'; 'First, the document does nothing to demonstrate a threat, let alone an imminent threat from Saddam ...' (see Doig, 2005).

The legal opinion was issued in March 2003, days before the invasion, by the Attorney-General. This provided the government with unequivocal advice that war was now legally justified under existing UN Resolutions. In his first and a number of subsequent opinions, the Attorney-General had initially suggested that there was the need for a new Resolution to provide 'sound legal cover' and avoid a challenge as to the legal basis for an invasion. Such advice was being given up to two months before the war when he warned that, even if there was no need for a Security Council decision, there was a need for a Council discussion. The reaction of Blair was clear: he annotated one letter with 'I just do not understand this'; one of his aides added '... specifically said we did not need further advice [on] this matter'. The Attorney-General reviewed his advice and then, three weeks before the invasion, issued a statement which said that war was justifiable on the basis of Resolution 678 on Iraq's need to remove any WMD, and of Resolution 1441 which gave Iraq one final opportunity to disarm, warning of the consequences if it did not.[11] Certainly there were concerns expressed at the inquiry about the lateness of such advice, what documentation was seen and how far the Attorney-General was questioned about his final decisions at a point when it was virtually politically impossible to turn back from the commitment to invade. It is suggested that the Cabinet never saw his evolving advice – there were no questions on receipt of the final advice – although the Attorney-General argued that this was more custom and practice than an intent to exclude him. Nevertheless, it has been argued that the earlier advice was not circulated by the government 'before the cabinet meeting to make the final decision, even though legally it should have done so', in part in case it 'raised more doubts and perhaps given a stronger basis for ministerial resignations' (O'Malley 2007: 10, 15).

The Chilcot Inquiry was the fifth of the official and parliamentary inquiries undertaken into the war.[12] The last completed report, the 2004 Butler Report, addressed the use of intelligence as the basis for invasion. The report was clear that the invasion was a long-developing strategy whose time had come but which required evidence of break-point circumstances to justify the specific need-to-act in early 2003.

For this, however, the report noted that the government 'would need to be convinced that Iraq was in breach of its obligations; that such proof would need to be incontrovertible and of large-scale activity; but that the intelligence then available was insufficiently robust to meet that criterion' (Butler 2004: 106). The report then noted that the Blair government, aware that there was no legal justification for the overthrow of the Iraq regime other than failure to comply with UN disarmament obligations, used 'intelligence on Iraqi nuclear, biological, chemical and ballistic missile programmes ... in support of the execution of this policy' to inform planning for a military campaign; to inform domestic and international opinion, in support of the Government's advocacy of its changing policy towards Iraq (Butler 2004: 106).

While the report did not review the legality of the invasion in terms of the UN Resolutions, the Attorney-General's advice, or the responsibility for determining the enforcement of Resolutions, it did note that the use of intelligence 'went to (although not beyond) the outer limits of the intelligence available', facilitated by 'the informality and circumscribed character of the Government's procedures which we saw in the context of policy-making towards Iraq risks reducing the scope for informed collective political judgement' (Butler 2004: para 331, 611).

Certainly, the lingering doubts about the need for war, about the lack of post-invasion planning, and the subsequent cost in lives and resources, led in 2009 to the Chilcot Inquiry, while two US state crime criminologists have argued that 'there is no need to reach beyond the existing body of international law in order to bring the Iraq War under the theoretical umbrella of state crime. Existing international law alone establishes the United States and the United Kingdom as guilty of state crime linked to the invasion and occupation of Iraq' (Kramer and Michalowski 2005: 448).

No doubt those with expertise in international law will be able to also comment, since the Chilcot Inquiry has asked international lawyers for their analysis of the arguments relied upon by the UK government as the legal basis for the military intervention in Iraq. This request appears to be part of a broad approach taken by the Inquiry, including visits to France and the USA, and a range of witnesses, with questioning that could hardly be described as meticulous or evidenced as that of Saville.

Certainly, while the inquiry references earlier inquiries it does not seem to have taken the findings either as context or as fact. Consequentially its approach appears to allow witnesses to present their information and assessments as though for the first time and relatively free from triangulation against previous findings. Thus, and while the inquiry is not yet complete, its overall perception of the lead-up to the invasion of Iraq was that everyone, including the UN Security Council, thought that the Iraqi regime had WMD. Caught between the neo-con resistance to a UN-led negotiated settlement and Iraqi refusal to cooperate over compliance, the UK increasingly felt that it had to act, knowing, as Jack Straw stated in a written memorandum, that 'neither self-defence nor overwhelming humanitarian necessity could provide a proper legal base for a possible invasion of Iraq. Regime change in itself was plainly unlawful.' (Chilcot 2010; Jack Straw, supplementary Memorandum: 2)

Indeed, most of the evidence so far appeared to reflect the UK's robust caution, keen to work through UN and more focused on WMD than regime change – a measured 'disarmament' approach (where regime change as a collateral consequence was acceptable but not sought). The caution also reflected the belief that the Prime Minister had influence over Bush in relation to working through the UN. This turned out not to be too influential because from mid-2002 onwards the UK was being informed that the US was planning for an invasion (it also knew that the purpose behind the US approach was the reverse to that of the UK in that the US believed that regime change was the precursor to disarmament).

Apparently still believing that the invasion planning lay alongside consideration of the UN route, the UK undertook contingency planning for a military role (based on varying levels of support) but also informed the US of the need for a 'proper public information campaign' to let the UK public know why the UK government believed that Saddam Hussein's regime had to be disarmed.[13] The dual approach was supported by the Prime Minister up to the 'very last weeks' before conflict broke out, but he committed to the military route when 'he believed he had exhausted the alternatives'.

So, there would be two issues for the inquiry to explore: the legality of the military route – whether 'military action to deal with Iraq's Weapons of Mass Destruction would be lawful' (Chilcot 2010: Jack Straw, Supplementary Memorandum, paras 8, 9) – and the education of the public.

This first issue in turn would then depend on the Attorney-General's decision on the lawfulness of the UK's participation in an invasion. What was needed was the legal option, about which, according to Jack Straw, 'it would be wholly improper of any Minister to challenge, or not accept' that decision. On the other hand, it would be up to the government 'to consider the moral and political case for that military action' (para 22).

The Attorney-General's opinion was an extended rerun of the Desert Fox justification. It was based on an interpretation of Resolution 1441, linked to 687. The former essentially told Iraq that it had one last opportunity to comply, and failure to comply triggered a consequence. In other words, failure to comply was in itself 'a justification for deriving authority' and 'sufficient to constitute a green light' for military action. The absence of any need to secure the necessary UN

Security Council resolution was achieved by relying on the disarming requirements of Resolution 678 which authorised Member States to use all necessary means to uphold and implement Resolution 660 (the legal authorisation to eject Iraq from Kuwait) and all relevant resolutions subsequent to Resolution 660 to restore international peace and security in the area. In pursuit of 678 and 660, all member states had to do was to keep the Security Council informed on their decisions. In other words, failure to comply with 1441 activated 687/660, which revoked the ceasefire and thus revived the war against Iraq without further reference to the UN Security Council.

Lord Goldsmith pointed out that 1441 stated that 'in its resolution 687 (1991) the Council declared that a ceasefire would be based on acceptance by Iraq of the provisions of that resolution, including the obligations on Iraq contained therein'. While 687 does not actually use the term ceasefire Lord Goldsmith took its mention in 1441 to argue that 'a ceasefire' was not the same as a 'termination of authority'. In other words, military action was suspended rather than ended, and any conduct by Iraq jeopardising the ceasefire, including non-compliance, allowed any state to act to 'restore international peace and security in the area', only telling the Security Council of what they decided to do.

Two further assumptions were made. First, the inter-linking of the Resolutions meant that acting to restore peace and security did not solely apply to the period following the Kuwait war but continued to remain in force. Second, the presence or absence of WMD was irrelevant; the material breach of the requirements was Iraq's demonstration of its compliance (as the former Prime Minister told the inquiry, he could not accept the 'risk' of Saddam Hussein 'reconstituting his weapons programme' (Chilcot 2010: Blair, verbal evidence, p. 90).

The Attorney-General's responsibility was to give the legal perspective; whether it was right to do so was the responsibility of others. In particular evaluation of the intelligence pointing to non-compliance was not his responsibility – 'I was dependent upon the assessment by the government which had all the resources it had, all the intelligence agencies' (Chilcot 2010: Goldsmith, verbal evidence, p. 164). Goldsmith thought that that lay with the Prime Minister ('who did have access to all that information'). He and the government were aware of the legal balancing act and, while a new Resolution was preferable, he proposed a 'reasonable case' – the legal 'green light'.[14]

As to the education of the public, this was linked in part to whether there was a material breach of 1441. The US did not care about any breach, since regime change was their main trigger for an invasion, but the UK did. Non-compliance was to be the grounds, but if not the presence of WMD then the capacity to develop and use WMD had to be argued as the basis for the need to ensure compliance. This perspective populated the two dossiers as the basis of the government's case, from the ability to launch them within 45 minutes to the search for ingredients (including the contentious claim about ingredients from Niger being 'sought' by Saddam's officials, which also turned up to the surprise of US intelligence agencies in Bush's 2003 State of the Union address).

The Director of International Security in the Foreign and Commonwealth Office (FCO) seemed to be clear-cut on such evidence; intelligence was limited, sporadic and patchy. On the other hand, the then Chair of the Joint Intelligence Committee (JIC), John Scarlett, told the inquiry that he did not feel that the language in the September dossier was too unequivocal, nor that he had been put under pressure to 'firm up' the language.

He was unaware of the concerns from within the Cabinet Office about the dossier, he did not know about concerns by a senior member of the Defence Intelligence Staff, there was no 'conscious intention' to manipulate the language or misrepresent the information, and the Prime Minister's foreword was 'overtly a political statement' and so received different attention from that he paid to the wording of the dossier itself. Alastair Campbell stated that he never applied pressure to anyone in the development of the dossier, he could not remember discussions about its weaknesses, the JIC were happy with everything in the dossier and, indeed, if there was any redrafting, then that was the responsibility of the JIC. Apart from the mistake in part of the February dossier, the September dossier was a 'very, very serious, solid piece of work' (Chilcot 2010: Campbell, verbal evidence, p. 84).[15]

To date, it would appear likely that the Chilcot Inquiry will add little new to what has already been said about the lead-up to the invasion; whether or not it would come to the same conclusion as the Dutch inquiry is debatable.

Some questions about crime, the state and the UK state

Five questions emerge here. First, exactly how and why does a liberal democracy actively engage in activities or decisions that are the subject of official inquiries that may or may not involve potential legality or illegality?

Second, at what point or level of official in either of the two inquiries would the label of *state crime* apply? If one accepts at face value the claims of a 'just' invasion of Iraq – to stop the possibility of the use of WMD by Iraq, WMD passing to terrorist groups and the repression of Iraqi citizens by the regime – would the invasion still be studied as a possible state crime, or is it possible to commit a state crime for the best of intentions?

Third, is a breach of international law sufficient to be labelled a *crime* – and, if so, is every breach of a law from international law all the way back to domestic crime law also the basis for a *state crime*?

Fourth, should the recognition by the Chilcot and Saville Inquiries that criminal acts may have taken place necessarily mean that the *state* – as opposed to state agents – has committed a *crime*, or at what point, and how, are the decisions and actions of public officials or agents of the state the responsibility of the state, to the point that they can be labelled state crime?

Fifth and finally, is it possible that different governments can come to different findings over the same body of information (such as the Irish and British governments over Bloody Sunday before Saville), or what may be deemed a breach of law in one country, such as the Netherlands, but not, so far, in the UK or the USA?[16]

This means that the terms *state* (and who is, or effectively working as, a state official) and term *crime* need to be clearly defined, as does exactly what may be encompassed by the term *state crime*, as well as who may be responsible for state crime.

As suggested above, these are not easy issues to address. Every first-year sociology and criminology course will point to the inherent difficulties in defining crime,[17] as an Open University module (DD100_1: The Meaning of Crime) points out:

> Crime has multiple meanings. Those meanings are socially constructed. The most important differences in the meanings of crime occur between strictly legal definitions and those that relate crime to the breaking of other codes and conventions – normative definitions. These may be formal moral codes like religions, or more informal codes of socially-acceptable behaviour. Both these ways of thinking about crime vary historically, across societies, and amongst different social groups. They are almost always in some kind of conflict. Many legally-defined crimes are considered to be legitimate acts in other contexts. This difference partly explains why many legally-defined criminal acts do not result in prosecution or imprisonment. So crime

19

can simultaneously be normal and abnormal. (http://openlearn. open.ac.uk/mod/resource; accessed 23 January 2010)

Laws define crime by indicating the unacceptability of certain conduct, providing a formal means of adjudication and imposing sanctions accordingly – but the broadness of that generality applies as much to car-parking as it does to murder. Whether everything that is labelled unlawful is also a crime in terms of state crime suggests that that

---

Box 1: A question of unlawfulness and the state

February 2008 – Sir Richard Dearlove, the head of MI6 at the time of the crash that killed Diana Windsor and Dodi El Fayed, was called to the coroner's inquest to give evidence as to whether the security services had ever considered murder as official policy.[18] A former MI6 agent, Richard Tomlinson, had previously given evidence that he had seen details of a plot to assassinate a Balkan leader by causing his car to crash. Dearlove was called to confirm or deny the plot. He explained that 'an officer working in one of the sections to do with the Balkans had suggested the possibility of assassinating another political personality who was involved in ethnic cleansing'. The proposal was 'killed stone dead' (*sic*) after it was committed to paper because it was 'out of touch with service practice, service ethos and it was not a proposal to which consideration would be given' (*Daily Telegraph*, 21 February 2008). However, he did add that MI6 was legally required to seek authorisation from the Foreign Secretary to carry out any operation which involved breaking the law. Whether or not this could include assassination was unclear – Dearlove simply stated, somewhat obliquely, that 'assassination played no part in the policy of Her Majesty's government' (*Daily Mail*, 21 February 2008).

November 2008 – Georgina Downs, who led the UK Pesticides Campaign, secured a judicial review hearing in the High Court against the Department for the Environment, Food and Rural Affairs over its policy on crop spraying. The judge ruled that the policy was unlawful, breaching a European directive to protect people from the possible harmful effects of exposure to toxic chemicals and failing to use an appropriate methodology for assessing harm to humans other than those directly involved in spraying (the case was overturned on appeal in 2009).

---

breadth will also have implications for defining a state crime (see Box 1).

Some criminologists argue that the social construction of crime may not be objective, or universal. They are concerned not only about whose laws to use (for example, domestic or international), or what types of law to use (such as criminal or regulatory): 'there are many forms of state organisational deviance that it would be inappropriate to label as "crimes". These include breaches of international economic regulations ... and deviations from rules which are themselves repressive' (Green and Ward 2004: 7; see, as a possible example, Box 2). They are thus selective over what types of crime they consider as coming within the scope of crime in terms of state crime.

Box 2: Illegal but not a state crime?

Sell-offs of state assets by the 1980's Conservative governments were intended not only to shrink the size of the state but to transfer to the private sector parts of the state sector which were profitable. Those that were not immediately attractive to the private sector had to be made so. Unlike the public utilities with monopoly positions and well-developed infrastructures from decades of investment ultimately underwritten by the taxpayer, lame-duck or risk-investment purchases by previous governments for political reasons are not simply a matter of share issues. To sustain the momentum of privatisation, therefore, many of the assets had to be dressed up for the sale and, in the case of the sale of Rover, the controversy was much more serious because the government took an active role in ensuring that it was sold.

The answer for Rover was a negotiated sell-off in 1990 to one interested buyer – British Aerospace (BAE) – with an offer of a £500 million contribution to assist the sale. The subsequent negotiations not only had to keep BAE interested but also satisfy the European Commission (EC), whose commissioner on competition and state aid had to agree on the level and nature of state assistance in the purchase. The EC ordered a cut in the level of state grants, which caused BAE to threaten to pull out of the sale unless other financial arrangements were made to offset the loss. In July the sale was agreed, although the government made concessions on the structure of the sale including a deferred purchase price, and writing-off Rover's debts plus £78

---

million regional assistance, and an agreement that BAE could take advantage of Rover's capital tax allowances and losses, a price the government thought took British Aerospace 'to the very brink'. In November the National Audit Office was somewhat critical as to whether the 'deal of the decade' was such a good deal for the taxpayer, a criticism heightened when a confidential memorandum written by the CAG was leaked, disclosing further undeclared government assistance with the purchase.

The row was pushed onto the political agenda by ministerial remarks that the deferral had to be arranged in such a way as to avoid the actual timing of the deferral being picked up by the EC and to avoid 'seriously' misleading Parliament. Furthermore, it appeared that BAE could make a great deal of money from the purchase. Both Sir Leon Brittan, the EC Commissioner, and the PAC announced inquiries, with the latter's hearings making it apparent that the secrecy over the deal was not just to protect the sale but was intended to last much longer to protect the 'Government's relations with the Commission'.

The Commission was to term some of the payments as illegal under competition rules (see Ranelagh 1991: 55). Calls for a 'new investigation into the sweeteners affair was launched in February 1992 immediately after the European Court of Justice in Luxembourg ruled, on a legal technicality, that BAE did not have to repay the money. The court upheld BAE's appeal against repayment on the grounds that the Commission had failed to follow correct EC procedures in demanding the return of the £44.4m. However, it did not reject the substance of the Commission's finding that the sweeteners amounted to illegal state aid' (*Independent*, 28 July 1992).

Other criminologists argue about whether law should be used at all as a framework for labelling actions or decisions as state crime because they see the state as a partisan and hostile agency which constructs a legislative framework, and controls its application, as both a reflection of the interests it serves and as a means of social control: 'intervening into and responding to the activities, criminal or otherwise, of the powerful ... has been and remains markedly different from the interventions into the lives of those without power, and the inevitable process of criminalisation that flows from these interventions' (Coleman *et al.* 2009: 5).[19]

In an approach which also helps address the question of which type of law and crime, some criminologists prefer to focus on who is affected in terms of the harm caused, rather than the type of law transgressed. This raises a spectrum of state crime moving beyond legal concepts to more subjective or normative criteria (see Box 3). Thus they consider that citizens, and not the state, are seen as also having a right to determine what is a state crime: 'if civil society plays a crucial role in legitimising the state in those societies where hegemonic rule prevails, it can also play a crucial role in defining state actions as illegitimate where they violate legal rules or shared moral beliefs' (Green and Ward 2004: 4).

Box 3: A spectrum of possible state crime or harm?

Illegal? In 2003, the Metropolitan Police Service was accused of 'state-created crime' in what the judge termed a 'massively illegal' undercover operation during which some £15m was brought to London hidden in suitcases, laundered by undercover police officers and then returned to alleged drug dealers over a three year period. Ten defendants were acquitted. It was argued that police had 'overstepped the line between legitimate crime detection and unacceptable crime creation' (*Guardian*, 29 July 2003).

The operation was directed at alleged drugs and tobacco-smuggling criminals in Spain and Gibraltar by offering them money-laundering facilities (or, as the judge put it, 'a wholly exceptional opportunity to others to commit crime ... I have come to the conclusion that what the police did amounted to state-created crime'). The police used a former UK criminal (*Independent on Sunday*, 2 August 2003) to make the introductions: 'in 1993, two undercover police officers, posing as husband and wife and pretending to be wealthy financial advisers able to move money around the world, went to Gibraltar ... The operation began 14 years ago and ran over a 10-year period. It was aimed at alleged drug barons using Gibraltar and other routes to launder their profits. The principal target of the operation was offered a 5 per cent fee for all the money he put through the fake firm. Once "cleaned", the cash was handed back to the suspected traffickers to allow police to continue gathering evidence. A financial company, set up with Scotland Yard's approval, came complete with bogus records filed by accountants who were granted immunity from prosecution. The firm had four staff based at offices in London, and false accounts lodged with Companies House' (*Independent*, 29 July 2003).

The money was laundered through London and back into Gibraltar banks, with cameras recording work in the office and surveillance teams following the defendants. This resulted in over 20 convictions for drug smuggling. It was the final trial, of ten defendants for money laundering, that led to charges of entrapment. While he did not accuse the police of acting in bad faith in setting up the arrangements, the judge felt that they were incompetent. Officers should have gone directly to the Director of Public Prosecutions, the head of the Crown Prosecution Service, or consulted Treasury counsel, senior barristers who advise the government. Instead, they contented themselves with a relatively low-level approach to the Crown Prosecution Service for guidance which was 'fatally flawed'. As a result, police effectively 'made up their own minds' that they were acting lawfully.

Unlawful? The Audit Commission, the public body auditing local government and the National Health Service, had the legal power to surcharge councillors (and still has the power to surcharge Board members of local public bodies) for unlawful or reckless expenditure. The big case was Dame Shirley Porter. Porter, heiress to the founder of the Tesco supermarket chain, was elected to Westminster Council in central London in 1974 and became leader of the controlling Conservative group in 1983. After narrowly retaining control in 1986 the group devised a policy that designated areas of council housing for privatisation rather than for let under council control (a continuing Conservative government theme on home ownership and implemented through the 1980 Housing Act's 'Right to Buy' policy which allowed council house tenants to buy their property at discounted rates).

This was a controversial policy, first because inner London had only a limited amount of affordable public housing. Second, the policy (called 'Building Stable Communities') was targeted on areas of marginal Conservative support and based on an assumption that home-owners were likely to be more predisposed to the council and more favourable in their voting habits. As a policy, it was successful in that it secured a clear majority in the 1990 elections. Porter gave up the leadership the following year.

In 1996 the District Auditor issued his final report, which confirmed 'his provisional view and surcharging Dame Shirley

Porter and others. This was on the basis that the sale of the Council homes had been for an improper purpose and therefore unlawful. Dame Shirley Porter and others became personally liable for the loss to the Council caused by their wilful misconduct' (Audit Commission 2007: 4; see also Hosken 2006).

Harmful? In the Victoria Climbié case, an eight-year-old girl was beaten by her relative and the relative's boyfriend for over a year – the child suffered 128 separate injuries – until she died. As the inquiry later pointed out, the evidence was 'not hidden away' but known to staff in three 'housing authorities, four social services departments, two child protection teams of the Metropolitan Police Service (MPS), a specialist centre managed by the NSPCC, and two hospitals' (Laming 2003: 3). The inquiry noted that there had been '12 key occasions when the relevant services had the opportunity to successfully intervene' but staff ignored all of them, less through ignorance and carelessness than through a wish to avoid the work and inter-agency negotiations to deal with it: 'it is clear to me that the agencies with responsibility for Victoria gave a low priority to the task of protecting children. They were under-funded, inadequately staffed and poorly led. Even so, there was plenty of evidence to show that scarce resources were not being put to good use' (Laming 2003: 4).

As a later Parliamentary Committee inquiry noted: 'Lord Laming told us that he continued to believe that the Children Act 1989 was "basically sound legislation". His recommendations do not argue for a major new legislative framework. However, he did not believe that the Act was being implemented in the way that had been envisaged for it, and, in his view, there was "a yawning gap at the present time between the aspirations and expectations of Parliament and the certainty of what is delivered at the front door ... As Lord Laming commented, not one of the agencies empowered by Parliament to protect children in positions such as Victoria's emerged from the Inquiry with much credit. What happened to Victoria, and her ultimate death, resulted from an inexcusable "gross failure of the system". Lord Laming's report expressed his amazement that nobody in the agencies "had the presence of mind to follow what are relatively straightforward procedures on how to respond to a child about whom there is concern of deliberate harm". We share Lord Laming's amazement that the system failed so comprehensively' (House of Commons Health Committee 2003: 14, 11).

Overall, the state crime arena is thus already one of definitional variation and subjectivity but allegations levelled at the state and its agents using a range of terms – such as illegal, illegitimate, unlawful, criminal – are made in a range of contexts. On the other hand, however, even the examples in Box 1 and Box 3 may lead some to argue that these are less examples of *state crime* than of unlawful or harmful acts or decisions by individuals or agencies rather by the *state*. What about the state itself?

Here the limited literature on the UK and state crime appears to focus on state crime within very narrow parameters. For example, Ross (2000b) argues that 'through the actions of the police, national security agencies and military branches' the UK state has 'often been accused of committing state crime both home and abroad' (2000b: 11). The agencies were identified as those 'having the highest amount of contact with citizens' and thus 'more prone to engage in acts of state crime than others' (2000b: 12). The 'state crimes' included: the violation of human rights of Northern Ireland detainees and shooting unarmed civilians in Northern Ireland; selling arms to countries with 'abysmal human rights records'; a possible military coup; disinformation campaigns by governments and assassinations by the security services; the destabilising of inquiries into the covert work of the security services; concealing evidence in court cases; surveillance of citizens; use of excessive police force; and the use of the police against trade unions and ethnic groups.

Much of the focus appears based on assumptions about a monolithic and top-down *state* that can undertake *criminal* activity or (as notes 17 and 19 suggest) a particular view of the nature of the state. Thus Ross and Pete Gill (who contributed a chapter relating to the UK in Ross 2000a) draw attention in their studies of the UK to a state which exercises control over resources; law that was 'increasingly insulated' from external control, and the nature of the British Establishment's capacity to neutralise scandals and protect itself; the shared 'assumptions' between government and the security services; and the concept of an invisible, covert or secret state that operates in parallel to the formal state.

For example, it has been argued that British state involvement in illegal activities in Northern Ireland has a long provenance, coexisting alongside more contemporary tenets of democracy, the rule of law, and so on. Thus Rolston suggests that 'dirty war and support for death squads in Northern Ireland represents an endemic response to political challenge by an authoritarian British state with a history of colonial oppression ... Within this mindset, democracy is an obstacle, standing in the way of getting the military job done. As such, it must be circumvented, all the while denying any derogation from the ideal' (Rolston 2005: 199).

This means looking at the state able to operate at more than one level or according to different, possibly contradictory perspectives:

> British state intervention in the North of Ireland cannot be considered in the same light as the application of its policies and laws within Britain. Since partition, and the formation of the Irish Free State, the six counties have experienced 'exceptional' state powers as the norm ...The due process of the rule of law has been regularly suspended, internment without trial repeatedly used, paramilitary policing consolidated and military rule imposed. In this neo-colonialist context, the democratic process has been partial, weakened and suspended ... Constantly justified on the grounds of state security, the authoritarianism implicit within the liberal state was always explicit in the state's intervention in the North of Ireland. (Rolston and Scraton 2005: 548–9)

To do this, however, requires consideration of the links, if any, between the different parts of the state, the levels and the perspectives. For example, another study of what has been termed the dirty war in Northern Ireland – involving activities up to extra-judicial killings – has suggested that the war 'was authorised at the highest levels of the state itself in terms of the chains of command which led back to chief constables, army generals, the secret services and political rulers' (Rolston 2005: 195).

Seeking explanations for how and why such a state should be involved in state crime, also raises questions about the balance between assumption and analysis, and the evidential basis on which they are based. Rolston notes that 'such chains of command ... were vehemently denied by all those involved' (2005: 195) and that all attempts to investigate the allegations would be disrupted or curtailed.

On the other hand, it is difficult, without such evidence, to move from assumptions that those in official positions and those in pro-state terrorist groups might share a common view on the problem to suggest, as a consequence, that it was government policy to initiate criminal activity through these groups in pursuit of that policy on the basis that 'the British state in Northern Ireland was intimately involved in terror' (2005: 199). Further, who or what comprises the 'highest levels of the state', what is the 'state', what comprises chains of command, are there separate or integrated chains of command, and who are the 'political rulers' (and from where do the chains of command start so that they lead *back* to the political rulers) all reflect conceptual and evidential issues about the nature and workings of the state.

Such issues were raised in the context of the invasion of Iraq. In 2007 a British politician, Norman Baker, wrote a book about the suicide of a UK civil servant, David Kelly. Kelly was a government scientist who was involved in the controversy over the alleged presence of WMD in Iraq. The allegations appeared in the September 2002 dossier discussing the threat being posed by Iraq. Kelly had expressed his scepticism to a journalist about the claims in the dossier. His views were later repeated, anonymously, by the BBC. Kelly committed suicide in July 2003, not long after the government confirmed him as the source of the media story, and after a grilling by a parliamentary committee[20] (and see p. 13 above).

Baker's argument was that Kelly may not have committed suicide but that he was murdered by those keen to silence him as a credible source who could disapprove the allegations. The rationale for this was based on the assumption that the 'evidence' for the existence of WMD came from Iraqi exiles. Undermining the dossier, went the argument, could be seen as threatening the credibility of the exiles. Keen to see an invasion take place that could result in them taking up positions of power in a new regime, they could have a motive in having Kelly silenced.

The argument goes further. The British government was insistent that they were legally right to join in the US-led invasion, and thus might be prompted to silence anyone who might undermine *their* credibility. The two may have thus had a common interest in ensuring that silence: 'The key question is whether the actions of the Iraqi group were self-generated, and subsequently covered up by the government, or whether a tiny cabal within the British establishment commissioned the assassins to undertake this. Perhaps it was somewhere in between, with a nod and a wink being unofficially offered' (Baker 2007: 348).

This is a somewhat pejorative statement, based on assumptions rather than actual evidence, but on that basis either way the government could have been a facilitator or commissioner of a serious criminal offence. Further, a 'tiny cabal within the British establishment' offers two further qualifiers to the statement, giving it the flavour of a conspiracy. 'Cabal'[21] implies a secretive group of plotters; 'establishment' broadens the scope of who might be involved, in that the term could cover any significant UK institution, public or private.

It could also imply a degree of shared assumptions and expectations; the cabal could be articulating the thoughts and wishes of others who, because of their official position, could not publicly or formally endorse such a course of action. The qualification of unofficial action, reflecting Baker's suggestion of a 'nod and a wink being unofficially offered', suggests the existence of communities of interest, informal networks and shared values. These might encourage others to interpret and execute – rightly or wrongly – the wishes of those in positions of power who did not want to be seen to act, or give orders to act, illegally or unethically ('deniability', as such conduct is usually described).

This is not to say that, in terms of who could be responsible either for the death of David Kelly or for the extra-judicial killings in Northern Ireland, senior political figures or senior public servants were *not* involved in instigating or authorising them. Similarly, it is not to say that those directly involved do so without instigation or authorisation but on the basis of knowing what was expected of them. It is arguable that crimes, certainly in the latter case, were committed to the benefit of the state and it may also be inferred that their initiation lay in non-formal and untraceable 'understandings' among those within, or linked to, state institutions. Governments may well react with hostility to those who threaten or frustrate their policies and plans. Indeed, there is no doubt that the British state has and can take a ruthless approach to achieve its policies and plans, including circumstances where its use of the law to achieve them has been considered unlawful (see Box 4).

On the other hand, to demonstrate that the state initiated, approved or authorised such a response in Northern Ireland as well as in relation to Iraq as state policy, whether overt or covert, the application of the term *state crime* requires a thorough discussion of the terms, actions and decisions involved, as well as the appropriate evidence.

This is not surprising; the term *state crime*, and what comprises a state crime, is considered by those who study it to be a contested definition, as well as a contested topic for academic study. As Barak notes, 'to begin with, the study of state criminality is problematic because the very concept itself is controversial. This is due, in part, to the debate over whether or not one should define "crime" in

Box 4: The Diego Garcia case study

In 1962 the US was looking for an island for communications surveillance of the USSR within the Pacific. In 1963 they and the UK opted for Diego Garcia, one island in the Chagos Archipelago which comprised over 60 islands with about 2,000 inhabitants. In 1965 the Labour government sent its Colonial Secretary, Anthony Greenwood, to Mauritius to buy out Mauritius's claim to the Archipelago with £3 million and the promise of independence. The UK then took direct control of the Archipelago and designated the islands the British Indian Ocean Territory (BIOT). In 1966 Lord Chalfont, on behalf of the Foreign Secretary George Brown, signed an agreement with the United States to allow the latter to lease the islands for defence purposes for between 50 and 70 years (part of the price was a discount on the purchase of US nuclear weapons, another activity that the Labour government concealed from Parliament and the public – see page 219). The treaty was not debated in Parliament. In 1972 another agreement was signed to establish a communications base on Diego Garcia but the US rapidly developed a major base there, despite government statements to the contrary (see Madeley 1982; Winchester 1985).

Between 1965 and 1973 the local residents of Diego Garcia were 'systematically' and compulsorily shipped out to Mauritius by a mix of deceit, bribes and threats, and local industries closed down. In 1971 the government issued an Immigration Ordinance – an Order-in-Council – that banned the islanders from returning.

Some 40 years later only about 500 of the original islanders were still alive (although there were about 4000 descendants), invariably living in poverty. The Ordinance was successfully challenged in 2000 by a judicial review on their behalf. The then Labour Foreign Secretary, Robin Cook, not only decided not to appeal but also issued an Order-in-Council to allow the islanders to return to any of the islands except Diego Garcia itself. The US government did not want any return on security grounds and leant on the UK government to rescind the Order. Since Diego Garcia was used for airforce strikes against Iraq and Afghanistan, it was hardly likely that the UK would object and in 2004 new Orders-in-Council – the British Indian Ocean Territory (Constitution) Order 2004 and the British Indian Ocean Territory (Immigration) Order 2004 – were issued, removing any right of abode and disentitling islanders from entry or presence without specific permission. The former was challenged in the courts on behalf of the islanders and their descendants, initially successfully (the Court of Appeal stated in 2007 that the orders were unlawfully made because both their content and the circumstances of their enactment constituted an abuse of power on the part of executive government). The Labour government appealed on two grounds: the cost of any resettlement was not in the public interest, and the security of the airbase was in the national interest.

In 2008 the House of Lords voted 3–2 to allow the government's appeal. It stated that the methods used – the Orders – were not, as other courts had previously determined, unlawful and an abuse of power.[22] Further, this method was not only acceptable to be used by the government against one of its own colonies but to do so against the interests of its inhabitants if it deemed those interests to be subordinate to those of the government: 'Her Majesty in Council is therefore entitled to legislate for a colony in the interests of the United Kingdom. No doubt she is also required to take into account the interest of the colony ... but there seems to me no doubt that in the event of a conflict of interest, she is entitled, on the advice of Her United Kingdom ministers, to prefer the interests of the United Kingdom' (Judgments – R (on the Application of Bancoult) v. Secretary of State for Foreign and Commonwealth Affairs, 2008, UKHL 61, para 49).

Even though the House of Lords accepted that the way of life of the islanders had been 'irreparably destroyed', it also argued that the destruction took place a long time ago and compensation had been paid. Any question of the islanders' rights 'had to be weighed against the state's diplomatic and defence interests', which were 'peculiarly within the competence of the executive' (Judgments – R (on the Application of Bancoult) v. Secretary of State for Foreign and Commonwealth Affairs, 2008, UKHL 61, paras 53, 58).

terms other than the law codes of individual nations' (Barak 1990: 33).

On the other hand, there are also as many arguments to focus on state crime as a specific area of study as there are addressing the problems of studying it. As Friedrichs points out:

a number of general observations can be made about state crime, and its somewhat paradoxical character or status. First, insofar as the state is the primary source of both the laws that define crime and the institutions of enforcement and adjudication, the concept of state crime is especially problematic and open to challenge. Second, for many of those who accept the claim that crimes in a meaningful sense are carried out on behalf of states or through the use of state resources, it is particularly disorientating to acknowledge this fundamental contradiction with the state's professed claim to advance and protect the general welfare. Third, if it is particularly true that conventional crime ... has been the primary focus of public fear of crime, it is surely disturbing to realise that the largest scale of criminal harm has been the consequence of state crimes. Fourth, the field of criminology has historically concerned itself primarily with the study of conventional crime and conventional offenders, and this is dismaying to confront the general neglect of the topic of state crime in the criminological literature. (Friedrichs 1998: xviii)

As noted above, there are issues over what is a crime and over legal frameworks, and who determines them. Friedrichs and Schwartz (2007) argue that 'a central theme of all of these strains of criminology has been on the power of privileged segments of society to define crime, and to support enforcement of laws in accord with their particular interests'. They also propose that 'definitions of crime ... would focus on objectively identifiable harm to human beings and violations of human rights as the criteria for labelling an activity a crime' or 'demonstrably harmful activities that fall in "the space between the laws," but that ought to be recognized as crime' (Friedrichs and Schwartz 2007: 4).

At the same time, the issue of state crime goes not only to the heart of the criminal justice process in addressing the conduct of those who propose, deliver and enforce the laws but also to the nature of the state itself, particularly those states which profess adherence to the rule of law and the principles of democracy, including the welfare, well-being and safety of those it governs. Indeed, the study of state crime will require an awareness not only of criminology but also history, politics, international relations and ideology. It may also include an ability to unravel the roles that these various perspectives play in relation to state crime and to understand the complexities and inter-relations of state activity and decisions that may comprise a state crime, and who may commit it (and how and why).

Such issues clearly lie at the heart of any discussion about the roles and responsibilities of the state and its officials or agents in a democratised and developed country, and whether these are illegal, unlawful or cause harm as part of or as a consequence of official policy. Whether all such actions or decisions may be labelled *state crime* is one issue, but more generally raises some key issues about the state and its conduct.

Yet state crime appears to have no place in today's mainstream models of criminal behaviour or democratic states. It is invariably ignored, overlooked or excluded from many academic textbooks and academic courses. Nevertheless, unless one is convinced that such issues can never happen in a liberal democracy, then state crime should be an integral part of contemporary political life and an essential aspect in the study of criminology, law, international relations, public policy and politics.

Summary

The questions that this book seeks to discuss are as follows. What are state crimes, or crimes by those employed by the state or working on behalf of the state? How far does state crime require evidence of official policy, initiated by those who are the leaders of the state, or state institutions, with their authority to approve, support and protect those who help it achieve its objectives officially or unofficially, including the commission of crime? Further, what actions and decisions may be encompassed by the term *state crime*, and what are the motivations for state crime, raise a number of other questions. Exactly what is a crime and what is the state, how are these defined, why and how do officials decide to break the law, how and why should a democratic state want to commit crimes against, or cause harm to, its own citizens or those of another country, who exactly decides that this should be official policy, and how and who adjudges on such conduct?

The structure of the book is thus based around six key issues to be explored: what is state crime according to the literature; what is the state; what is a crime; what are the drivers for the state to commit a crime; what are the roles of the various institutions of the state in being involved in state crime; and what, in terms of monitoring or investigating state crime or unethical conduct, are the roles of those institutions, from the police through to Parliament, responsible for holding governments and state institutions to account?

Unusually for books on state crime, this book looks at a specific country, and one claiming to be a liberal democracy as the context within which to explore these issues. Further, it looks not only at crime but also at the structure of the modern state and thus provides a balanced and rigorous perspective with which to study the concept of state crime. This is particularly relevant to the work of other disciplines, and also to the study of those states – the western liberal democratic state – where state crime should be, by definition, deviant conduct but which also appears a regular occurrence. Overall, this book seeks to provide an introduction to state crime for contemporary developed states, which will facilitate the study of such issues as part of mainstream academic study across a number of disciplines.

Notes

1   Although in the case of some, this required an appeal process, and some could not be discussed in public – see *Daily Telegraph*, 4 February 2010.
2   Whether this includes a conclusion about the legality or otherwise of the decision to invade is debatable. When, in July 2010, the UK Coalition government Deputy Prime Minister described the invasion as an 'illegal invasion', the inquiry issued a statement saying that it was examining the legal issues in the run-up to the war but would not make a judgement about the legality of the war.
3   This might not come as a surprise, given that the Minister of Defence at the time, Lord Carrington, later wrote in his written submission to the Saville Inquiry that, 'I seem to remember that at the time his military background was seen as an advantage because he would have a better understanding of what was going on in the minds of the troops ...' (Evidence KC6, p. 3: http://www.bloody-sunday-inquiry.org.uk: evidence and statements).
4   A 'breed like rabbits' statement, allegedly made by a senior Protestant politician, reflected a generally held view that the propensity for large Catholic families could eventually shift the balance of voters in a sufficient number of constituencies to give them an overall majority. The alleged policy was a redrawing of constituency boundaries to try and ensure that increases in Catholic votes were added to or retained within the limited number of constituencies where they were already a majority.
5   It should be remembered that Article 3 of the Irish Constitution stated that 'it is the firm will of the Irish Nation, in harmony and friendship, to unite all the people who share the territory of the island of Ireland, in all the diversity of their identities and traditions'.

6 In his submission to the Saville Inquiry, Lord Carrington wrote that 'we would never have agreed to any course of action which involved the deliberate loss of civilian life ... I can state quite categorically that it was never policy to shoot unless a target had been identified as a threat. It is ridiculous to suggest there was a plot. People always find plots in everything. I suspect the army was frustrated at the time with the situation in Northern Ireland at the time [sic] but to suggest that there was a deliberate plot to shoot civilians is ludicrous and something no politician would ever agree to' (Evidence KC6, p. 12: www.bloody-sunday-inquiry.org.uk: evidence and statements).

7 Iraq was subject to a number of Resolutions before and after the invasion. Two of these related to the Iraq invasion of Kuwait. Adopted in 1990, 678 called for 'all necessary measures' to ensure peace in the area (and the basis of the US-led support to Kuwait to remove the Iraqi army); 687 (1991) laid down the conditions for the ceasefire and included the destruction of WMD; 1441 (2002) warned that Iraq was still 'in material breach' of the earlier Resolutions and could be subject to 'serious consequences' if it did not respond appropriately.

8 Operation Desert Fox was a number of US and UK air strikes in December 1998. At the time, the US justification was that the strikes were intended to disable his WMD capacity while UK Prime Minister Tony Blair argued that the use of military action was the only option. In many ways, the legal justification used by the UK government at that time heralded that to be used for the 2003 invasion. Robin Cook, the Foreign Secretary, was to argue that the authority derived from Saddam Hussein's failure to do what the existing Resolutions had told him to do, although the general government position was that 'a further resolution declaring Iraq to be in "material breach" of the 1991 cease-fire terms, though not in its view legally necessary, would be desirable' (Youngs and Oakes 1999: 26).

   Indeed, on the basis of the November 1998 Resolution (1205, condemning Iraq for a 'flagrant violation of resolution 687 (1991) and other relevant resolutions') Robin Cook argued on the day of the attack that 'we are absolutely clear that we have thorough clear backing in UN resolutions ... Last February Saddam was warned in the Security Council resolution that there would be the severest consequences if he broke his undertakings' (Youngs and Oakes 1999: 27).

9 Indeed, the Attorney-General was later to tell the Chilcot Inquiry that 'we did have an advice which the legal adviser to the United Nations had given to the Secretary General in 1993 ... in which he confirmed that the original authority to use force in Resolution 678 could revive, if there was a material breach, but said that it was for the Security Council to determine' (Chilcot 2010: Goldsmith evidence, p. 10).

   Addressing the General Assembly on 23 September 2003, the United Nations Secretary-General himself stated that states retained the inherent right of self-defence but that, when they 'decide to use force to deal with broader threats to international peace and security, they need the unique legitimacy provided by the United Nations. Now, some say this understanding is no longer tenable, since "armed attack" with weapons of mass destruction could be launched at any time, without warning, or by a clandestine group. Rather than wait for that to happen, they argue, States have the right and obligation to use force pre-emptively, even on the territory of other States, and even while weapons systems that might be used to attack them are still being developed. According to this argument, States are not obliged to wait until there is agreement in the Security Council. Instead, they reserve the right to act unilaterally, or in *ad hoc* coalitions. This logic represents a fundamental challenge to the principles on which, however imperfectly, world peace and stability have rested for the last 58 years' (quoted in Bethlehem 2004).

10 This dossier was apparently 'largely culled from Amnesty International reports' with Amnesty International accusing the UK government of 'being "opportunistic and selective" in its use of material' (Foley 2010: 15).

11 The Attorney-General later queried the lawfulness of the invading forces remaining in Iraq, since the use of the Resolutions was about dealing with the regime for 'failing' to comply with their requirements on WMD. Without a UN mandate, running the country once the objectives of the Resolutions had been achieved by military action could also have been illegal under international law governing the authority of the occupying power (see Kampfner 2004: 317–18). The authorisation came with Resolution 1483 in May 2003.

12 The four completed to date are: the Hutton Inquiry (2004, www.the-Hutton-Inquiry.org.uk); the Butler Inquiry (*Review of Intelligence on Weapons of Mass Destruction*, 2004, www.the-Butler-Inquiry.org.uk, HC898); the Intelligence and Security Committee, 2003, *Iraqi Weapons of Mass Destruction – Intelligence and Assessments*, Cm 5972; the House of Commons Foreign Affairs Committee, 2003, *The Decision to go to War in Iraq*, HC813.

13 Although apparently Blair did not go so far as to explain his intentions to Parliament. He was asked by the Chilcot Inquiry why when asked by the House of Commons Liaison Committee in July 2002, 'Are we preparing for possible military action against Iraq?', he had said 'No, there are no decisions that have been taken about military action', when a number of decisions were being taken about military options. The former Prime Minister explained to the Chilcot Inquiry that he was still considering the UN route and that 'Parliament can be quite a tricky forum in which to engage in a nuanced exercise.'

14 Not everyone was as certain. The FCO's legal adviser had warned in October 2002 that to advocate the use of force without a credible legal base would be to advocate the commission of a crime of aggression

and would expose members of the armed forces to charges of murder. Following the Attorney-General's opinion, the First Sea Lord took his own legal advice as to whether the invasion was lawful.

15 He was also to say that the actions and decisions of the UK government were done 'because we think it is in the British national interest' (p. 47).

16 Similar inter-state divergences happen elsewhere. Maher Arar is a Syrian-born Canadian. He was incorrectly reported by the Canadians to have possible links to terrorism, and was arrested in the US while in transit. Despite the Canadians still being equivocal about their information and without explaining what they intended to do with him, the US government authorised his rendition to Syria where he was imprisoned and tortured. Later released and the subject of a comprehensive public inquiry in Canada, he was offered an official apology and substantial compensation. Under the Bush administration, the US refused to cooperate in the inquiry and apologise. When Arar sought to sue those involved, the US courts refused to take on the case because of national security issues. The grounds for this were that Arar's rendition involved 'special factors' that included 'considerations of "diplomacy, foreign policy and the security of the nation" – matters it suggested were best left to the executive and legislative branches' (Los Angeles Times, 21 June 2010; see also The New York Review of Books, 15 June 2010). When the case went to the Supreme Court, the Obama administration argued that the courts should not hear the case; the Court agreed.

17 Just as every first politics course will, like the equivalent OU module DD203_1, discuss a state as one which 'exercises the monopoly of the legitimate use of force within a demarcated territory' – a single-function focus that in part has persuaded many state crime authors to focus on the illegitimate use of force as one of the core components of state crime.

18 Mohammed Al Fayed, Dodi's father, was convinced that the possibility of the mother of the future monarch being married to his Egyptian-born playboy son was something the state wanted to avoid at all costs. This included their deaths being arranged by the British security services on behalf of the monarchy.

19 The authors describe the UK state as a strong, interventionalist, law and order state and the work of their book's contributors as focusing on the 'on-going intensification in the authoritarian interventions of a numerically-expansionist, surveillance-oriented, highly militarised and nakedly aggressive state form' (Coleman et al. 2009: 4).

20 The government set up the Hutton Inquiry, also designating the inquiry as an inquest under the Coroners Act by the Lord Chancellor. Hutton's report included findings analogous to those that a coroner would make. Hutton exonerated the government from having in any way contributed to Kelly's death, blaming instead the BBC for making and then defending

a false claim – that the government 'sexed up' the September dossier and especially in relation to the 45 minutes claim. Hutton also concluded that Kelly committed suicide and made a request for the records provided to the inquiry, not produced in evidence, to be closed for 30 years, and that medical (including post-mortem) reports and photographs be closed for 70 years. In October 2010 the government released the post-mortem report which confirmed a death consistent with suicide.

21 The term 'cabal' is formed from the surnames of five plotters in the reign of Charles I.

22 It is also worth noting here the handing down of both 'lawful' and 'unlawful' judgements in relation to government decisions affecting Diego Garcia where different adjudication venues at different times may produce different results while considering essentially the same body of fact.

Chapter 2

Themes from the state crime literature: labels

Introduction

Currently the study of state crime is primarily the preserve of criminologists, not least because of the term 'crime', the use of deviant organisational behaviour to explain public institutional misconduct, and the work done in this area by those sociologists and criminologists who style themselves radical sociologists and criminologists. The latter have a particular view of the communities of interest among the rich and powerful, including those in corporate and public life, which may lead to claims of 'the state within the state' and other somewhat prescriptive approaches.

At the same time, those criminologists and sociologists who *do* study state crime tend to stay within the conceptual and theoretical perspectives of their discipline. They do not appear to have drawn much material from the other disciplines – despite long-time students of state crime such as Greg Barak arguing that the study of state criminality involves the study of 'power, ideology, law, and public and foreign policy' (Barak 1991: 5).

This chapter looks at state crime literature themes and issues from within the main disciplines (criminology and sociology) and from other disciplines.

Themes and issues from within the discipline

How is state crime defined?

One of the continuing themes has been that of definition. The spectrum of acts within the range of definitions discussed above only serves to underline the elasticity and diffuse nature of what could be labelled state crime, encouraging attempts to further refine the definition. One consequence is to further subdivide concepts and definitions.

Friedrichs argues that 'a good deal of confusion surrounds the use of the concept "state crime" and "governmental crime"' (Friedrichs 2000: 53). He therefore proposes a range of descriptions to distinguish between types of state crime:

> *Governmental crime* is the broad, all-encompassing term for a range of illegal and demonstrably harmful activities carried out from within, or in association with, governmental status. The conventional term *political crime* has been used to embrace crimes committed by those within the government and by those acting against the state, and is probably more readily associated with the latter type of activity. The term *state crime*, which has been quite widely quoted in more recent times, refers only to one major class of crimes that can be committed by those acting within a government. (Friedrichs 2000: 74)

Ross uses the term political crime: 'in general, an actor has committed a political crime if he or she has a political or ideological intention or motivation to cause harm ... State political crime consists of an action perpetrated by the government to illegally minimise or eliminate threats to its rule' (Ross 2003: 4). He then goes on to claim that 'crimes committed by the state are somewhat unique because they include illegalities committed by the government as a whole, by organisational units of the state, and by individual officials who break the law for their own or their agency's gain ... These types of crime differ because the former is organisationally based whereas the latter is regarded as individual crimes of occupational corruption' (Ross 2003: 10).

Barak also uses the term 'political crime', but from a different perspective: 'acts committed by and/or on behalf of the state and its dominant ruling elites are political crimes essentially because they have been rationalised or justified in order to preserve and maintain the status quo. In this sense, all of these crimes by the state become repressive means directed at the real and imagined enemies of a given state and the associated political and economic arrangements' (1991: 275).

Most authors recognise that one of the defining characteristics is that *personal* gain is not one of the drivers. Kauzlarich *et al.* argue that 'most scholars working in the area agree that governmental or state crimes are illegal, socially injurious, or unjust acts which are committed for the benefit of a state or its agencies, and not for the personal gain of some individual agent of the state' (2001: 175). A definitional approach that reflects a majority of authors has been proposed by Bill Chambliss (1989):

> The most important type of criminality organized by the state consists of acts defined by law as criminal and committed by state officials in the pursuit of their jobs as representatives of the state ... State-organized crime does not include criminal acts that benefit only individual officeholders, such as the acceptance of bribes or the illegal use of violence by the police against individuals, unless such acts violate existing criminal law and are official policy.

What is included in the study of state crime?

Within sociology and criminology the relevance of the study of state crime would appear self-evident, if not always recognised as such. This is a recurring theme for those sociologists and criminologists who study state crime and want to see their chosen topic move more into the mainstream of their own discipline where they note a lack of enthusiasm. As Barak notes: 'the criminological journey towards the development of a criminology of state criminality will not be accomplished without resistance from both inside and outside the boundaries of academic criminology. Simply put, there are a number of disciplinary biases and the political obstacles to overcome' (1990: 33).

The reason for this, he argues, is the discipline's reluctance to accept the breadth of the subject as defined by critical criminology, the aspect of the discipline most associated with the study of state crime. Critical criminology has not limited itself to illegal conduct, as defined by law, but to conduct resulting in harm or injury which is recognised in the 'higher criteria established in various international treatise, covenants, or laws. Therefore, for the purposes of this discussion, crimes by and of the state, like those crimes against the

---

Box 5: Traditional state crime (1)?

In Canada in 1977 a Royal Commission of Inquiry into Certain Activities of the Royal Canadian Mounted Police (RCMP) (the McDonald Commission) was held after allegations of break-ins, unauthorised mail-opening and wiretapping following the Quebec separatist crisis. It was known about by senior officers who also claimed that the information collected went to ministers (the security intelligence service was at that time part of the RCMP and staffed by RCMP officers):

> The government requested the RCMP to undertake a 'proactive' strategy in this area – to try and get advance information as to the intentions and activities of nationalist organizations and, if possible, to prevent or 'counter' disruptive acts. This the Security Service proceeded to do. It embarked on an extensive campaign of intelligence-gathering, infiltration, harassment and disruption directed at virtually all stripes of nationalist sentiment in Quebec. In many circumstances, the Service committed clearly illegal acts ... Operations such as these had not, the McDonald Commission found, been ordered by the government. They were generated from within the Service in response to government directions to find out more about separatism. Quite aside from being illegal, these operations showed a lack of discrimination between true threats and legitimate dissent. None had any major effect on the organizations targeted, and none brought in intelligence of much importance.
> Although the most spectacular acts of the Security Service were committed in Quebec, they certainly were not limited to that province. Throughout Canada, the Service engaged in a whole series of illegal or improper activities, particularly in relation to left-wing or radical groups ... The abuses of the Security Service were not limited to the 1970s, or to excesses in 'countering' nationalist or radical threats. It was revealed by the McDonald Commission that some activities such as surreptitious entry, mail-opening, and the gaining of access to supposedly confidential information in the possession of the government, had gone on for many years, in relation to various aspects of national security – from espionage and counter-intelligence to subversion. (Rosen 2000: 4–5)

---

state, may be viewed similarly as involving exploits of both a violent and non violent nature ... state criminality may include the more general transgression of both domestic and international laws, not to mention the more subtle institutional relations or behaviours which cause social injury' (Barak 1990: 33).

Another aspect relates to the definitional variation. Friedrichs, like a number of other state crime authors, considers that the term *state crime* is best applied to 'harmful acts carried out by state officials on behalf of the state ... in this context, it is necessary to recognise the difference between acts deemed to be in violation of international law, acts deemed to be in violation of state law and acts deemed to be harmful by some other criterion (for example, by the standards of some international human rights organisation, such as Amnesty International)' (Friedrichs 1998: xvii).

This width – from breaches of international law to harm – and the increasingly subjective definitions of the latter attracts some criticism for the breadth of such definitional and conceptual perspectives. Sharkansky suggests that its proponents 'have produced a boundless array of actions that might be labelled as state crimes, but the term has been so broadened as to render it just another epithet for *undesirable activities*' (Sharkansky 2000: 39). He argues that:

> there is no doubt that some state officials act in ways that are illegal and/or distasteful to domestic and foreign observers. Yet there are no clear linkages between terms like *distasteful* or *nasty* on the one hand and *criminal* or *illegal* on the other. Not all official actions that are distasteful are illegal, and not all that is illegal is distasteful. Moreover, some actions committed by state officials are clearly not those of the state. Some violations of the laws by state officials are the rogue actions of individuals at the bottom of administrative hierarchies. Others may not be officially declared as policy, but may be perceived as having at least the tacit encouragement of policymakers. (Sharkansky 2000: 35)

This raises two themes, in terms of what parts of the state may be included within state crime and, where injury results, whether or not this may be caused intentionally. Much of the crime by the state discussed in the literature relates to the misuse of the instruments of state power, such as surveillance, violence and repression, and reflects the state as the legitimate monopoly exercise of force. Here the traditional motive is relatively clear; such instruments are about the relationship between the rulers and the ruled, and when exercised by the former against the latter are hardly likely to reflect good intentions or motives. Use within a liberal democracy will be substantively regulated and thus misuse is more than likely to be considered illegal.

Widening the definition of crime to actions or decisions that (and before the question of intention is raised) lead to injury or harm may widen what parts of the state should be included in any study of state crime. They may include those actions and decisions done with good intentions by those directly involved, and intentions by others which, by focusing on different objectives, create circumstances in which the likelihood of injury or harm occurring is increased – but again without intent to do so.

The study of state crime needs to address such issues and parameters, and decide if the term could become applicable to conduct – and the regulatory framework within which it works – that does lead to injury or death but which would not traditionally be considered for labelling as state crime[1] (see Box 6).

Whether it is the question of definition of state crime, or specialist demarcations within the discipline, or even what is or should be encompassed by the term state crime it is true that the study of state crime continues to be a niche activity. Even within that niche, however, there are divergences on a number of issues.

Nevertheless, there has been a continuing minority academic interest in *state crime*. Much of the limited literature is derived from US academics who divide primarily between one main perspective – those studying *state crime* – and a lesser variant – those studying *state-corporate crime*.

What is the state in state crime?

State crime is essentially crime by and for the benefit of the state. The definition of what is a state can be elastic and one of the most elastic comes from Green and Ward who describe the state as: a '"public power" comprising personnel organised and equipped for the use of force, "material adjuncts prisons and institutions of coercion of all kinds" and agencies that levy taxes', but then go on to include those 'political entities ... which deploy organised force, control substantial territories and levy formal and informal taxes but are not accepted members of the international society of states. We shall refer to such entities as "proto-states"' (2004: 3). Since this could include revolutionary groups, terrorist organisations and self-proclaimed independent movements, then such a definition may be too diffuse.

Box 6: Healthcare: institutional harm or potential state crime?

The chair of the Healthcare Commission noted of the investigation into Mid-Staffordshire NHS Foundation Trust (2009) that there were 'appalling standards of care and chaotic systems for looking after patients. There were inadequacies at almost every stage of the care of patients' and 'there is no doubt that patients will have suffered and some of them will have died as a result' (*Guardian*, 17 March 2010).

The inquiry, triggered by an apparently high number of deaths among patients admitted as emergencies, found poor staffing, lack of training, poor communication and poor use of monitoring equipment, poor monitoring of patients, and lack of operational supervision. Operational conditions were unsuitable. In many of the cases involving emergency patients 'at least one element of the clinical management or monitoring of their condition was unsatisfactory. Areas of concern included infrequent reviews of patients by doctors, the lack of systematic monitoring of whether the patients were recovering or deteriorating, and the failure to respond adequately to signs of deterioration. There was inadequate monitoring to identify common complications of surgery' (2009: 7).

Overall, in the Board's 'drive to become a foundation trust, it appears to have lost sight of its real priorities. The trust was galvanised into radical action by the imperative to save money and did not properly consider the effect of reductions in staff on the quality of care. It took a decision to significantly reduce staff without adequately assessing the consequences. Its strategic focus was on financial and business matters at a time when the quality of care of its patients admitted as emergencies was well below acceptable standards' (2009: 11).

Most state crime authors focus on the state as, variously, governments, the executive and various public agencies. A number now include those private sector agencies that deliver public services or functions through government-funded contracts. As Dave Whyte notes in relation to the increasing use of private military companies (PMC), this 'does not imply a decline of the political decision-making processes … in other words PMCs do not work in a political vacuum, but are dependent upon the consent of governments for their livelihood' (Whyte 2003: 584; see Jamieson and McEvoy 2005).

Friedrichs notes the need to make some distinctions in relation to the nature of state crime as follows: 'one issue with state-organised crime is the degree to which it is sanctioned by authority figures, or is carried out quite autonomously by state agents. A second issue is the extent to which this type of crime is motivated by a disinterested commitment to the perceived interests of the state, or government, or is motivated by personal career-related aspirations' (Friedrichs 2000: 73).

What is crime in state crime?

A traditionalist state crime approach would argue that a crime is a consequence of breaking domestic or international law:

> criminologists have been successful in using existing laws to identify a broad range of state harms as crimes. While states are not quick to define their own actions as criminal, criminologists should not ignore the fact that sometimes states violate their own laws ... When states violate their own laws, clearly state crimes are being committed. Likewise, criminologists have also argued that when states violate international laws and other formal agreements, they are also committing crimes. The question of state crime, for criminologists working within a legalistic framework, is not whether it is a real phenomenon, but rather which legal definition(s) to use. (Matthews and Kauzlarich 2007: 47)

As noted above, the social construction of law means that many state crime authors are concerned that states can control what is 'defined by law as criminal'. Some state crime commentators argue that domestic law limits 'the study of state crime to harms that political states *had chosen* to criminalise ... the study of state crime must include governmental acts that violate international law, even when they do not violate domestic law' (Kramer and Michalowksi 2005: 447, emphasis in original).

They have therefore sought to extend the concept of state crime as widely as possible. Ross has argued that state crime included both illegal acts and those 'that have not reached the point where a formal law prohibits them'. Thus, state crime includes 'crimes of commission and omission ... In an effort to focus future research and policy, state crime, as defined here, is limited to cover-ups, corruption, disinformation, unaccountability, and violations of domestic and/

or international laws. It also includes those practices that, although they fall short of being officially declared illegal, are perceived by the majority of the population as illegal or socially harmful' (Ross 2000a: 74; Ross 2003: 87).

Is harm a state crime?

The concept of harm or injury by the state as the basis for labelling decisions or actions as a state crime widens the question of who or what defines state crime. It also moves its study outside of what is seen as a restrictive legal framework:

> many events and incidents which cause serious harm are either not covered by criminal law or, if they could be or are encompassed within its ambit, are either ignored or handled without resort to it: corporate crime and state crime are obvious, heterogeneous categories of offence that remain largely marginal to dominant legal, policy, enforcement, and indeed academic, agendas, while at the same time creating widespread harm, not least amongst already relatively disadvantaged and powerless peoples. (Hillyard and Tombs 2007: 12)

Using social harm or injury widens the scope to encompass universally defined human rights (such as food, shelter, self-determination).[2] Green and Ward define state crime as 'restricted' to 'the area of overlap between two distinct phenomena: (1) violations of human rights and (2) 'state organisational deviance'. The former are those rights incorporating 'freedom and well-being that human beings need to exert and develop their capacities for purposive action'. Green and Ward define the term 'state organisational deviance' as 'conduct by persons working for state agencies, in pursuit of organisational goals, that if it were to become known to some social audience would expose the individuals or agencies to a sufficiently serious risk of formal or informal censure and sanctions to affect their conduct significantly (for example, by inducing them to conceal or lie about their activities) (2000: 110).

Others are broader still. Matthews and Kauzlarich argue that state harm covers 'state crimes, state crimes that technically do not include law breaking, and social harms caused by the state ... state harms would include all behaviours for which no legal definition of criminality exists, nor any analogous definition of crime exists' (2007: 51).

Is harm helpful?

Approaching the issue of state crime from the perspective of harm has a number of advantages. First, the study of harm 'permits a much wider investigation into who or what might be responsible for the harm done, unrestricted by the narrow individualistic notion of responsibility or proxy measures of intent sought by the criminal justice process. It allows, for example, productive considerations of corporate and collective responsibility. A study of harm also allows – requires – a sharper focus on political responsibility' (Hillyard and Tombs 2007: 19).

Second, it moves away from the state's own legal framework to a wider – usually rights-based – framework: 'international and domestic laws and human rights standards can be used to define certain state activities as criminal. Thus, in defining the activities of a state as criminal, one may employ ratified international law and customary international law (i.e., which may or may not be codified) in addition to domestic law or human rights standards' (Kauzlarich et al. 2002: 176).

Third, it takes a significant responsibility away from the state in terms of *who* decides what is a harm as opposed to a crime, for two reasons. First, it looks at state crime from the perspective of those who are harmed – those 'individuals or groups of individuals who have experienced economic, cultural, or physical harm, pain, exclusion, or exploitation because of tacit or explicit state actions or policies which violate law or generally defined human rights' (Kauzlarich et al. 2001: 176). Second, a people-focused perspective offers a balance for those who see domestic legislation as constructed by ruling elites.[3] Since the state invariably exercises control over any adjudication process, as well as determination of procedures and memberships, then what is defined as state crime may be very much under the influence of the state itself: 'when state institutions and their employees are under scrutiny, the operation of official inquiries and processes of investigation and accountability constitute a terrain on which the "battle for truth" is contested' (Rolston and Scraton 2005: 550). If states exercise that control, then it may be argued that they proscribe the roles of non-state individuals and organisations in such a 'battle' over definitions, thus eroding 'the ability of civil society to expose, name and sanction state crime' (McCulloch and Pickering 2005: 482).

If, as Green and Ward suggest, what is classed as a state crime may be determined through informal or formal censure, then control over the means of censure could significantly determine the outcome (or at least address the asymmetry following on from state control over the process). This is seen as especially important in those states – generally democracies – which tend to be those states with strong civil societies. These provide, as Green and Ward argue, 'a major constraint on state crime' because they include a range of associations which are independent of the state and which are capable of 'articulating norms against which the legitimacy of state actions can be judged' (2004: 186, 187).[4]

On the other hand, harm is a term with wide application. It may relate to enduring adverse consequences to health or career advancement, and involve individuals or groups. At its broadest, it may be ideological discrimination against social groupings; 'we should define crime in terms of needs-based social harms inflicted by the powerful on less powerful people, independent of formal legal institutions; accordingly, actions that contribute to the denial of food, clothing and shelter – and the realization of human potential – should be recognized as crime' (Friedrichs and Schwartz 2007: 4).

In the UK, outside the legal context, defining harm could be problematic. Pemberton notes that 'it is proposed that an individual is harmed through the non-fulfilment of their needs' (2007: 35–6). On the other hand, 'the harm principle is that each person should be allowed to do and say what he or she likes provided that this does not harm the interests of others. Simply because an activity is seen as immoral or harmful to the actor is not a good enough reason to justify criminalising it' (Herring 2004: 21).

What offences are included in state crime and from which countries are they drawn?

Barak defines state crime as 'crimes by the state (that) involve violence and property and include such diverse behaviours as murder, rape, espionage, cover-up, burglary, illegal wiretapping, illegal break-in, disinformation, kidnapping, piracy, assassination, counter- and state terrorism, bankrupting and destroying whole economies, secrecy, unaccountability [sic], corruption, exporting arms illegally, obstruction of justice, perjury, deception, fraud, conspiracy, and the general violation of both domestic and international law' (1991: 274; see Box 7 for an example).

Chambliss (1989) gives examples that include complicity in piracy, smuggling, assassinations, criminal conspiracies, acting as an accessory before or after the fact, and violating laws that limit their

---

Box 7: State kidnapping?

The aftermath of the invasion of Afghanistan had a number of consequences. Several hundred, largely Afghan, nationals (but also including a few UK citizens) were captured or seized and transported round the world, either to Guantanamo Bay in Cuba or to compliant nations, using allied airspace and airports for transit purposes (termed *rendition*), so that they could be interrogated by the CIA, FBI and US military personnel. The President, the Pentagon and the Justice Department all agreed that these were combatants, and thus exempt from US law and any international law and conventions.

    The issue of torture or cruel, inhumane or degrading treatment was another issue since the US had ratified the UN Convention Against Torture in 1994. Like the abuse at Abu Ghraib prison in Iraq, those involved in what amounted to physical and psychological abuse pointed upward to senior armed forces' officials as the instigators; they in turn took their guidance from the administration whose commitment to treatment 'consistent with military necessity' (Bush's phrase) was also matched by a clear if implied message that a war on terror took precedence over the rule of law and human rights. That message was protected by being wrapped in 'grossly inadequate legal advice' and by bypassing 'any legal advice that would have stopped the abuse, short-circuiting the normal decision-making processes' (Sands 2009: 293).

---

activities, including the use of illegal methods of spying on citizens, and diverting funds in ways prohibited by law (illegal campaign contributions), selling arms to countries prohibited by law, and supporting terrorist activities; see Box 8 for an example.

    Many of the types of state crime mentioned by state crime authors are unreferenced or unsupported by specific country instances. Indeed, one of the interesting disconnects is between the types of offences and the countries used as illustrations of country examples.

    Of the nearly 70 countries mentioned by Green and Ward in their book *State Crime* (2004) only 11 could be described as modern democratic states (and a number of the others would be hard to describe as functioning states with any pretence to being anything other than repressive regimes where state crime, however defined, was the norm rather than the exception).

Box 8: Traditional state crime (2)?

'Irangate' began in the 1980s with attempts by the US Government to open a covert dialogue with the Iranian regime, partly in the hope to use this influence with Lebanese terrorist groups to release US hostages in Beirut and partly to pre-empt Russian meddling in any succession crisis that would follow the death of the aged Khomeini. The task of devising a policy towards Iran fell to the National Security Council (NSC), an advisory body that coordinated executive departments' policies relating to national security, advised the President and monitored policy implementation. The NSC way into Iran was to propose a limited sale of arms. After a failure to secure cooperation with the relevant departments, the NSC chose to mount their own operation through the Israeli government and several businessmen intermediaries. The plan, formulated in mid-1985, was for Israelis to sell the arms Iran wanted and for the US to replenish the Israeli stocks.

President Ronald Reagan approved the deal as long as the amounts were modest, did not involve 'major weapons systems' and did not change the military balance in the Iran–Iraq war. If there were any objections, said Reagan, he would take 'all the heat for that' (of the precise timetabling of shipments and presidential approval he later said: 'I don't remember – period'). During 1985 and 1986, with the involvement now of the NSC staff officer responsible for anti-terrorism policy, Lt Col. Oliver North, various shipments were made and profits hidden in Swiss bank accounts (in the event three US hostages were released and three more were taken).

Reagan then wanted congressional funding for the right-wing Contra rebels in Nicaragua. North, who also had responsibility for the Contras within the NSC, was concerned over delays, so at least $12 million from the bank accounts went to the Contras. This was done through North's private funding network for 'Project Democracy', a supply and transport organisation which provided the Contras with weaponry – in direct contravention of Congress's ban on the CIA, the Defense Department and other government agencies funding military operations by the Contras.

When the Iran story broke, Reagan set up an inquiry; there were also three congressional committees and the Special Prosecutor (a Watergate innovation) inquiry. Reagan would admit to mistakes, praising the efforts of NSC senior staff, while the inquiries noted that once Reagan had indicated his support for the Iran initiative, the NSC became enmeshed in a private foreign policy outside the 'traditional jurisdictions' of other agencies – 'a chilling story, a story of deceit and duplicity and the arrogant disregard of the rule of law', according to Daniel Inouye (Chair of the special congressional committee), that developed from the Executive's 'ability to pursue its own ideas of the national interest, free from all checks and balances and free from the law itself'.

In November 1987 the congressional report condemned Reagan for not knowing what was happening when he was responsible for having 'created or at least tolerated an environment where those who did know of the diversion believed with certainty that they were carrying out the President's policies'. The report also objected to his silence during the inquiries which created 'the impression that he does not find these actions objectionable,' actions in which the law was seen as raising impediments to White House goals and as needing to be subordinated to those goals (see Wroe 1992; Report of the Congressional Committees 1987; Tower Commission 1987; Bradlee 1988).

In relation to democratic states, what is surprising is the low level of many of the examples; in a number of cases, there is no evidence that the examples were examples of *state crime*. Thus both the UK and Australia are commented on for police shootings of people with mental health problems. Other examples from other liberal democracies are equally old, episodic or well-worn: removal of Aboriginal children (Australia), torture by France, UK and Greece, death squads in Spain and the UK, state links with organised crime in Italy and Japan, and the involvement of the US, UK, Germany and France in the arms trade (the book also suggests that Belgium was guilty of a state crime of gross negligence in the Dutroux child abuse case).[5]

In relation to modern states, Ross suggests that the most common types of state crime on the basis of chapter contributions from a number of 'advanced industrialised democracies' were: military violence, human rights violations, tax evasion by politicians, torture, illegal domestic surveillance, illegal police violence, corruption and bribery, and cover-ups (Ross 2000b: 5). Other authors draw on specific historical events – Nazi Germany, the US in Vietnam and

Latin America or the French in Algeria – or to well-known cases other criminologists discuss (Italy, Japan and organised crime), low-level (and not necessarily officially-endorsed) police corruption (Australia and the UK), or tangential issues (such as the use of US tax authorities to selectively audit political and other opponents).

Elsewhere in the literature, the discussion is even more limited. Ermann and Lundman (2001) offer the ordinary obedience of a South African police officer and apartheid torturer, the Los Angeles Police Department Rampart Division scandal, and the Challenger space shuttle disaster. Michalowski and Kramer's book on state-corporate crime (2006) discusses primarily corporate misconduct (ranging from Nazi Germany and gender issues to the Exxon Valdez oil spill and the Challenger space shuttle disaster) with nuclear power and the Iraq invasion among the limited examples of state misconduct.

The latest state crime anthology (Chambliss *et al.* 2010) includes examples of crimes and countries as follows:

Offences: torture, bombing, death squads, environmental damage, executions, genocide, war, human rights violations, kidnapping, use of nuclear weapons.

Countries (in the context of state crime): Afghanistan, China, USA, Argentina, Armenia, Brazil, Southern Sudan (Darfur), Democratic Republic of Congo, Ecuador, England, Rwanda, Germany, Japan, Indonesia, Iraq, Iran, Korea, Nicaragua, Chile, Senegal, Somalia, Vietnam.

For those who recognise that the state is not monolithic, the tendency has been to argue that state crime is primarily related to the repressive functions of the state such as national security, where the state, and those agencies of the state responsible for such areas, can, given the purposes of the state, be considered as 'state criminogenic organisations' (Ross 2003: 16). Ross's edited books bring together a number of papers on democratic states – UK, US, Canada, France, Italy, Japan. The crimes include the organised crime and corruption relations with the latter two states, unauthorised intelligence activities in Canada and the US, and state-sponsored violence or terrorism in Israel and France (see Box 9 for an example).

What offences aren't included?

One of the major problems with state crime, of course, is the

53

Box 9: State-sponsored terrorism?

In 1985 the Greenpeace ship *Rainbow Warrior* was sunk, with the loss of one life, off New Zealand. The ship was in the area to monitor French nuclear weapons tests in the South Pacific, a right the French had consistently and vigorously defended. Soon after, two French people were picked up by New Zealand police; one had a false passport, and they made several calls to what was eventually discovered to be the Paris telephone number of the DGSE (the French secret service). They were charged with conspiracy to commit arson, bombing and murder. The New Zealand police tried to unravel how many French personnel had been involved in the operation; the Greenpeace office in New Zealand had been infiltrated and there were sightings of a yachtful of French people in the area, but all those under suspicion managed to leave ahead of the police.

The police had called on other countries for help – the French government originally flatly denied any involvement – but 'there were strong suspicions among members of the New Zealand government, intelligence agencies and police, that cooperation with American and British authorities was being limited because of New Zealand's non-nuclear policy. This suspicion was enhanced by the unwillingness of both allied governments to condemn the bombing, even when it was acknowledged to have been the work of the French government' (King 1986: 193–4; see also *Sunday Times* Insight 1986).

The arrest of the two French agents, together with increasingly strong accusations in the French press as to the origins of the bombing plan, prompted President Mitterrand to set up an independent inquiry under Bernard Tricot, a senior civil servant. Tricot interviewed the Defence Minister, the head of the DGSE, his deputy, Mitterrand's military chief of staff and the agents who had been on the disappearing yacht. This report, intended to be made public, argued that six DGSE agents were sent to collect information on Greenpeace's South Pacific activities and that there was no plan to sink the *Rainbow Warrior*. According to Tricot, there may have been an unlikely misinterpretation of orders, or orders given verbally, and the possibility that officials might have conspired 'to keep part of the truth from me'.

Both the Defence Minister and the head of the DGSE resigned on the grounds that each was concealing information from the other, but both were blamed by the government for the attack;

> the government in turn never initiated a promised inquiry, refused to apologise and certainly had no intention of handing over the agents named in Tricot's report for trial. Indeed the government was eventually successful in ensuring that the two arrested agents, who were sentenced to ten years' imprisonment, served their sentence on a French military base in the Pacific.

availability of evidence. Two issues pertain here; the source of evidence of actions or decisions to be labelled state crime and, in the words of Donald Rumsfeld in 2002, the unknown unknowns (or, as he rephrased it: 'simply because you do not have evidence that something exists does not mean that you have evidence that it doesn't exist' (Press Conference, NATO HQ, 6 June 2002)).

To use his range of felicitous phrases, most state authors know about the known knowns – publicly available information from a number of sources. The problem for many state crime authors is that those sources tend to be limited to official papers or records and the limited geographic and subject matter focus of the material produced by activist NGOs such as Amnesty International, Human Rights Watch and Global Witness. Indeed, many authors have to draw upon official reports and inquiries, set up as often as not by the states themselves as a consequence of public or other extra-state pressure.

While they might not like it, such material may be all that is available until archives and other historical sources are researched. One response by state crime authors is thus to assume the known unknowns – that state crime is an integral aspect of state conduct even if there is no evidence to support the assertion, taking into account the assumptions to be made about criminogenic organisations or, as discussed below, the nature of state-corporate crime.

Indeed, their scepticism is often confirmed retrospectively. In 1957, for example, the core of a nuclear reactor at Windscale nuclear processing plant in the UK caught fire. During the lengthy attempts to put the fire out, it produced clouds of radioactive contamination. The official response was to play down the significance of the fire, and its aftermath, with only a short-term milk production ban. A 'thorough-going' inquiry by Sir William Penney was commissioned but, in raising possible charges of faulty judgement by staff, and faulty instruments, the report was seen as a threat to continuing US cooperation in developing the UK nuclear weapons programme by 'shaking confidence in British technical ability' (Horne 1989: 54). As Alistair Horne, Harold Macmillan's official biographer, later showed, some of its findings were put into a White Paper and the rest buried; the Prime Minister personally 'instructed the Atomic Energy Authority not to permit any leakage of the Penney Report, to the extent that all prints of it obtained from the Stationery Office were to be destroyed; so even was the type sent to the printers' (Horne 1989: 54).

The real difficulty is how to address the unknown unknowns – the possibility or presence of state crime in areas of state activity where none has been suggested or evidenced or expected. For example, it has been argued that organisational deviance may occur in 'a society with a strong competitive *ethos* … a socially developed fear of failure … an increasing commodification of all human relationships and practices, an ever increasing number and frequency of transactions which at the same time are less open to scrutiny, and a capitalist economy constantly pushing people with targets to hit, promotions to seek and demotions to avoid, recessions to try and survive, and so on, can thus be seen as a society likely to engender corporate crime' (Slapper and Tombs 1999: 161–2).

If one transfers such themes to the public sector, and if one acknowledges harm or injury, irrespective of intention, as the basis for the study of state crime, then the inquiry into the Mid Staffordshire NHS Foundation Trust may well suggest to state crime authors that the health service could be one of the unknown unknowns now worthy of study; the third in a series of inquiries was announced in June 2010 to look into what the government minister called 'a tragic story of targets being put before clinical judgement and patient care, focusing on the cost and volume of treatment not the quality'.

As the first inquiry reported:

> We noted that much of the board's time was taken with the process of the application to become a foundation trust, including considering issues such as business development and marketing. Members of the trust's board were adamant that the quality of care had always been a top priority for the trust. They were not, however, able to point to evidence of any significant scrutiny of standards of care of patients that they had undertaken. Many members of staff at all levels and in different professions told us that the trust's priorities had been finance and achieving foundation trust status … (Healthcare Commission 2009: 111)

While it may not have led to the quoted 'excess' number of deaths reported by the first inquiry, it certainly led to harm – what the second inquiry termed 'so many accounts of bad care, denial of dignity and unnecessary suffering' (Francis 2010: 50).

The irony is that when such perspectives are identified they, like the more traditional areas, are not seized upon by state crime authors for original or empirical research into state crime. Ironically the latest state crime anthology includes a call not for more empirical work (of which there is little) but for more conceptualisation (for which there is still a need but less so than the empirical work necessary to evidence the concepts):

> ... if all we ever do as critical criminologists is produce powerful quasi-sociological, or perhaps quasi-journalistic reframings of press, NGO and court reports on crimes by the powerful, that may be enough. If, however, our goal is to develop sociological analyses of state crime that move beyond debunking the image of the sovereign states as a beneficent provider of social well-being, we may need some additional theoretical tools. (Michalowski 2010: 29)

Themes and issues from other disciplines

Some criminologists acknowledge that they may have arrived late to an area of study where 'many of the key contributions to the study of state crime have come from outside the discipline of criminology: notably from political science, international relations and anthropology' (Green and Ward 2005: 431). The point about the contributions from 'outside the discipline' – and they are not restricted to political science, international relations and anthropology – is not that they consider state crime as a core component of their discipline, or label the issues they discuss as state crime (although they use their own equivalent terms). The relevance is the range of relevant perspectives that they bring to the debate on activities, decisions, motives and issues that involve states and criminality, as well as examples from those perspectives.

International relations

The conduct of states – and what is a state – is clearly a longstanding issue for those studying international relations. The discipline brings three important dimensions to the study of state crime: state-to-state relations, offences states can commit, and who is responsible

57

for adjudication. This is particularly true this century, when the development of international law sought to curtail wars originating through unilateral state 'aggression'. To do this, it has specifically had to address what is a state, and what crimes it could commit:

> the outstanding feature of the last half a century is the decisive change from a legal regime of indifference to the occasion for war, in which it was regarded primarily as a jewel, a means of settling a private difference, to a legal regime which has placed substantial limitations on the competence of states to resort to force ... by 1939 a norm of illegality had appeared as part of customary law based upon a considerable state practice and instruments the obligations of which were accepted by virtually all states ... in particular the acceptance by the majority of states of the criminal character of illegal resort to force, or at least the major forms of resort to force, has considerable significance in supporting, and raising to a higher power, the norm of illegality. (Brownlie 1963: 424)

A number of conventions and treaties occurred during the twentieth century, beginning with the end of World War Two because the 'dramatic results of the failure to maintain peace by a system of alliances, the geographical extent of the war and the enormous loss of life, the chaos which followed, all these tended to create a climate favourable to a new approach' (Brownlie 1963: 51). The focus on war as an international crime against mankind was developed through regional treaties, such as the North Atlantic treaty or the International Conferences of American States, extended to encompass genocide (1948) and developed following major events such as the Nuremberg Tribunal (whose principles on crimes against peace, war crimes and crimes against humanity were later codified into international law by the International Law Commission of the United Nations in 1950).

The clarity of international law (as well as the roles of a permanent international body (the United Nations) and, later, an international court – the International Court of Justice that deals with state-to-state issues) and the conduct of states has been substantially, but not entirely, addressed. The question of what is a state has been defined, since the issues of criminality that international law seeks to address only apply to those countries or regions or population groups accepted by each other as states.[6]

Of particular interest, therefore, has been the concept of the state. This applies in terms of both who may be a perpetrator of offences under international law and who may be afforded protection against such perpetrators:

> a considerable number of conflicts in recent times have raised the question of whether a particular entity was a sovereign state or merely part of the state accused of aggression ... questions which have arisen or may arise include the possibility of unrecognised states and *de facto* governments committing aggression, the necessity to protect territories under special regimes under the law, and the nature of the geographic limits of state sovereignty for the purpose of determining what is an unlawful infringement of that sovereignty. (Brownlie 1963: 379)

The point of the international law dimension is that once a state is recognised as a state, then questions of neutrality, right to self-defence, and the right to collective self-defence, can be determined as part of the process in trying to define what is or is not a crime in terms of one state's conduct towards another. Thus, the study of international relations has sought to address what crimes a state might commit in breach of international law, how these are adjudicated, and what sanctions may be imposed as a consequence.

In international relations, state crime – 'which are directly imputable to the state' – would be those crimes identifiable by the fact that 'the act is carried out as part of a state policy', involving those exercising government authority and covering 'government's actions, or those of its officials or private individuals performed at the government's command or with its authorisation' (Jorgensen 2000: 77, 70).

Of course, states can commit illegal acts against non-states,[7] and it should be noted that international relations now seeks to address states' conduct towards non-states, its own citizens and citizens of other countries. This is because international or transnational bodies have issued guidance on issues beyond state sovereignty. Thus the UN has developed what is described as the International Bill of Human Rights, while the Council of Europe developed the European Convention of Human Rights (a number of whose articles have significant implications for state crime).

There are three dimensions to international law: how states deal with other states, how states deal with their citizens, and how states deal with those states whose conduct towards their citizens is seen to be unacceptable under international law. Breaches may be considered illegal acts and, in certain circumstances, the perpetrators as war criminals. In terms of the UN,

59

the scope for the use of force is closely circumscribed under international law and Article 2(4) of the UN charter states: All members shall refrain in their international disputes from the threat or use of force against the territorial integrity or political independence of any state, or in any other manner inconsistent with the Purposes of the United Nations. The exceptions to this are the use of force when mandated by a competent organ of the UN (usually the Security Council acting under Article 42 of the Charter) or the use of force in self-defence (under Article 51). Self-defence is itself subject to qualification. Proportionality of response is also a key concept in determining the legality of the use of force. (Youngs and Oakes 1999: 25)

Under the UN Charter, non-violent measures may be taken to address what the Charter calls 'any threat to the peace, breach of the peace, or act of aggression'. If these fail to work, the UN may authorise under Article 42 'such action by air, sea, or land forces as may be necessary to maintain or restore international peace and security' (subject, of course, to the requirements of Article 51 whereby any state can undertake individual or collective self-defence if an armed attack occurs against them).

Written international law, and international conventions translated into domestic law, provide the basis of a universal standard – and a possible useful benchmark against which to judge those countries of an equivalent level of development which do not sign up to them. For example, the US has made it plain that it 'could pick and choose those rules which it wished to follow, and in other areas dispense with multilateral rules and proceed according to its own interests' (Sands 2005: 20; see Box 10).

Caution needs, however, to be exercised in relation to customary international law – law that is uncodified. Nevertheless, the Statute of the International Court of Justice notes that the court will apply 'international custom, as evidence of a general practice accepted as law, and the general principles of law recognized by civilized nations' – for example, conduct such as the general diplomatic immunities or slavery.

Given the efforts at international level to control the conduct between states, these have also been extended to deal with intra-state issues – for example, when a state acts against its citizens, or against those citizens who form a significantly homogenous group to support demands for self-determination or secession. On the other hand, the relationship between international law and conduct of

Box 10: Friendly fire?

In 1979 Grenada had been the subject of a bloodless coup by the New Jewel Movement (NJM), an amalgamation of socialist groups seeking the removal of the corrupt democratic regime. NJM metamorphosed itself into the People's Revolutionary Government (PRG) with Maurice Bishop as Prime Minister. PRG was not enthusiastic about parliamentary democracy or human rights, but keen to promote economic self-sufficiency, with grudging support for the latter from the World Bank and the UK House of Commons Foreign Affairs Committee (which both acknowledged, as the former noted, was performing economically and fiscally better than its predecessor whose mismanagement of the economy, abuse of human rights and corruption precipitated the coup).

The relatively pragmatic approach of its politics and the issue of power-sharing split the PRG. A bloody coup ended with Bishop's death and the establishment of a Revolutionary Military Council (RMC) in October 1983. Cuba condemned the RMC; other Caribbean countries, particularly those belonging to the Organisation of Eastern Caribbean States (OECS), wanted more concrete action to block the threat of instability and Marxism spreading outward. While their formal relationship hardly gave any of them 'the right to call for an invasion of another state under any circumstances' (O'Shaughnessy 1984: 156), they quickly overrode the plans of the larger Caribbean heads of government groups to handle the matter internally by 'inviting' the US to join in a combined military invasion. The US government had already directed a task force heading to the Lebanon towards the island to 'reassure' the 1,000 US students at medical school on the island, resolving en route to intervene militarily. This justification, like other claims about arms caches and Cuban military build-up, was unsubstantiated; see Zunes 2003).

The UK government had already discussed the issue and dismissed any idea that they would join in an invasion led by neighbouring countries (see Wilkinson 2009). Geoffrey Howe, the Conservative Foreign Secretary, also announced that he knew of no intention of a US military invasion, but that 'it is only prudent that when Governments of democratic countries are faced with such circumstances they take steps to provide for the rescue of their citizens if necessary. That is the reason for the presence of the naval vessels.' He also, unfortunately,

61

mentioned that his government was 'keeping in the closest possible touch with the United States Government'. This was either a mistake or a misunderstanding because a few hours later the marines were landing; the Reagan administration had 'deliberately misled the British' (O'Shaughnessy 1984: 171) and US officials 'were acting under strict instructions not even to allow any suspicion to get out' (Smith 1990: 128).

The United Nations passed Resolution 38/7, which deeply deplored what it termed 'a flagrant violation of international law and of the independence, sovereignty and territorial integrity of that State'. Privately, the furious British Prime Minister, Margaret Thatcher, was to say: 'we in the Western countries, the Western democracies, use our force to defend our way of life. We do not use it to walk into other people's countries, independent sovereign territories' (Smith 1990: 131; see also Urban 1996). In public, however, the Conservative government refused to condemn the intervention, disingenuously arguing that the Americans' action was the result of 'applying their judgement to the circumstances as they saw them', but that their action was not the 'correct action' that the British government would have chosen.

sovereign states towards their own citizens is less clear-cut. In many cases the perpetrators of such actions are 'not considered criminal by those in their own society, since their behaviour conforms with the expectations of others in that society. To call their behaviour deviant only makes sense with reference to some standard at a superior level (e.g., international law and universal norms)' (Neubacher 2006: 788).

Is international law universally applicable, however, and should it apply to those states which do not ratify or endorse its purpose or use? In such circumstances are states that do not ratify or endorse international law deviant in not so doing or only when they act in a way that breaches the law? Who determines what type of intra-state conduct should be subject to international standards, and under what conditions? Russia took three years to decide that the Chechen Republic was to remain part of the Russian Federation (see Jorgensen 2000: 135–7). It was later to claim that the conflict – which could be seen by others as a 'blatant denial of the right of a people to self-determination' (Jorgensen 2000: 137) – was both an internal disturbance and terrorist-inspired. Russia's conduct in relation to Chechnya, and certainly its interference in the sovereign state of Georgia on behalf of Russian-speaking Georgians living in

South Ossetia and Abkhazia (allegedly at the latter's request), could be seen as breaches of international law. As a member of the Council of Europe, Russia would also appear to have broken every article in the European Convention of Human Rights, but in neither case has its conduct been subject to formal censure.[8]

Further, the intervention of one state into the affairs of another, whether or not sanctioned by the United Nations, raises issues as to what may be considered 'deviant' or 'acceptable' in terms of the general intention of international law. It also raises the contradictory issue of whether self-determination, protection of minorities and human rights may take precedence over state sovereignty.

In terms of 'acceptable' state aggression or violation of another sovereign state, the criteria are usually: right intention ('for the common good, not for self-aggrandisement or because of hatred of the enemy'), a just cause ('self-defence, defence of others, restoration of peace, defence of rights and the punishment of wrongdoers'), proportionality of ends ('whether the overall harm likely to be caused by the war is less than that caused by the wrong that is being righted'), and last resort ('is the use of force the only, or the most proportionate, way that the wrong is likely to be righted') (see Bellamy 2006: 122–3). Thus, 'in addition to self-defence and UN authorised action, it is increasingly, although by no means commonly, accepted that the unilateral use of force by a state may be justified on grounds of overwhelming humanitarian necessity where there is convincing evidence, generally accepted by the international community as a whole, of extreme humanitarian distress on a large scale which requires immediate and urgent relief' (Bethlehem 2004: para 14; see also Foley 2010; see Box 11).

The potential contradiction in relation to international relations has not gone unnoticed:

humanitarian intervention is one of the most controversial concepts in world politics. It opposes directly the sacred rule of sovereignty. After the end of the cold war, however, it has been perceived as a possible instrument of international community aiming at changing the world for the better ... the system of states has its own logic, which is not necessarily humanitarian. Its basic premise is that states, especially great powers, are still centred on their power and welfare. As a result, the use of force in pursuit of human rights seems to stand in opposition to the national interests of key actors in international relations. (Domagala 2004: 3)

Box 11: UK intervention in Kosovo

The UK stance from the start of the break-up of Yugoslavia in the early 1990s was an orchestrated policy by John Major's government designed to fend off the need for intervention, based on what one critic termed 'an unsustainably narrow conception of the national interest' (Simms 2002: 343). This policy was reversed under the incoming Labour government of 1997 who saw the importance of doing something about Bosnia as 'primarily that of cementing a relationship with the US' (Chandler 2000: 187). In relation to Kosovo and the basis for NATO's intervention and the UN's subsequent support, the unilateral declaration of independence on the basis of ethnic self-determination, and the subsequent humanitarian crisis it initiated, were recognised as the prime considerations. The UK, as part of NATO, was involved in the bombing of Serbian civilian and military targets in 1999 to put pressure on the Serbian government, followed by the invasion of Kosovo, to end Serbian ethnic cleansing.

The use of NATO military force has been criticised, since the 1949 North Atlantic Treaty is about a collective self-help in face of attack, rather than the other way around: 'in order more effectively to achieve the objectives of this Treaty, the Parties, separately and jointly, by means of continuous and effective self-help and mutual aid, will maintain and develop their individual and collective capacity to resist armed attack'. Further the bombings were not supported by the UN Security Council although the NATO presence in Kosovo was undertaken under a UN mandate following a Resolution (1244) two days before the troops arrived. Serbia has unsuccessfully challenged the actions as a war crime.

In other words, what triggers a 'just war' intervention is not straightforward, not always altruistic, and not always free from allegations of a war crime or the 'the sacred rule of sovereignty'. Thus the question of state interference to protect others is not only a contentious issue, it also raises questions of intent and opportunity (for example, Charles Haughey established his Republican credentials by planning shipments of weapons to Northern Ireland to support the beleaguered Roman Catholic minority; see Box 12).

Thornberry (2005) writes that the 'concept of humanitarian intervention deserves more serious consideration for the future, although

Box 12: Governmental gun-running

At the onset of his ministerial career in Ireland Charles Haughey led a plan to arm a minority group in another sovereign country (see Joyce and Murtagh 1986; Walsh 1986; Sachs 1976; *Magill* 1980; Kelly 1971; O'Brien 2000). In 1969 an experienced intelligence officer in the Irish Army, James Kelly, was in Derry to witness the violent police reaction to Catholic unrest. Senior Cabinet ministers, including Haughey, were demanding that the Prime Minister, Jack Lynch, do something to protect the Northern Ireland Catholic population. Although aware of the military and economic consequences of direct intervention, Lynch, arguing that the Irish government could not stand by and see innocent people 'injured and perhaps worse', had hoped for some form of UN intervention. While this failed to materialise, the government had also decided to set up field hospitals in the border areas, considered the re-equipment of the army, publicised information on events in the North to attract international attention, and set up a £100,000 fund for the 'relief of distress' suffered by victims of the continuing violence.

These measures did not satisfy some members of the Cabinet – who thought Lynch was refusing to consider the use of force to end partition – and many members of the public. On the other hand, Northern Ireland activists took Lynch's words of 'no longer standing by' as evidence that concrete help would be forthcoming. A series of emissaries journeyed south to lobby politicians and particular members of the Cabinet sub-committee dealing with the North, including the Minister of Defence and Haughey. The latter had sole responsibility for the funds for the 'relief of distress' which were intended for distribution through the Irish Red Cross.

Kelly made his reports to Neil Blaney, the Minister of Agriculture, and Haughey after his visits to the North. Kelly had no reason to doubt that his intelligence gathering was officially authorised. He had been sent North by the Director of Intelligence, and on one occasion had been accompanied by an official from the government's propaganda unit formed to create an international awareness of events in the North. Kelly had a meeting in October 1969 with 'representatives of defence committees' from the North who 'considered the acquisition of arms for defence purposes a necessity'. After this, he arranged for Haughey to pay much of the relief money into a Dublin account for a Northern Ireland community committee, from where Kelly intended to draw the money necessary for the purchase of arms. In April 1970, after some delays organising transport, Kelly arranged for 6.8 tons of arms and ammunition to be flown by charter plane to Dublin. Kelly, still thinking he was on an official mission, made no secret of the shipment and asked the Department of Transportation to 'facilitate the flight'.

The Department passed the information to the Ministry of Justice, whose minister ordered the shipment to be seized on arrival (Kelly got wind of this and cancelled the shipment). The Ministry's senior civil servant, believing that 'at most, a caucus was involved and that Government qua Government were not behind the arms conspiracy', went to the President and then to the Prime Minister. Kelly was arrested some days later on charges of trying to import arms illegally, as were Haughey and Blaney, who were sacked as ministers after they refused to resign. The case came to court in 1970; charges against Blaney were dismissed, and the remaining defendants were acquitted after the jury essentially accepted that whatever the legalities, the planned importation of arms was generally assumed to be an official government strategy that was legally acceptable. Later the Irish Parliament's Committee of Public Accounts looked at the expenditure of the 'relief of distress' funds but found no one 'guilty' of the misuse of public funds.

its application is also fraught with dangers to international stability. He continues:

> One of the greatest challenges for the international community is to provide an instrumental framework to give substance to its glimpse of the essential oneness of humanity through the gauze of multiple sovereignties and cultural and national diversities. Human rights are strong on principle, strong on mechanisms for dialogue with governments, but relatively weak on 'emergencies' of a humanitarian nature. This imbalance has the potential to encourage adventures beyond the legal framework on the basis of claims that the system is irredeemably sclerotic. But unilateral rescue exercises raise issues of motive and authority ... (Thornberry 2005: 129)

Another important dimension that international law brings to the study of state crime is offences. Article 5 of the Rome Statute relating to the International Criminal Court spells out the offences over which the ICC has jurisdiction – genocide, crimes against humanity, war crimes, and the crime of aggression (see Box 13 for a recent inquiry in possible offences). Aggression had been excluded until the international community agreed a definition and the conditions under which the court will exercise jurisdiction; in June 2010 this was finally achieved. A 'crime of aggression' is now defined as the planning, preparation, initiation or execution, by a person in a position effectively to exercise control over or to direct the political or military action of a state, of an act of aggression which obviously breaches the UN Charter. The 'act of aggression' means the use of armed force by a state against the sovereignty, territorial integrity or political independence of another state. These include: the invasion or attack by the armed forces of a state of the territory of another state, or any military occupation, however temporary, resulting from such invasion or attack, or any annexation by the use of force of all or part of the territory of another state; bombardment, blockade or an attack by the armed forces of a state on the land, sea or air forces, or marine and air fleets of another state, using guerrillas or mercenaries to carry out aggression on their behalf.

As an investigable offence it reinforces the definition of who may be held responsible, but in terms of its use (and thus a potential state crime), it does not take effect until one year after ratification by 30 states – which in practice means not before 2017.

The final dimension is the question of who is the perpetrator under international law. There is no doubt that individual public officials, or groups of officials, can commit crime. The United Nations War Crimes Commission and the Nuremberg Tribunal are important because they raised the question of state crime, in the sense of a 'country' committing crime – collective criminality – and whether a country can be punished. The concept was not unknown – the discussions on genocide included having criminal responsibility extended to states, as well as governments and governmental institutions (see Brownlie 1963: 152).

Some commentators have argued that a criminal state is a 'nonsense': 'Drost rejects the concept of the criminal responsibility of a state under international law, but believes that it is possible to imagine a criminal government' (Jorgensen 2000: 69). However, as Jorgensen points out, 'states, like corporations, can only function by means of natural persons, their agents. It has been demonstrated that criminal law principles do not preclude imputing the acts and intentions of the individual to the corporation, as if it were a natural

67

Box 13: Crimes under international law?

The continuous Israeli–Palestinian conflict has led to both sides resorting to the use of force in ways that do not comply with the various international conventions and laws on armed conflict and which also involve indiscriminate actions against civilian groups.

In addition, Israel has waged economic warfare against the nascent Palestinian state to ensure that as a matter of state policy Palestine could never offer either a sustainable state or an economic base for state formation. The conflict has decimated the economy of the latter: 'in general, it has been estimated by the Palestinian Economic Council for the Development and Reconstruction (PECDAR) that the Palestinian economy has suffered a total loss of $19.9 billion, due to the Israeli policy of closures and incursions from September 2000 to September 2004' (AMAN Coalition for Integrity and Accountability 2007a: 8).

Reconstruction of the Palestinian state also attracted millions of dollars of donor aid, much of it wasted when 'all the efforts towards improving living conditions, building roads, building water treatment plants, electricity plants and garbage dumpsites, constructing schools, hospitals and clinics, even traffic lights which were all donated by the international community from 1993–2000, were systematically destroyed across the West Bank and Gaza strip by the Israeli occupation during the second Intifada' (AMAN Coalition for Integrity and Accountability 2007b: 18).

Both the incursion of Israeli settlements and the building of a wall have continued to restrain any economic and political development. The UN Human Rights Council set up an independent fact-finding mission under Richard Goldstone, which noted both the military and economic activities of the Israeli government:

> From the facts gathered, the Mission found that the following grave breaches of the Fourth Geneva Convention were committed by Israeli forces in Gaza: wilful killing, torture or inhuman treatment, wilfully causing great suffering or serious injury to body or health, and extensive destruction of property, not justified by military necessity and carried out unlawfully and wantonly. As grave breaches these acts give rise to individual criminal responsibility. The Mission

notes that the use of human shields also constitutes a war crime under the Rome Statute of the International Criminal Court.

The Mission further considers that the series of acts that deprive Palestinians in the Gaza Strip of their means of subsistence, employment, housing and water, that deny their freedom of movement and their right to leave and enter their own country, that limit their rights to access a court of law and an effective remedy, could lead a competent court to find that the crime of persecution, a crime against humanity, has been committed. (Human Rights Council 2009: paras 1732, 1733)

Of course, as the Mission noted, neither domestic nor international courts were particularly effective when it comes to dealing with such states. In the case of the wall:

In 2004, the International Court of Justice issued an advisory opinion on the legality of the Wall being built by Israel, at the request of the United Nations General Assembly. The Court stated that Israel must cease construction of the barrier, dismantle the parts of the barrier that were built inside the West Bank, revoke the orders issued relating to its construction and compensate the Palestinians who suffered losses as a result of the barrier. Israel disregarded the views of the Court and construction of the Wall continued. In 2004 and 2005, the Israeli Supreme Court, sitting as the High Court of Justice, ruled that some parts of the route of the Wall violated the principle of 'proportionality' in both Israeli and international law, causing harm to an 'occupied population' and that the construction of the structure should be done in a way to lessen the prejudicial impact on the rights of the resident Palestinians. The Israeli Court ordered the rerouting of different portions of the Wall, but considered the structure legal in principle. (Human Rights Council 2009: 54–5)

person. The question is which wrongful acts and states of mind may be imputed to the state so as to make the state criminally liable' (2000: 76).

In case of Nazi Germany, where the 'only effective sanction for crimes against peace is the punishment of the individuals and members of governments directly involved', the International Military Tribunal at Nuremberg expressed the matter clearly: 'crimes against international law are committed by men, not by abstract entities, and only by punishing individuals who commit such crimes can the provisions of international law be enforced' (Brownlie 1963: 154). The Nuremberg Tribunal considered the applicability of the concept of criminal organisations to 'condemn the entire state apparatus' but with sanctions imposed on those directly responsible rather than a collective punishment (1963: 151).

Further, the Tribunal articulated the concept of criminal organisation as a group (by involvement or knowledge) 'bound together and organised for a common purpose' or with a common plan of action, where the members could be accused both of involvement and of knowledge. This in turn meant that 'the notion of organisational criminality goes further in making each individual within an organisation susceptible to punishment, rather than directing the punishment toward the organisation as a legal entity' (Jorgensen 2000: 69). Thus 'a declaration of criminality against an organisation such as a state need not expose the entire population to the threat of punishment, but enables the members of the government and significant numbers of key criminals to be tried individually' (2000: 69).

Politics, political philosophy and anthropology

Why states act criminally within and between recognised geographic boundaries, and the underlying institutional and decision-making processes, have also been of interest to those studying politics and political philosophy. Here the academic focus has been on both policy-making and political motivation. Of particular interest are the dichotomies relating to issues of ethics and morality in everyday life, politics and public life. This may include discussion ranging from whether individuals are innately good or driven by self-interest, to the behaviour of the rulers and their treatment of their own citizens or those of other states.

While political scientists publish extensively on state formation, what comprises a state, policy-making and decision-making, power and the executive, and so on, they have not spent much time discussing state crime – even where some of the issues have a resonance with aspects of organisational deviance. Much orthodox politics and political science research takes the state at face value, with a focus on legal and institutional aspects.

Where allegations of 'illegal' or 'unlawful' acts take place, the absence of an appropriate conceptual or methodological framework means that the discipline tends to class them at the least as atypical or, more usually, as a force of circumstance. If the allegation is pursued, and even if there is any consequential official inquiry, then both politicians and political scientists have tended to dismiss the conduct as an irrelevant *ad hoc* necessity, with little focus on why such conduct occurs from the perspective of the person as an official or one of the leaders of the state of which they are a part (see Box 14).

Box 14: Force of circumstance? Sinking the *Belgrano*

The return of the Falklands Islands to Argentina had always been on the Argentine agenda (see Burns 1987) ever since a 1968 draft (but unsigned) Memorandum of Understanding recognised the possibility of a British government ceding the Islands' sovereignty to the Argentines. This would be subject to the safeguarding of the interests of the islanders, who wholeheartedly rejected any ties with or takeover by Argentina. For Argentina, the issue was more than a question of a return – it was about unresolved history and a useful rabble-rousing call for politicians – and so they were never likely let the issue rest. On the other hand, the British were happy to maintain contact, since an ongoing process postponed the inevitable compromise.

To successive British governments this compromise had to be leaseback – the transfer of sovereignty with the islands administered by the UK for a given period. This could not be announced publicly as it was recognised that such an option would also require prolonged discussions to 're-educate' British public opinion and the islanders in its favour. Continuing Argentinian pressure was regarded as a priority for the collection of intelligence information, but within that priority was ranked 'in a relatively low category' within the FCO, as was the need for a UK presence in the area.

When an Argentinian invasion was launched, followed by the dispatch of a UK military Task Force to retake the islands (during ineffective US-led discussions over a potential peace deal), a military threat from an Argentinian aircraft carrier led to changes in the UK Rules of Engagement (ROE) to allow it to be attacked. When it was lost by the UK submarine that was following it, the target was replaced by the Argentinian *Belgrano*

---

cruiser, which was sunk, committing both sides to military action.

While there may be no link between the continuation of the peace plan process and the sinking, there was controversy over the gap between the existing British ROE (see Cardosoo *et al.* 1983; Dillon 1989; Gavshon and Rice 1984) and the attack. Lord Lewin said later that in war 'opportunities must be taken while they exist; there may not be a second time' (Freedman and Gamba-Stonehouse 1990: 265–6). The controversy arose from the British Prime Minister's comments broadcast on the radio after the event, about the location, direction and threat posed by the *Belgrano*. This raised the question as to whether the ROE were changed, whether the Argentinians knew about the change and whether the cruiser was sunk within or outside the international law governing the right of the British government to retake the islands under the provisions of Article 51.

The argument that such an attack was seen by both sides as a legitimate act of war should be qualified by the argument that the UK was not at war. The sinking took place not under rules of war but under UN Articles 73 and 51 whereby the British Government was, under Article 73, the recognised administering authority for the Falklands, and had an 'inherent right of self defence under Article 51' with the right to use the minimum force necessary to deal with the Argentinians.

Margaret Thatcher's comments then required ministers and civil servants to consider how to defend her line that the cruiser was a legitimate target within the ROE and thus lawfully sunk within the terms of international law. The ROE had been changed a number of times during the Task Force's journey to retake the Falklands, including addressing the aircraft carrier as the threat to the Task Force; 'it is clear ... that ministers wished to ensure that any attack should be mounted only if there was evidence of a direct threat to the task force ...' (Freedman and Gamba-Stonehouse 1990: 252).

Francis Pym, the Foreign Secretary, who was responsible for peace negotiations, wrote to the Prime Minister about the last warning change (on 23 April, warning of an attack to any approach that 'could amount to a threat to interfere with the mission of the British forces'). Both he and other ministers were less concerned with the subsequent ROE changes – which they thought fell within the 23 April warning – than whether they would be fully understood externally. Hence he and the

Attorney-General wanted to ensure a 'way in which our action would have to be publicly defended and its legality defended', less because they were concerned about the legality of the attack on the *Belgrano* than about public and international perceptions. Consequently a further warning was issued on 7 May, to 'reduce the possibility of misunderstanding' and be more explicit about the geographic area to which the 23 April warning applied (see Foreign Affairs Committee, 1985).

There followed ministerial meetings with senior civil servants to manage government statements on the alleged progression of timely warnings of changes to the ROE and how the *Belgrano* fell within their scope. This was later the subject of a court case; one of the civil servants involved (Clive Ponting) leaked information on the meetings on the grounds that the government had manipulated its ROE to fit its military purposes, misled Parliament and continued to give an incorrect impression about the threat posed by the *Belgrano*: 'we were not telling a direct lie ... it was all right to imply this as long as we did not explicitly state it as being correct' (Ponting 1985: 133). The sinking of the Belgrano was investigated by the Conservative-dominated Commons Foreign Affairs Committee which concluded that it was the responsibility of Ministers to decide what information to withhold on national security grounds and that the sinking of the *Belgrano* was rightly authorised for 'legitimate military purposes'.

The question of utility or pragmatism, where the end may justify the means, is one much discussed by political scientists and political philosophers. Certainly for liberal democracies, the morality and motivations of rulers and the influences or environment that affect them are studied by both anthropologists and philosophers. Indeed, one perspective from the former goes back to a basic building block of political life – often termed 'small politics' – and one which also has resonance in terms of harm and human rights.

This involves the routines and interactions of everyday life in any community. Frederick Bailey, a social anthropologist, noted in his research that 'a central concern of the enquiry has been definitions of the moral being: finding out and explaining where people think it proper to draw the line between treating man as an instrument and granting him the status of a human being' (Bailey 1971: 4). Just how far leaders of a community or a society are expected to be moral beings, he argues, however, is less important than the point of leadership:

73

everyone claims to be acting for the general good, and I
suppose many would not be able to act with such passionate
intensity if they did not also sincerely believe that they were
fuelled on altruism. But the fact remains that even such people
will encounter others whom they perceive as motivated by self-
interest, who advocate opposing policies, and who therefore
must be tripped up, knifed in the back, or in some other
way disposed of so that the general good may be served. No
statesman is effective unless he knows the rules of attack and
defence in the political ring. (Bailey 1969: xii)

This becomes a dilemma that has continuously engaged political
philosophers. From Aristotle and Plato, through Augustine and
Machiavelli to Hobbes, Locke, Paine and Rousseau, the roles and
responsibilities of the rulers are invariably considered in terms of
the capacity of the rulers to resort to any means to achieve their
objectives (or, on occasion and invariably coincidently, objectives that
benefit those over whom they ruled). This would include their being
prepared to become 'involved in, or invited to such things as: lying, or
at least concealment and the making of misleading statements; breaking
promises; special pleading; temporary coalition with the distasteful;
sacrifice of the interests of worthy persons to those of unworthy persons
...' (Williams 1978: 59). As Williams suggests, it is 'a predictable and
probable hazard of public life that there will be these situations in
which something morally disagreeable is clearly required' (1978: 62).

On the other hand, and especially for the study of state crime in
a liberal democracy, motive is important. Much attention has been
given in the political philosophy literature not only to the self-interest
of human beings but also how far such drivers are inherent in the
conduct of rulers and how far they are shaped, revised or curtailed
according to the nature of the political, legal and institutional context.
As Nagel suggests (1978: 76):

There is, I think, a problem about the moral effects of public
roles and offices. Certainly they have a profound effect on the
behaviour of the individuals who fill them, an effect partly
restrictive and significantly liberating. Sometimes they confer
great power, but even where they do not ... they can produce
a feeling of moral insulation that has strong attractions. The
combination of special requirements and release from some of
the usual restrictions, the ability to say that one is only following
orders or doing one's job or meeting one's responsibilities, the

sense that one is the agent of vast impersonal forces or the servant of institutions larger than any individual – all these ideas form a heady and sometimes corrupting brew.

Another label? State crimes in other disciplines

The 'brew' Nagel refers to above is not labelled *state crime* but clearly addresses aspects of that issue. Indeed, one of the features of using other disciplines is being able to identify the themes which, within the state crime context, would be seen as relevant aspects. For example, political philosophy recognises the concept of organisational deviance, even if it is not called that. Nagel's comments about moral insulation are echoed in the corporate sector literature; Punch notes that 'size, complexity and differentiation in large corporations can contribute to lack of control and poor communication, to obfuscation of authority, and to deviant subcultures' (Punch 2000: 274). Similarly, Nagel's argument that 'public acts are diffused over many actors and sub-institutions; there is a division of labour both in execution and in decision. All this results in a different balance between the morality of outcomes and the morality of actions' (Nagel 1978: 83), also reflects Punch's view that 'corporate affairs may be conducted in such a way that managers feel far removed from the consequences of their actions and depersonalise the effects of their decisions' (Punch 2000: 274).

In the study of international relations, the label is determined by offences, for which the generic term *war crime* is normally used instead of state crime, if only because the crimes invariably involve violent conduct by a state against its own citizens or those of another state. The components of each crime are generally defined and understood in international law:

- *Genocide* means any act – killing, causing serious bodily or mental harm, preventing births, removing children and 'deliberately inflicting on the group conditions of life calculated to bring about its physical destruction in whole or in part' – which is intended to destroy, in whole or in part, a national, ethnic, racial or religious group.

- *Crime against humanity* means any act – murder, extermination, enslavement, deportation, imprisonment, sexual abuse, persecution on political, racial, national, ethnic, cultural, religious, gender grounds, apartheid, enforced disappearance, and so on – as part of a widespread or systematic attack directed against any civilian population, with knowledge of the attack.

- *War crimes* mean 'grave' breaches of the Geneva Conventions during conflict, including murder, torture, 'wilfully causing great suffering, or serious injury to body or health, destruction of property, not justified by military necessity, denying prisoners 'of the rights of fair and regular trial', unlawful deportation or transfer or unlawful confinement, attacking civilian populations not actively engaged in fighting, incidental loss of life or injury to civilians and to the natural environment, using gas or poison or other types of weaponry, rape, causing starvation, and so on.

At the same time, and again not using the term *state crime*, much of the political discipline-related debate on what would be regarded as state crime by criminologists is about what political science calls 'dirty hands'. John Parrish suggests that among those who have practised the trade of politics or reflected on the character of public life, 'it has long been a truism that significant moral dilemmas arise more frequently within the political arena than they do anywhere else. Power seems to invite its practitioners to do what would be unthinkable to them in ordinary life: indeed, it often seems to insist that doing the unthinkable has, because of their public responsibility, become not merely their prerogative but their duty' (Parrish 2007: 2).

The term 'dirty hands' is used for such duty, but more about state crime as a means rather than an end: 'sometimes political actors ought to sacrifice their own moral integrity in order to achieve some overriding moral good' (Dovi 2005: 129). It is possible that this inevitability dissuades a focus on the act or decision and encourages attention on the tensions between politics, especially democratic politics, and the question of ends versus means where that end is to the benefit of the citizens or the avoidance of harm.

Here the discussion in the literature is not on the crime but on the contradictions associated with such conduct: 'paradoxically, moral leadership sometimes requires doing wrong in order to do right, and that understanding this marks a practical appreciation, on the parts of both political actors and objective observers, of an awkward, limited, but realistic pairing of ethics and politics' (Shugarman 2000: 11; see also Walzer 1973).

Summary

The literature on state crime proposes a wide range of crimes that are or have been committed by the state. Similarly, the international relations, political science and political philosophy literature also discusses activities and decisions that are state crimes, even if they are labelled differently.

Overall, the common theme to the definitions is that it is crime initiated, approved, committed or condoned by the state for state purposes; here the state comprises those responsible for its policies, direction and so on. In most definitions that follow the theme, this rules out crime by public officials for personal or partisan policies. It does not necessarily rule out those who commit state crime on the basis of a misinterpretation of the intentions of the state or on a unilateral perception of what the state requires of them.

The framework used to determine what is a state crime could include codified international law, customary international law, domestic law and the concept of harm. Concept of harm helps address whether or not breaches of regulatory or administrative law, or indeed any official conduct, whether or not it breaches any formal legal rule, should be classed as a 'crime', because it is the harm or the abuse of human rights that may form the basis of determining the crime. On the other hand, these latter two concepts can be difficult to apply because their status as universal standards may be as much a social construct as the laws they may supersede as the basis for determining what is a state crime.

In any discipline, the concept of crime by the state is not a significant discipline topic. Apart from the international relations and criminology disciplines, other disciplines see such conduct from a perspective that is more about political imperatives and necessities than legal breaches. There is limited crossover use of material from the various disciplines.

The state crime literature carries few examples relevant to the liberal democratic state; much of the literature either focuses on the same examples or draws on countries where such examples are commonplace and the only benchmark would be universal harm and human rights standards. The topic, as it stands, is more concentrated on the definitional quagmire than on an evidence-based approach grounded in empirical research.

The state crime literature spends little time drawing on other disciplines to define the state but abrogates to itself the focus on crime, for which it often takes a traditional perspective in terms of

77

a focus on state repression or coercion. The literature outside the discipline also recognises the capacity of the state to commit crime, collectively and individually, at domestic and international levels. On the other hand, much of the relevant political science and political philosophy literature argues that what may be labelled state crime may be instigated or undertaken for the best, as well as the worst, of intentions. They thus bring some very different perspectives to those generally used in the state crime literature on *why* – the motives for state crime.

Notes

1 One related issue, discussed further on p. 43 ff, is not just the question of what is a state, but also who is a state official. The United Nations Convention against Corruption is the latest official attempt to define a state official as: (i) any person holding a legislative, executive, administrative or judicial office of a State Party, whether appointed or elected, whether permanent or temporary, whether paid or unpaid, irrespective of that person's seniority; (ii) any other person who performs a public function, including for a public agency or public enterprise, or provides a public service, as defined in the domestic law of the State Party and as applied in the pertinent area of law of that State Party; (iii) any other person defined as a 'public official' in the domestic law of a State Party.

2 There is, however, a debate to be had (but not here) about whether human rights are a construct of agreements between rulers and the ruled or should be considered an innate universal right. Some argue that, 'as rights are won through political struggle they represent the interests of a number of social groups and, consequently are contradictory by their very nature. Therefore, there are probably too many tensions inherent within a human rights framework to make it a useful normative base for social harm' (Pemberton 2007: 35–6). While there may also be debates about what such a standard should contain, most state crime commentators appear to follow the view of human rights as universal and 'that people have such rights even in societies in which the rights are neither recognised nor respected' (Raz 1996: 255).

3 This may be an important perspective for those criminologists who believe the state constrains what is a state crime through its control over legislation and then seeks to evade responsibility and accountability for those actions and decisions which could be considered as state crime.

4 This also assumes a coherence among civil society about what is a crime. However, there may be as many labelling issues here as there are about what comprises state crime among academic authors. For example, a British Social Attitudes survey (Johnston and Wood 1985) noted that, in

relation to everyday financial misuse (such as paying in cash, cheating the benefits system) 'looking for explanations of censoriousness or tolerance, we do not find formal props, such as the legality or illegality of the action, very helpful ... when laws or rules are known to be at odds with common practice ... people in all subgroups tended to come down in favour of practice; or at least they did not judge breaches of the rules very harshly' (1985: 138). In the area of benefits fraud, many claimants 'were willing to admit that their activity had been illegal but they did not feel that it had been "criminal". They were angry at being treated in exactly the same way as "real criminals" such as murderers' (Rowlingson et al. 1997: 114, 116).

5 Given that the Vatican City is classed as an independent country, it might also be worth considering if the various country allegations of cover-ups of sex abuse cases and protection of those involved could be viewed as state crimes.

6 For example, Taiwan (which claims to be the legal government of China following the flight there of the national government in 1949 after defeat at the hands of the communists) is not recognised as an independent state by many countries, although it keeps indicating its intention to declare itself to be one. China, which displaced Taiwan in the UN and lays claim to it on the basis of a one-China policy, has threatened to 'employ non-peaceful means and other necessary measures to protect China's sovereignty and territorial integrity' against the island. The 1971 UN Resolution (2758) stated that 'the representatives of the Government of the People's Republic of China are the only lawful representatives of China to the United Nations' and 'to expel forthwith the representatives of Chiang Kai-shek from the place which they unlawfully occupy at the United Nations and in all the organizations related to it'.

7 For example, Tibet self-proclaimed independence in 1911 but it was never recognised as an independent state, although it was operating as one until the Chinese invaded in 1950 and reclaimed the territory as its own.

8 In 2006 the Parliamentary Assembly of the Council of Europe passed a clear rebuke, accusing Russia of murder, enforced disappearances, torture, hostage-taking, and arbitrary detention in Chechnya. It also stated that 'a fair number of governments, member states, and the Committee of Ministers of Europe have failed to address the ongoing human rights violations in a regular, serious, and intensive manner, despite the fact that such violations still occur on a massive scale'. Russia, which responded by saying that its intervention had led to 'huge' progress in human rights in Chechnya, remains a member of the Council of Europe.

Chapter 3

Themes from the state crime literature: motives

Introduction

Within broad terms of motive, the state crime discipline has two perspectives. The lesser perspective of state-corporate crime also includes motive in that the relationship between the state and the corporate sector determines both the propensity to crime and also who acts on behalf of whom and how in the relationship. Most state crime authors look outside such a relationship for explanations of drivers or motives for state crime, primarily to organisational deviance. It is a usual perspective, more generally applicable across a range of crimes and countries, but it does have the drawback, certainly in terms of the perspectives of political science and political philosophy, of assuming that conduct that may be labelled a state crime is deviant behaviour by those involved, or by those adjudicating on the behaviour.

State-corporate crime

The concept of state-corporate crime adds three dimensions to the study of state crime. First, it argues for a broad interpretation of crime in that the types of offences range across a number of the state's activities, responsibilities and obligations. Second, it distinguishes between an intention for the crime to take place, and allowing it to take place. In other words, it argues for a dual approach in terms of how the crime can happen and thus provides a context that is more flexible in terms of looking at state crime in developed societies. Third, it provides the explanation of the motive. In this last dimension, however, it is also more restrictive in its use since it takes a partisan view of the basis of state crime.

The state-corporate crime perspective can trace its provenance to the early literature on white collar crime: 'a crime committed by a person of respectability and high social status in the course of his occupation' (Sutherland 1983: 7). From the outset, Sutherland's argument when he first published on the subject was that criminal behaviour, when linked to wealth and power, and in the hands of those senior enough to make the necessary decisions, meant that many cases would never get to court, given the complicit relationship between the political and economic elites (see Doig 2006).

Friedrichs argues, in relation to the relationship between what he calls governmental crime (see above, p. 40) and white collar crime, that the former 'has both important parallels with traditional forms of white collar crime – in its corporate and occupational forms – and not infrequently important interlocks and interconnections with such crime' (Friedrichs 2000: 74). He suggests that 'governmental crime can clearly produce structural conditions and generate an ambience that facilitates or promotes various forms of white collar crime. The notion of state-corporate crime ... is an important conceptual advance, insofar as it allows for a much clearer exploration of the symbiotic relationship between major forms of governmental crime and white collar crime' (Friedrichs 2000: 74–5).

Kramer and Michalowski (2006) do not see this as restricted to 'major forms', but that the state-corporate approach

> directs attention toward the way in which deviant organisational outcomes are not discrete acts, but rather the outcome of relationships between different social institutions. Second, by focussing on the relational character of the state, the concept of state-corporate crime foregrounds the ways in which horizontal relationships between economic and political institutions contain powerful potential for the production of socially injurious actions. This relational approach, we suggest, provides a more nuanced understanding of the processes leading to deviant organisational outcomes than approaches that treat either businesses or governments as closed systems. Third, the relational character of state-corporate crime also directs us to consider the vertical relationships between different levels of organisational action: the individual, the institutional, and the political-economic. (Kramer and Michalowski 2006: 22).

They go on to argue that the relationship between the corporate sector and the state provides two perspectives on the involvement of the latter. Thus state-corporate crimes are:

> illegal or socially-injurious actions that result from a mutually reinforcing interaction between (1) policies and/or practices in pursuit of the goals of one or more institutions of political governance and (2) policies and/or practices in pursuit of the goals of one or more institutions of economic production and distribution ... The deviant inter-organisational relationships that serve as the basis for state-corporate crime can take two forms. One is state-initiated corporate crime, and the other is state-facilitated corporate crime. State-initiated corporate crime occurs when corporations employed by a government engage in organisational deviance at the direction of, or with the tacit approval of, that government. State-facilitated corporate crime occurs when government institutions of social control are guilty of clear failure to create regulatory institutions capable of restraining deviant business activities, either because of direct collusion between business and government or because they adhere to shared goals whose attainment would be hampered by aggressive regulation (Kramer and Michalowski 2006: 20, 21).

This state-corporate crime interpretation places the corporate sector as the source of criminality, either on behalf of the state or under the protection of the state. With Kauzlarich, Kramer and Michalowski go on to explain the distinction between initiation and facilitation. State-initiated state-corporate crime means that 'the state is actively and explicitly involved in crime commission'. State-facilitated state-corporate crime involves state complicity 'because it or one of its agencies has failed to protect people vulnerable to potentially harmful organisational practices' (Kramer et al. 2002: 278).

The state-corporate crime perspective generally argues that it is the corporate sector that is the predominant partner in the relationship, and is the driving influence in terms of criminal intent. The basis for that, they argue, is rooted firmly in 'the political and economic processes that enable state and corporate managers to pursue plans and policies – often in concert with one another – that result in death, injury, ill health, financial loss, and increasingly in the globalised capitalist economy, cultural destruction, all the while being insulated from the full weight of criminalisation for these actions' (Kramer et al. 2002: 266).

Ross takes a similar approach:

> state-corporate crime ... results from interactions among corporate and state policies, practices and outcomes ... State-corporate crimes are committed by individuals who abuse their state authority or who fail to exercise it when working with people and organisations in the private sector. Their actions and inactions, and the resulting social harms, emanate from these mutually reinforcing interactions among corporate and state policies, practices, and outcomes. (Ross 2003: 148)

Here the state-corporate crime approach seeks to widen the legal framework to be breached, beyond the traditional state crime perspective of criminal law. The distinction between criminal and regulatory law is rejected, although it is argued that, 'from a juridical standpoint violations of regulatory law are not crime'. This is because, despite the acquiescence by a liberal democratic state to competing demands (such as regulatory law addressing health and safety at work), such laws are ostensibly intended 'to address harms that can only be caused by corporate and governmental elites'. They are therefore selectively introduced and applied to satisfy the ruling elites they are 'designed to control' (Michalowski and Kramer 2006: 4). Much of this is related to the (ineffectual or absent) implementation of the public regulatory environment and the resulting 'legal violations that are driven by political and private agendas' (Ross 2003: 154; see Box 15).

Box 15: Unlawful state-business benefits

The possibility of a hydro-electric dam on the Pergau river had been on the Malaysian government's wish-list for some time but first appeared as a firm proposal in a 1987 World Bank power sector report. Although this favoured gas-fired stations, a firm of Australian consultants costed the hydro-electric project at approximately £150 million in 1988. In that year a consortium comprising Balfour Beatty and Cementation International first proposed it as an ATP project (aid for trade, where the aid should be spent on UK suppliers) to the UK Department of Trade and Industry (DTI). The latter's role, if they supported the project, was to pass the proposal to the UK Overseas Development Agency (ODA) to be considered under their aid

---

criteria. Balfour Beatty and GEC had been chasing possible hydro-electric schemes in Malaysia and the Malaysian Electricity Authority pointed to the dam scheme as their 'selected priority project'. The consortium price was initially £200–300 million. The project was also supported by the FCO and passed to the ODA, a department within the FCO at that time, even though the ODA was 'not looking for aid projects in Malaysia which was not among the most needy countries' (Committee of Public Accounts 1994: pvii).

In an arms deal negotiated by Prime Minister Margaret Thatcher in 1988, funding for the dam was included at the insistence of the Malaysian government to offset the costs. A formal protocol signed by an MOD government minister contained a statement that the MOD would use its resources to secure 'aid in support of non-military aspects under the programme' to at least 20 per cent of the £1 billion to be spent on arms purchases (coincidentally and fortuitously the amount that the UK finally paid up for the dam). Unfortunately, Whitehall scrutiny of the document triggered off concern because it was 'policy' not to link arms sales to aid. The law governing the ODA specifically stated what aid money was to be used for: 'the Secretary of State shall have power, for the purpose of promoting the development or maintaining the economy of a country or territory outside the United Kingdom, or the welfare of its people, to furnish any person or body with assistance, whether financial, technical or of any other nature'.

Publicly delinked, the project was landed on the ODA as costs escalated. Cautious because of the size of the project in terms of its budget, the ODA indicated that a full appraisal was required but later claimed it had been discouraged because the contractors, the DTI and the British High Commission had not wanted to disturb 'commercial negotiations' about the dam, especially in terms of opening up opportunities for the power generation equipment industry.

Apart from the enthusiasm of the UK commercial companies, who were pressing the government for a firm decision and had the support of the Prime Minister, and although both sides were aware of the rising costs of the project, both sides also recognised the 'serious' consequences for UK business if the government decided to pull out just before the visit of the Malaysian Prime

Minister and his meeting with Mrs Thatcher at which he was expected to raise the issue. It also coincided with the ODA's decision to send a two-person appraisal team to Malaysia. Their short visit supported the project in developmental terms but the team believed that the project's economic viability was marginal – but 'just about acceptable' at the £316 million price tag. To appraise a multi-million pound project in two days, the ODA said later, was apparently 'a lamentable slip up'. Nevertheless, on the basis of its findings, the Prime Minister made the aid offer to her visitor towards the cost of the dam. Shortly after, the consortium put in a revised project submission of £397 million, claiming to take account of adverse geological faults and other additional costs, as the Malaysian Electricity Authority – Tenaga Nasional – signed a deal with the Balfour Beatty/ Cementation International consortium, with projected costs now £417 million.

The ODA's accounting officer first raised his concerns one month after the 'letter of award' had been made to the consortium and refused to approve the funds. In February 1991 he formally wrote to the Foreign Secretary, Douglas Hurd, twice stating that the project was not value for money (a ministry accounting officer is required to state their objections in writing as well as notifying the CAG; if the minister still intends to proceed, the accounting officer would require 'a written instruction to take the actions in question'). As expected, he was overruled by the Foreign Secretary and the Prime Minister. The concerns reached the NAO after the expenditure of the money had been made, triggering off a report that brought the issue retrospectively into the public domain and to the attention of two parliamentary committees, the Committee of Public Accounts (PAC) and the Foreign Affairs Committee.

The PAC was unhappy with the deal but failed to secure the attendance of the persons responsible for the commitments and the expenditure. This was left to the Foreign Affairs Committee. Mrs Thatcher refused to attend its hearings – she argued that a convention, 'established since 1945', allowed serving and former Prime Ministers not to give evidence to Select Committees on specific issues – while the Committee had some difficulties accessing personnel, material and information, including the forgetfulness of Lord Howe, the Foreign Secretary (by now a non-executive director of BICC, Balfour Beatty's parent company) in recalling whether or not he was consulted about the dam and its cost ('I just cannot remember').

An action for judicial review was then brought by the World Development Movement, a UK NGO, on the grounds that the legislation governing the ODA precluded expenditure unless there was a genuine developmental basis to the project. The court ruled that the project was so uneconomically sound that it put it outside the scope of the law, finding that the Foreign Secretary had acted *ultra vires* and thus unlawfully in allocating funds that had no 'economic or humanitarian benefit for the Malaysian people' (see also International Development Committee 2000–01; Brazier 1997). The response of Douglas Hurd, the Foreign Secretary, to the Foreign Affairs Committee was that: 'Ministers of the Crown and senior members of the public service have the responsibility of judging where the interests lie ... I think that all of us should be a little careful about saying that they should have followed every exactitude of procedure, even if it meant losing the deal ... One has to be a bit careful about rushing to judgement on that matter' (Foreign Affairs Committee 1994: 38).

The deviance approach

A number of mainstream criminologists would argue that the undifferentiated assumptions underpinning the state-corporate crime perspective are too universal (or simplistic). In relation to the corporate side of crime, some argue that to see all business as potentially criminogenic all of the time, 'as an inevitable consequence of capitalism', is too sweeping a generalisation. Nelken suggests that

> it is well to bear in mind some reservations about the idea that capitalism as such is criminogenic. The argument appears to predict too much crime and makes it difficult to explain the relative stability of economic trade within and between nations, given the large number of economic transactions, the many opportunities for committing business crimes, the large gains to be made, and the relative unlikelihood of punishment. This theory also has difficulty in accounting for improvements in safety and increases in the quality of goods under capitalism. (Nelken 2007: 747)

At the same time, and given that the state-corporate crime proponents believe that the state is a facilitator of crime, it is also not 'convincing to assume that all businesses act as "amoral calculators" and would choose to offend but for the availability of serious sanctions' (Nelken 2007: 747). Nelken goes on:

> The desires to continue in business and to maintain self-respect and the good will of fellow businessmen, go a long way to explaining reluctance to seize opportunities for a once-only windfall ... Trading competitors (as well as organized consumer groups, unions, and others) can serve as a control on illicit behaviour for their own reasons. Law-abidingness can often be definitely in the competitive interests of companies. Marxist theory has no need to assume that all business crime will be tolerated. Many forms of business misbehaviour made into crimes may reflect changing forms of capitalism or inter-class conflict. At any given period, some corporate crimes, such as anti-trust offences, will not be in the interest of capitalism as a whole, so it is important to distinguish what is in the interests of capitalism from what suits particular capitalists. Even if the latter may succeed in blocking legislation or effective enforcement, at least in the short term, this does not prove that it is capitalism as such which requires the continuation of specific forms of misbehaviour. (Nelken 2007: 747, 748)

Of course, what is organisational deviance is, like state crime, also subject to definitional variation; for example, see the variations in the literature that focuses on workplace conduct undertaken by employees (Kidwell and Martin 2005: 5). Much of the focus of the literature is on self-regarding activity by low-status employees, whether stealing stock, manipulating the opportunities presented at the workplace, or defrauding the company or customers in an organisational context (see, for example, Ditton 1977; Mars 1983). The other focus continues to regard business as an aspect of organizational deviance or as providing a 'criminogenic arena' – 'the organisation as a weapon, a target, an offender, a scene of crime, a justification, an opportunity, a means, and as a victim' (Punch 1996: 271).

Much of the organisational deviance literature looks at managers and executives who may act deviantly not only on behalf of the organisation but also against it. In looking at the private sector, Punch discusses a number of contextual possibilities that may trigger corporate deviance in pursuit of corporate objectives. These may be structural – markets (either competition or anti-competition factors); size of organisations (which dilutes both control and responsibility); achieving organisational goals; opportunity; total loyalty to the company; corporate culture – and personal – depersonalisation in deference to the corporate ideologies and practices; corporate-focused rationalisation; business as war; risk-taking; dominant personalities; necessary dirty hands as part of corporate competition; pressure and rewards – which lead to the development of a 'corporate mind'. The mind is attuned to the 'signals' from the corporate environment (what they are expected to do, or what others are also doing, or what it takes to succeed) that are set by the 'fundamental concerns of senior management ... centred on corporate survival, continuity, power, reputation/face, and profits' (Punch 1996: 239).

Further, to fit into and rise up within a company, managers will conform in style and conduct, and collectively will adhere to 'group-think', a reinforcing dynamic that gives managers the rationale for what they are doing and comfort that they are doing what others are doing and what will bring the approval of peers and superiors. The managerial mind thus becomes programmed to 'function in relation to underlying precepts about what business is about as an economic activity – maximising profits, providing a sound return on investment, reducing unit cost, performance in relation to the competition, investing for the future to ensure continuity, and so on. It is not necessarily the case that managers are obsessed with these matters on a daily basis is but rather that they underpin decision-making at crucial moments. By almost automatically drawing upon them executives may consciously, or even imperceptibly, turn to a deviant solution for a business problem' (Punch 1996: 240; see Box 16 for a state example).

The usefulness of the occupational or organisational deviance dimension is, in terms of collective as well as individual activity, responsibility and punishment, in addressing the understanding of *how*, by adding a more general theme of self-regarding activity by organisations and management. The deviant behaviour here is often for the benefit of the organization as opposed specifically for the individual and may also be applicable to public sector agencies and officials.

In such cases state crime could share many of the (not necessarily complementary or related) features associated with such a perspective because, as Croall (2001) notes, occupational offences in institutions often share the same organisational characteristics:

Box 16: Iraq – the state-corporate mind and group thinking

The September 2001 attack by Al-Qaeda on the World Trade Center in New York provided the 'cause' on which President George Bush could hang his long-held desire to invade Iraq. Whatever the reasons – such as the longstanding issue deriving from the inconclusive nature of the Gulf War, the oil-related perspective for ensuring the regime never posed a threat to Kuwait and Saudi Arabia, or a failure to submit to post-Gulf sanctions (see Klare 2004; Gordon and Trainor 2007) – the need to 'create the conditions for the removal of Saddam Hussein from power' triggered off a core, unequivocal and uncompromising source of executive influence and 'the use of preemptive military action to combat terrorism. Preemption would emerge as the overriding idea behind the Administration's foreign policy' (Hersh 2005: 167–8). While 'Rumsfeld pushed and pressured the CIA on covert operations after 9/11, Deputy Defence Secretary Paul Wolfowitz and other neo-conservatives at the Pentagon, and their allies in the office of Vice President Dick Cheney, pushed and pressured the CIA on the toxic issue of Iraq' (Risen 2007: 71).

Once the objective had been determined, the advocacy was variously based on the need to curb a potentially rogue state in the Middle East as a lesson to others (notably Syria and Libya); ensuring a compliant regime in a country with significant oil reserves; re-emphasising a world order based on US strategic interests and those of its allies; bringing democracy to a repressive regime. Whichever perspective (or permutation of perspectives) one takes, the one that was always at the forefront and detailed in specific terms was that relating to WMD. In pursuit of this the neo-conservatives undermined the work of the weapons inspectors, played up partial and unsubstantiated information (including the UK's MI6 report on seeking uranium from Africa) both in relation to WMD and to the Iraq–Al-Qaeda links. They also worked through a non-standard unit (the Office of Special Plans) that 'bypassed the checks and balances of the intelligence community' (Hersh 2005: 222) to provide their version of intelligence to the President and his advisers.

The consequence was not only pressure on the CIA to fall into line but also the CIA senior management's willingness to avoid upsetting the President and 'create a climate within the CIA in

89

which warnings that the available evidence on Iraqi WMD was weak were either ignored or censored' (Risen, 2007: 109). In 2002 the US National Intelligence Estimate was unequivocal about the existence of WMD, further compounding the organisational climate because, as the 2004 Senate inquiry noted, 'the analysis in the National Intelligence Estimate suffers from a "layering" effect whereby assessments were built based on previous judgments without carrying forward the uncertainties of the underlying judgments' (US Senate Select Committee on Intelligence 2004).

Given that the US government had public support, had no interest in the UN (except in how it was thinking[1]) and was happy to go alone (although the UK government was trying to set up either a wider coalition or UN support as part of its self-imposed role of unwavering ally), the WMD issue became the catalyst as common ground to unite the state apparatus. This included Congress, which voted in October 2002 to authorise the use of military force, if all else failed to secure the regime's compliance, behind the inevitability of the invasion (see Cornish 2004); 'in its doctrine of pre-emption (presidentially adjudicated and, if need be, unilateral), the Bush administration challenged not only the prerogatives of the US Congress but also the norms and conventions of international law and society' (Dumbrell 2005: 45).

Initially the official inquiries argued that the intelligence was poor, or poorly analysed, rather then politically influenced. The Senate, however, returned to the topic after some delay. Its second inquiry was published in 2008. After providing an extensive set of quotes from the major political players – Bush, Rumsfeld, Cheney and Powell – it noted that each had used information unequivocally even if it was contested within the intelligence community, used material selectively, and on more than one occasion made unsubstantiated claims (anything specific tended to be incorrect since the intelligence community had few sources on the ground).

The Chair of the committee, talking of rogue actions, 'improper' actions and a 'disturbing picture', noted that their source, primarily the Office of Special Plans in the Pentagon, 'had expanded its role and mission from formulating policy and had inappropriately disseminated an alternative analysis, linking Iraq to Al-Qaeda' that 'the Intelligence Community was unable to substantiate', in order 'to shape and politicise intelligence in order to bolster the Administration's policy of invasion' (US Senate Select Committee on Intelligence 2008: 89). Not that the intelligence community was in conflict with this approach. As the 2004 Senate inquiry noted, the intelligence community 'suffered from a collective presumption that Iraq had an active and growing weapons of mass destruction (WMD) program. This "group think" dynamic led Intelligence Community analysts, collectors and managers to both interpret ambiguous evidence as conclusively indicative of a WMD program as well as ignore or minimize evidence that Iraq did not have active and expanding weapons of mass destruction programs' (US Senate Select Committee on Intelligence, 2004: 18).

The Chair of the 2008 Senate inquiry also noted that

> the Administration's misuse of intelligence prior to the war was aided by the selective declassification of intelligence reporting. The Executive Branch historically exercises the prerogative to classify information in order to protect national security and, unlike Congress, it can declassify information unilaterally and with ease. The Administration exploited this declassification authority up to the war and disclosed intelligence at a time and in a manner of its own choosing with impunity, knowing that others attempting to disclose additional details that might provide balance or improve accuracy would be prevented from doing so under the threat of prosecution. This unlevel playing field allowed senior officials to disclose and discuss sensitive intelligence reports when it supported the Administration's policy objectives and keep out of the public discourse information which did not. (US Senate Select Committee on Intelligence 2008: 92).

Overall, he argued that the leading proponents of war 'spoke in declarative and unequivocal terms about Iraq's weapons of mass destruction programs and support for terrorists. Administration officials often failed to accurately portray what was known, what was not known, and what was suspected about Iraq and the threat it represented to our national security ... Representing to the American people that the two had an operational partnership

> and posed a single, indistinguishable threat was fundamentally misleading and led the Nation to war on false pretences' (US Senate Select Committee on Intelligence 2008: 91).

- because they take place in the private sphere of the workplace they are relatively *invisible* and can be concealed more easily;
- because they are committed during the course of an occupation, they involve an abuse of the *trust* inherent in an occupational role;
- offences are possible by the use of some form of *technical* or *'insider'* knowledge;
- this makes many offences *complex*, and the extent, duration and details of offending are difficult to determine;
- offences may be sins of 'omission' or 'commission', with a long 'paper trail' and cover-ups often being involved;
- many are highly *organised* and involve several participants with differing levels of responsibility;
- in many cases, determining who is responsible is difficult because of the *diffusion of responsibility* in organisations;
- offences also involve different patterns of victimisation, and many offences are characterised as victimless ... in other cases, effects are immeasurable and indirect (Croall 2001: 8–9, italics in original).

On the one hand the state-corporate crime approach may suggest that the propensity for the state to become criminally engaged is determined by corporate imperatives. Others recognise that the state is capable of acting accordingly without external drivers: 'all organizations, and not only the corporate form of trading, can be criminogenic in so far as they tend to reward achievement even at the expense of the outer environment ... This would help to explain why public organizations such as the army, the police, or government bureaucracies also generate crime and corruption (these behaviours are increasingly being included in textbooks on white-collar crime)' (Nelken 2007: 748).

Further, it is important to recognise the organisational structure of government: 'the state does not always or even in the majority of cases act as a unitary force. The state comprises an ensemble of institutions which do not necessarily share a single set of interests and goals ... The same will often be true of large institutional structures within the state' (Green and Ward 2004: 5). At the same time, an awareness of the state less as a monolithic structure and more as an aggregation of organisational components is also important for how it provides explanations of why state crime takes place but also because it recognises the differentiated nature of the state: 'the goals of different organisational units within any government may contradict those of other units. To the extent that pursuit of organisational goals by one governmental unit blocks the attainments of organisational goals by another, the blocked unit may experience pressure toward deviant strategies' (Kramer and Michalowski 2006: 23).

Thus the argument by Kauzlarich *et al.* (2001) about organisational deviance and state crime being less the consequence 'of a few people engaging in immoral, unethical and/or illegal behaviour' than 'state crime as the product of organisational pressures to achieve organisational goals' also makes the point about the relevance of organisational deviance approaches as much to the state as to the corporate sector:

> ... many forms of state crime persist for long periods of time ... and are carried out by many different actors. If the unethical, immoral, and/or illegal behaviour in question were the result of a handful of people, then one would presume that either the activities would desist once those people left the organisation or that there would be other people waiting to fill those roles. Since many state crimes persist over time with different people filling various roles, one can only assume that either there are a lot of immoral people who come to positions of power to carry out the immoral or unethical behaviour, or that there is something about the organisational culture itself which fosters such immorality. In the best case, the organisation itself has a problem screening out immoral/unethical decision-makers. In the worst case, the organisational climate itself fosters, facilitates, or encourages such behaviour. (Kauzlarich *et al.* 2001: 188–9)

This point is worth noting; it raises the question of the *why*, particularly in terms of a liberal democratic state, as well as specific organisations within it. In any case, the organisational deviance perspective is helpful when looking at state crime in the context of the changing nature of the contemporary state. The emphasis on decentralisation and agency autonomy, as well as the changes to the public–private sector boundaries in the past two decades and their increasing closeness of working, has had a significant effect on organisational cultures, and for the potential of organisational deviance and state crime, including in those areas of the state not traditionally associated with either.

Certainly, changes to the contemporary state, and the loci of decision-making, would suggest the increasing 'wider network of governance within states, between states and outside the state/s' which 'provides us with a corrective to the monolithic and unidimensional *feel* to some of the traditional state crime literature' (Jamieson and McEvoy 2005: 519).

Included here (and noting the state-corporate crime argument in relation to state-facilitated corporate crime) is the level of privatisation of state functions as well as the increase in state supervision of those areas where the state retains residual responsibility either on behalf of its citizens or because of the strategic nature of the activity or service. This may require a reassessment of the 'value of new forms of privatisation and (re)regulation, not simply in light of how they restrict access to markets for corporate actors and prevent the production of harms, but also for their ability to encourage or facilitate the production of social harms and crimes via particular forms of regulation' (Whyte 2003: 582).

Nevertheless, delivering state services or functions through third parties or proxies raises issues of whether the state initiates or may be held responsible for state crime through third parties (see Jamieson and McEvoy 2005, on 'othering') and whether, unlike the traditional state-corporate crime perspective, it involves the state as the dominant partner, using the corporate sector to achieve its objectives (see Box 17).

Summary: labelling and motivation – what is included in state crime?

This chapter suggests that there are two main strands: one sees state crime as primarily driven by organisational deviance, and the other sees it as a consequence of its subservience to corporate interests. The former strand addresses the nature of organisations, where public and private sectors share many similarities in terms of a criminogenic organisation. It also complements the material from other disciplines that discusses the state as an organisation of individuals whose collective conduct contributes to state crime, or a collection of public sector organisations which may also be engaged in state crime.

Box 17: Othering offences

Civilians in Iraq in the aftermath of war were unfortunate in terms of the rule of law and human rights, especially in relation to the PMCs:

> ... the contractors escaped scrutiny because they functioned in a legally sanctioned grey area. Under an order issued by the Coalition Provisional Authority, which stayed in effect under successive Iraqi governments, contractors accused of wrongdoing were supposed to be tried in their home countries. The order essentially gave the contractors immunity from Iraqi courts but it did not obligate the United States or any country to carry out prosecutions. Nor were there civil remedies in the case of property damage or wrongful death. Some security contractors had informal compensation programs which paid out cash to aggrieved parties, but such payments were entirely voluntary and haphazard ... The legal ambiguity surrounding contractors was markedly different from the system for the U.S. military. The army set up a formal commission, with offices in the Green Zone, which reviewed damages claims and made payments when troops were determined to have erred in opening fire on property or people. American troops suspected of shooting at Iraqis also faced trial in military tribunals. More than twenty U.S. service members were accused of crimes leading to the deaths of Iraqis, and at least ten were convicted. The military system wasn't perfect, of course. But it provided at least a path to justice. With the contractors, there was nothing but a dead end' (Miller, 2007: 169).

The second strand – state-corporate crime – provides a more focused but more restricted approach in that its assumption about the role of the state driven by corporate interests may be too broad. On the other hand, the development of concepts of state-commissioned and state-facilitated corporate crime provides a more flexible perspective in looking at the state as it develops its roles, in relation both to privatisation and to its responsibilities for regulation of the corporate sector on behalf of those for whom the state, at least in a democratic context, is supposed to work.

Both raise the question of what type of crime is committed, with both strands looking if not to international law then to breaches of domestic law, including regulatory law, or even to harm caused, as the criteria for determining criminality.

Overall, however, where does this leave us in terms of what is state crime and what are its causes? A number of themes are discernible from the literature. First, there are two distinct strands – those that focus on the state and those who see a wider state-corporate nexus (thus opening up the question of an 'establishment' or communities of interest between the state and the corporate sector). Given the complexity of state functions, the role of the private sector in delivering state functions or services, and the role of the state in committing crime through the private sector, some commentators acknowledge the need to be aware of the restrictions of legal frameworks and also the potential for state crime through the failure to act or to enforce legal requirements as much as actively seeking to breach legal frameworks or to inflict harm or injury.

Of course, it may be that within the context of the contemporary state, state crime and state-corporate crime, state-facilitated or state-commissioned state crime, and the organisational deviance approaches may be relevant, depending on which type of, or part of, a state is involved. Further, the literature draws attention to the need to have regard to the informal as well as the formal workings of the state, and those it interacts with; to be aware that the state may act as a single entity or that individual parts may act independently; and to recognise that the crimes that may be committed are extensive and varied.

A number of themes and issues need to be highlighted to provide some contextual issues for assessing state crime in the UK. First, state crime concerns activities that benefit the state. It may include, as Kramer and Michalowski suggest, both breaches of the law *and* failure to exercise due diligence over the official conduct of state officials: 'state crime is any action that violates public international law, international criminal law, or domestic law when these actions are committed by individuals acting in official or covert capacity as agents of the state pursuant to expressed or implied orders of the state, or resulting from state failure to exercise due diligence over the actions of its agents' (Kramer and Michalowksi 2005: 448). This extends the areas of possible state crime because it would include all aspects of the state and all state officials – not only those usually identified as being involved in the traditional types of (coercive or repressive) activity associated with state crime. It may also be worth noting that, as the SCAD approach suggests,[2] whether that means the state *as the state*, as opposed to the democratic state on behalf of its citizens, needs to be considered. Thus, the question of state interest as non-deviant behaviour, or at least non-deviant behaviour within the state, as opposed to the democratic state, should be borne in mind. In other words, what is a state and what are its interests?

Second, in terms of the range of crimes in the literature, most concern the coercive role of the state; fewer relate to the question of crime or harm as a consequence of the subservience of the state to economic interests. Even fewer address crime or harm from other services or functions of the state whose delivery has a beneficial rather than a repressive purpose. This second issue concerns the distinction between state-initiated and state-facilitated crime. It must also recognise the impact of business practices on the public sector in terms of the potential for organisational deviance.

Thus, and particularly in relation to the issue of harm, state crime could encompass both crimes of commission (decisions or actions in pursuit of the state's objectives by illicit means) and crimes of omission (regulatory or other failures by or through the state that fail to stop crime or harm occurring). In other words, what is covered by 'crime', in the legal-harm continuum?

Indeed, the temptation to encompass all state failings as criminal needs to be addressed. In relation to the spy scandals of the 1950s and 1960s, for example, Ross argues that the UK state was 'negligent' in protecting its citizens' national security, thus 'causing a crime of omission, and thus committing a state crime' (Ross 2000b: 15). Such perspectives, however, raise the question of whether more formal frameworks may be more useful to avoid definitional elasticity.

Finally, there is the question of state crime catching up with its operating environment, particularly in terms of the liberal democratic state. It is possible that, given the size and complexity of the modern state and the significant changes to the delivery of public functions and services, insufficient attention has been given to the increase in what may be described as 'routine' unlawful acts or decisions as a consequence of wider official policies and where issues of negligence and failure to act may be more likely to occur:

What is missing is literature about less major offences or 'everyday' violations of rules and general standards by public bodies. Most researchers are more interested in the cases that attract a lot of attention such as large scale corruption, political murder, illegal arms-trading, prison torture, et cetera. Even though that focus is understandable because of the seriousness of the cases, it clearly hinders the development of a body of knowledge on the amount and character of rule and law breaking by government bodies. As a consequence, there is little or no contemporary empirical research available on rule breaking in a broader sense.

We do not know, for example, how often government organisations and officials break environmental and safety laws, nor do we know how their quality or rate of compliance compares to private citizens and companies. Research on these topics is exceptional ... we simply do not know how often (Western democratic) states break the laws and rules that they make. This lack of knowledge is problematic for theories of political and administrative crime, as well as for the body of knowledge of political and administrative ethics and integrity ... This also illustrates the practical importance of the phenomenon. Governmental rule and law breaking is potentially very damaging for the integrity and credibility of the state in general and law and rule enforcement by the state in particular. (Huberts *et al.* 2006: 16).

In other words, what is the scope of state crime in the modern state and what are the different drivers? One of the purposes of this book, unlike most other material on state crime or state-corporate crime, is to look at these issues in a single-country context, and to do so in relation to a contemporary liberal democratic state (and this type of state may be the *least* likely to be involved in state crime). First, however, in order to begin to explore these issues and for the purposes of understanding *state crime*, a sensible start is to unpick the two words and understand what is a *state* and what is a *crime* in the context of such a state.

Notes

1 In February 2004 Clare Short, former Secretary of State at the Department of International Development who resigned after the war ended, announced that the UK government had assisted the US National Security Agency (NSA) in eavesdropping on members of the UN Security Council. Confirmation had come from the sacking of a translator at GCHQ for leaking an email from the NSA. The translator was charged but not prosecuted under the UK Official Secrets Act; Ms Short was implicitly

warned over the confidentiality and collective responsibility pertaining to her ministerial and Privy Council status.

2 'State crimes against democracy' (SCAD) is a state crime concept variant that allows consideration of those actions or decisions that benefit the state as the state rather than the citizens (on whose behalf, in the context of a liberal democratic state, the state is supposed to work). This type of 'harm' is described as 'concerted actions or inactions by public officials that are intended to weaken or subvert popular control of their government', or 'the use of state authority and resources by public officials to achieve political objectives through illegal or extra-legal means' (de Haven-Smith 2006: 333, 334).

Chapter 4

What is a state in the UK context?

Introduction

The following two chapters look at the *state* and *crime* in practice in relation to one state. This chapter is intended to describe and discuss the term *state* and its development within the UK context. For all that the term is used regularly in the state crime literature, it is used very casually and often without a full appreciation of what the component means when applied to a specific country. Rather than using the various approaches to assess examples from the UK, this chapter first discusses the genesis of the state and its development trajectory towards democratisation, before describing the loci of legitimate power within the state. The intention is to understand exactly what may be a *state* in terms of *state crime* and from where the actions and decisions derive that could be labelled state crime.

What do we mean by a state?

The emergence of the state

The concept of a state in the UK emerged from the sixteenth century onwards with the transformation of 'semi-feudal clusters of highly idiosyncratic loyalty networks based on kinship, lordship, and an atavistic attachment to one's immediate locale ... into something resembling a nation to which all subjects gave their undivided loyalty and from which they derived their status as well as their security'

(Smith 1986: 187). The acceptance of a single dynastic authority, however, was nonetheless uneven, marked by the constant fear of threats over the transfer of loyalty to, and the continued stability of, the Crown.

The aggregation of spiritual as well as temporal leadership by Henry VIII offered both supporters and opponents a rallying-point, with the former realising that only the preservation of the new order guaranteed their place in it, while opponents were provided with the rationale for challenging the authority of the Crown. The Crown was convinced that its tenure would be lost without constant vigilance and ruthlessness (whether dealing with internal plots or with external threats). Once identified, real or imagined conspiracies, and the manipulation and exploitation they offered the Crown and its supporters, were based on the premise that not only could the enemy overthrow the Crown but that the Crown alone could identify, confront and defeat the threat (see Smith 1986; Maybray-King 1967).

The monopolisation of military force and coercive taxation, together with the use of dynastic marriages and the judicial exercise of patronage, land and honours as the basis of a mutual self-interest in maintaining the existing order, wedded more and more of the propertied classes to the primacy of the Crown. The Crown was not, however, universally recognised for a number of centuries as legitimate or permanent by those who opposed it, nor was it seen as unchallengeable by those who supported it. Indeed, the history of the UK state was not only about repressing opponents (real or imagined[1]). It was about accommodation and negotiation between the rulers and those of the ruled whose wealth and property ownership allowed them a say in the relationship and whose support was crucial in terms of mutual dependency to preserve the status quo.

The lengthening stability of Crown successions established rules and routines of interdependence between it and its supporters on the right to exercise political power and its exercise in the interests of both. This evolved into an embryonic concept of a more formal relationship and institutions through which that relationship was cemented. That relationship also extended as the state learned to accommodate unrest rather then ruthlessly suppress it, as it did in the early nineteenth century (see Box 18).

The development trajectory then took on (often grudgingly) the reforms necessary to absorb the challenge from first the middle class and then the working class for political recognition in Parliament and channelling it into support for existing institutions and away from radicalism (see Porter 1989: 65–80). Political inclusion as an alternative

---

Box 18: Peterloo and Cato Street conspiracy

The French Revolution offered, as did the later Chartist movement, the threat of mass agitation for reform premised on principles that were alien to the political leadership, who fervently believed that unthinking and unswerving loyalty to the Crown, Parliament and the Church was all that was asked of society at large (see Thompson 1984). Demands for economic and political change were met with repressive state action, culminating in mounted soldiers charging a mass gathering of radical supporters at Peterloo in Manchester in 1819. While there has been argument over whether the Government precipitated the massacre to justify the introduction of repressive legislation (see Walmsley 1969: 37–9, 278–82; see also Marlow 1970), there was no doubt that in the subsequent stand-off the government found a perfect opportunity to present the radicals as the cause of greater violence than themselves by manipulating the Cato Street conspiracy. In a rundown central London stable, some 18 men armed with guns and swords met with the intention of murdering the entire Cabinet at an evening dinner. They were ambushed by a party of policemen and soldiers on the orders of the Home Secretary, who had been forewarned by an informant close to the conspirators' leader, Dr Thistlewood.

The government protected its involvement in the events of 1819–20 by refusing to hold an inquiry into Peterloo and denying any knowledge of its informants' activities. The call by a London MP, Alderman Matthew Wood, for an inquiry into the activities of one of the informants (see Stanhope 1962) was brushed aside by the government on the grounds that, so long as people like Thistlewood existed, the government not only had to use such informants but would be 'highly culpable if they neglected to do so'. Speaking in the House, George Canning defended 'all governments that had ever existed in this or in any other civilised country, for taking the means which circumstances rendered necessary to defeat by the prostitution of wicked men, the plots of men as wicked'. Days later, when the call for an inquiry was finally voted down, Canning argued that such an inquiry would put the government on trial; why, he asked, had he not heard any thanks for 'having incidentally saved the country by their efforts to save themselves' (HCP, New Series, Vol. 1, 1820, cols 54–63, 242–94).

to revolution was paralleled with the exploitation of 'tradition', the monarchy, and the Church to emphasise the importance of the continuing hierarchical nature of politics and society. The first issue to note in relation to the development of the state is the balance of state power and negotiation, intended to ensure the primacy, legitimacy and monopoly of key functions to achieve the maintenance of its existence.

State functions

In terms of understanding the *state*, the focus of state development on establishing and defending geographic boundaries, as well as control and then management of a given space, has been the determinant: 'frontiers define nation-states. They mark the edge of national authority ... They are the object of national defence, they mark the boundaries of national resources' (Horsman and Marshall 1995: 44, 45). The emergence of a state has a number of specific features: 'the growing coincidence of territorial boundaries with a uniform system of rule'; 'the creation of mechanisms of law-making and enforcement'; 'the centralisation of administrative power'; 'the alteration and extension of fiscal management'; 'the formalisation of relations among states through the development of diplomacy and diplomatic institutions'; and 'the introduction of a standing army' (Held 1995: 36).

In terms of state development, however, it should be remembered that 'the state preceded democracy by some four or five centuries' when 'its initial functions were external security, internal law enforcement, and the management of the country's finances' (Bealey 1988: 6). In political shorthand, these might be described as the 'high politics' perspective of the state, those activities and interests that are to be pursued in order to further or protect the viability and status of the state as an independent, geographically defined, functioning entity by those who exercised leadership (see Bulpitt 1983).

As core responsibilities these do not disappear, but their significance or visibility, as well as their short-term or long-term implications and the relative priorities they may be given by elected or appointed officials, may vary. Nevertheless, they will remain central to the role of the state in protecting its identity and primacy. Indeed, Susan Strange's list of the ten 'more important powers or responsibilities attributed to the state, and still claimed for it by many political leaders' (Strange 1996: 73), continues to show an emphasis towards 'high politics' issues (see Box 19).

Box 19: High and low – the roles of the state

- The right to sacrifice the lives of individual citizens is clearly related to the state's responsibility for defending national territory against foreign invasion.

- Maintaining the value of the currency.

- Choosing the appropriate form of capitalist development is generally thought to be a major responsibility of the state.

- Correcting the tendency of market economies to cyclical booms and slumps has been another major responsibility assigned to the state, and accepted from the 1930s onwards by governments of many developed countries.

- Providing a safety net for those least able to survive successfully in a market economy – the old and the young, the sick and disabled, and the unemployed. If the state was no longer so important to civil society as a shield against military attack, it was perhaps still essential as a shield against economic security.

- Responsibility for taxation.

- Responsibility for the control over foreign trade, especially imports.

- Responsibility for the building of the economic infrastructure, from ports to roads, to posts and telegraphs.

- Competitiveness in the world market requires a competitive environment in the national market.

- Marxist writers always counted as the most important attribute of the state a special kind of monopoly – that of the legitimate use of violence against the citizen or any group of citizens.

Source: drawn from Strange 1996: 73–82.

Thus the second issue to understand about a state, is that a state and a democratic state are not necessarily exactly the same thing. Any understanding of state crime has to appreciate that every current liberal democratic state, of which the UK is one, has a history. That history does not necessarily mean that such a current liberal democratic state comes with the same or a specific set of components, nor that the 'democratic' term defines the whole state or all its interests. State formation and development adds or adapts rather than removes or replaces layers.

Opening up the state – moving towards democratisation

Some of Strange's responsibilities of the state would emerge when the state began to change or adapt its relationship with the population, over and above coercion and repression, towards accommodation, protection and inclusion (although often more a consequence of a grudging willingness to make concessions to preserve the continuing basis of the existing system rather than a consequence of either confrontation and conflict, or democratising influences). The evolution of the state, certainly in the western liberal democratic model, followed on from a number of developments in the nineteenth and early twentieth centuries:

> Firstly, the process of urbanisation drew governments increasingly into the planning and provision of public amenities and municipal services and the regulation of the market economy – both to facilitate production and trade as well as check abuses. … Secondly, and inextricably bound up with this process, was the expansion of trade and commerce which both expressed and made possible the rise of a bourgeois class.
>
> This, thirdly, gave rise to the emergence of civil society and the emergence of a public domain, an area of social space between the state and the private sphere in which citizens are able to articulate and pursue their interests in association with others … [and] engendered a growing consciousness which manifested itself in increasing pressure on the state initially for political citizenship (the extension of the franchise and other political rights).
>
> However, the admission of the working class to the political arena eventually produced an escalation of demands to incorporate social citizenship – in other words, demands for both greater access to the fruits of the industrial system as well as greater protection from the vagaries of the market …
> In underwriting the well-being of its citizens the modern state seals its contract with civil society whose interests are its primary purpose to serve. (Doig and Theobald 1999: 16–17)

Broadly, the changes encompassed the role of the state in promoting the well-being of society, the right of citizens to participate in the decision-making processes, and the individual rights of citizens. The changes generally addressed what is sometimes termed the 'low politics' dimension, to contrast with, as discussed, 'high politics', and involved 'civil rights in the eighteenth century, political rights in the nineteenth century, and social and economic rights in the present century' (Blackburn 1993: 2).

The rights, and the basis of the contract, included, according to T. H. Marshall:

> the rights necessary for individual freedom – liberty of the person, freedom of speech, thought and faith, the right to own property and to conclude valid contracts, and the right to justice ... the right to participate in the exercise of political power, as a member of a body invested with political authority or as an elector of the members of such a body ... the right to a modicum of economic welfare and security [and] the right to share to the full in the social heritage and to live the life of a civilised being according to the standards prevailing in the society. (Quoted in Blackburn 1993: 2–3).

Rights and democracy

In relation to political rights, the development of the concept of the democratic state was based upon 'the assumption that citizens have the ultimate say in how they are governed and what decisions are taken in their name ... the institutions of representative democracy are seen as both the most practical and the most desirable methods of giving effect to the popular will' (Greenaway *et al.* 1992: 47). The nineteenth and early twentieth centuries are shaped by the expansion of the electorate, and the increasing impact of organised labour (especially on the introduction of social and welfare legislation), the expansion of the machinery of government to give form and support to the expectations of citizens and interests (from education to trade), and the introduction of policy-based party politics.

Overall, the predominant shift of democratisation was an acceptance that political power is vested in the electorate and their political representatives. With this has come the concept of the public interest as a cumulative response, or giving a purpose, to the various reforms. These include universal suffrage, the increasing interventionist role of governments and the rights of the public – which have shaped the changing formal relationship of the state and the citizens. The ideology of democracy therefore largely shapes what the state does (and the how and why of what it does) by defining both principles and process.

Such a state 'is seen as the institutional embodiment of a concern with the identification and realisation of public interest, with a rational analysis of norms in a disinterested and benevolent manner' (Dyson 1980: 275). It is also seen as having a single, public interest role: 'the state seeks its own legitimation in terms of the common interests of a community. It defines a common culture, and common goals' (Jordan 1985: 2). There is now, among academics, commentators and (officially) practitioners, 'almost certainly a consensus, if not unanimity, that democracy is essentially a decision-making system, assuming certain absences of restriction on free expression, with a hugely developed form of citizenship. Democracy combines freedom of criticism of authority with the rights to organise in opposition to authority and to participate in the making of decisions for the whole community' (Bealey 1988: 1).

In the UK context, whose representative democratic system is one variant of the liberal democratic model,

> policy makers are selected through elections ... though leaders (ministers, etc.) are selected usually by election or appointment within Parliament ... There is a strong element of popular control in this model. Though the people don't actually make policy, they do, through their representative, have some kind of broad influence on policy decisions. Clearly then it is the role of government, according to the conventional view, to carry on the demands of the citizenry as interpreted by their representatives ... The conventional view is very much the accepted way of talking about the British system of government ... Many academic textbooks emphasise elections, the sovereignty of Parliament, and the idea of accountable ministers (advised by expert civil servants) as key policy makers. Practitioners such as politicians, civil servants and local government officers often put forward this view, at least in public. It is frequently used as a language for justifying their activities. (Burch and Wood 1990: 34–5).

The standard orthodoxy would also argue that such democracies are part and parcel of pluralistic societies which have a high level of trust on the part of citizens in, and thus providing legitimacy for, the political systems and their decision-making processes. As Almond and Verba (1965) attempted to claim for the UK, such societies could be seen as 'civic' cultures with a highly developed participant role: 'exposure to politics, interest, involvement and a sense of competence are relatively high. There are norms supporting political activity, as well as emotional involvement in elections ... And the attachment to the system is a balanced one: there is general system pride as well as satisfaction with specific government performance' (1965: 315).

Democratic societies may be aspirational rather than actual in terms of Dahlian goals of 'effective participation' (the fullest means of expressing choice), 'enlightened understanding' (the fullest information for choice), 'control over the agenda', 'voting equality at decisive stages', and 'inclusiveness' (Held 1995: 207), but the rhetoric infuses expectations and agreements between the ruled and the rulers.

Indeed, most liberal democratic countries would profess adherence to participatory, transparent and accountable procedures, to promoting economic development and liberalisation, to improving the social, health and educational prospects of the citizens and providing a responsible and responsive normative political and legal framework. There may be no single checklist of a democratic framework but the textbooks repeat lists of key principles – tolerance, equity, service: probity, and so on – and themes: political legitimacy for the state through democratic elections and peaceful transfer of power; an effective political opposition and representative government; accountability through transparency of decision-making and the provision of information; separation of powers; effective scrutiny of financial expenditure; effective standards of conduct in public office; official competency such as trained public servants; realistic social policies and low defence expenditure; human rights as indicated by freedom of religion and movement; impartial and accessible criminal justice systems; and the absence of the use of arbitrary government power.

The power of the Executive

The current prevailing orthodoxy is that the UK is a democratic state, although it should be remembered that 'democracy is one form of the state' (Dyson 1980: 208). In particular the next issue to appreciate is how the state accepted the process of democratisation, not least because of its ability to deploy the capacity to assimilate the principles and control the process, as well as the roles and responsibilities that legitimised its relationship with the expanding electorate. In this way the state also expanded and realigned itself, but not always in ways that made it subservient to the electorate. In other words, the process of accommodation and inclusion was as much about ensuring the continued primacy of the state, albeit that its identity was modified, so that it maintained its high politics responsibilities while at the same time sealing the contract with civil society by bringing to the fore its low politics roles.

Embedding executive dominance

Until the seventeenth century and the English Civil War, the Crown was the state, and the state was the Crown. In other words, power and authority, including the source of legislation, and all appointments, lay with the Crown. The Crown's authority was divinely derived but its tenure depended precariously on the avoidance of capricious or arbitrary conduct towards, and the expectation of consultation with, those on whom the Crown depended for funds and military support. The coercive powers – such as the right to raise an army or taxation or protect boundaries – resided with the Crown. While the Civil War broke the concept of the divine rights of the monarch it did not break the preference for a hierarchical political structure focused on the Crown as reflecting the interests of the state. What it did was formalise the framework for negotiation and working relationship between leaders and their supporters, whose shared values and interests reflected a relatively cohesive elite.

The 'independence' of Parliament as the voice of the people (or those limited number of qualified property holders eligible to be elected) made it the forum where the conduct of the state and the authority for the exercise of its powers would and should be acknowledged. Parliament was not, however, seen as an independent source of political authority. Rather it was seen as a legitimating source that was to be the arena of perennial negotiation for the next three centuries to maintain a balance between the actions of the rulers and the consent of the ruled (primarily from the elite grouping) but with an overriding duty 'to advance the "national interest" or the "common good" through upholding the independence of government and its primacy in determining policy' (Kettell 2006: 14).

It was accepted that authority lay with an Executive appointed by the Crown but within which the roles and purpose of the state remain largely unaltered. Tant (1993) argues that in the shift from Absolute Monarchy to the advent of parliamentary democracy the debate about government ... focused very largely upon **who** should govern, and on what basis of authority, rather than upon **how** government should be carried on. Initially the main concern was with whether authority should rest with the monarch alone or be shared between the monarch and the unreformed parliament. Subsequently the focus shifted and it was accepted that authority lay with an Executive drawn from the reformed parliament. However, the concept of governmental office and the role of government itself, has remained very largely consistent. Throughout, the office of government has been deemed to involve the reconciliation of the various 'particular' interests in society, with what today tends to be referred to as the 'national interest'; government policy, once made, thereby becomes sacrosanct. (Tant 1993: 89–90, bold in original).

Victorian political leaders followed the views of Prime Ministers like Peel:

[Peel] believed that the executive must give a strong lead to the House of Commons rather than be subservient to it ... Although the Commons retained a reserve power of veto over Ministers, Peel's Cabinet expected to hold the initiative in the conduct of affairs, entirely so with regard to executive action, and largely so with regard to proposals for legislation ... he treated his elevation to the highest office as placing the responsibility upon backbenchers to support the Queen's Ministers in policies which the Government chose to recommend in the national interest. The party behind him existed in his view to make majorities, not to make difficulties. (Read 1987: 98)

Governments were able to continue to exercise political power through the acquiescence of the electorate who were collectively wedded to the existing order through the integration of the symbolic and deferential aspects of society (see Hobsbawm and Ranger 1983). The consequence was a democratisation veneer over a modified but functioning traditional state framework:

the development of a constitutional monarchy meant that governments, while maintaining the fiction of serving the Crown, were also able to gain independence from the Crown whilst at the same time inheriting its old prerogative powers and at the same time appearing to acknowledge the centrality and importance of Parliament. This, plus the increased legitimacy resulting from the creation of a more democratic franchise, meant that the United Kingdom Centre was able to claim authority from both democratic and more traditional constitutional sources. (Bulpitt 1983: 121; see also Kettell 2004: 15)

The development of a party system and the evolution of political parties (which neither had nor have any constitutional or legal status) were never intended to be sources of grass-roots democracy, governmental policies, political control or even party funding. They were in existence to support the candidate, and the party whose leadership was still in the hands of a small political elite which also dominated Parliament and the government (see Pugh 2002; McKenzie and Silver 1968). The role of the former was to allow the latter 'a certain freedom of manoeuvre in order to be able to perform effectively and to be able to take and implement the difficult and unpopular decisions that would invariably be needed to protect the interests of the nation' (Kettell 2006: 14).

The expansion of the roles and responsibilities of the state led, however, to a need for professional competence and a hierarchical civil service structure whose (mainly) male recruitment provided the basis for service, precedence and conformity, underpinned by a common purpose and also cemented in support of elite dominance through class and education imbued from the top down (see Sutherland 1972; Wright 1969).

This was reinforced by an unquestioning service to, and subservience to the interests of, what they perceived to be the state. Indeed, the civil service later formally proclaimed its role as the servant of the State in the 1920s: proclaiming that 'the first duty of a Civil Servant is to give his undivided allegiance to the State at all times and on all occasions when the State has a claim upon his services'. The allegiance and homogeneity was strengthened by shared backgrounds and attitudes that permeated its development, defining its cohesion, its loyalty, its culture and its capacity to coalesce and cooperate to address perceived threats to the state (see Box 20).

The ties that bound the political and administrative world were paradoxically strengthened as that world expanded. As the traditional uses and role of direct individual personal patronage, influence or contact were gradually weakening, background increasingly provided the common link. Furthermore, a shared educational and social

Box 20: Destabilising Parnell

Charles Stewart Parnell (1846–91) was the charismatic leader of the pro-independence Irish Party controlling both parliamentary and extra-parliamentary nationalism that threatened violence in Ireland and chaos in Westminster. While this placed him in a position of immense influence it also left him open to criticism by both extremists and moderates as to where his true loyalties – and thus the choice of means towards achieving Home Rule – lay. In 1882 he sought an agreement with Gladstone that tied him to the constitutional route to Home Rule, a goal Gladstone also accepted. It was opposed by the Conservatives; this view was held not just by the politicians but generally throughout the civil service in Ireland.

After Gladstone's government fell, Parnell was the focus of much attention from the incoming Conservative government and when the opportunity to attack his political reputation presented itself, they were quick to exploit it. In 1887, fortuitously at the time that a special powers law, which the Irish MPs were trying to block, was having its second reading in the House, *The Times* published a series of articles on Parnell's links with terrorism, partly provided by a British intelligence officer (later to become a Home Office 'adviser on political crime' and then Head of the Metropolitan Police CID[2]). This included a bombshell – a letter allegedly written by Parnell in 1882 that suggested he had, for political reasons, condemned the Phoenix Park murders of that year where two senior British officials were killed by Irish nationalists, but that he actually believed that one of those killed 'got no more than his deserts'.

Parnell did not sue the newspaper but a fellow Irish MP did. The defence barrister who also happened to be the Conservative Attorney-General (lawyers in government office were then allowed to pursue private practice; this was ended after this controversial conflict of interest) took the opportunity of court privilege to read out in court other correspondence, all portraying Parnell in the same light as the letter in *The Times*. The letter published in *The Times*, however, later turned out to be a forgery.

Parnell demanded – and got – an official inquiry, whose terms of reference and use of civil servants to trawl for damaging information very much reflected a government determined to use the inquiry for political purposes (see Chilston 1960). As one

> Irish civil servant noted: 'the Government decided I should give
> my services to the new development of the political campaign,
> to wit, to act as Chief Agent on behalf of the Government in
> surreptitiously procuring such evidence and materials as would
> enable *The Times* to sustain, if that were possible, the accuracy of
> the allegations' (O'Brion 1971: 21; see also Cole 1984; Egremont
> 1980). The whole business led to calls by the Liberal opposition
> that it would expose the collusion, a pledge it reneged on after
> winning the next election after 'a clear understanding had been
> arrived at to this effect with prospective successors' (O'Brion
> 1971: 132).

background instilled the qualities which reflect, or were sought by,
those within the political world and which could be taken for granted
without personal assessment or recommendation (see Rosenthal 1986;
Mangan and Walvin 1987; Banks 1981).

These threads ran upward to universities, into the professions,
armed forces, the established Church and the civil service, embedding
an ethos that could transcend public politics:

> the new role of the public schools and ancient universities as
> tutors in leadership provided a common code and grounding
> which always threatened to carry them beyond political parties
> 'in the national interest'. Here, the interpretation of the national
> interest lay not in the emerging democratic state at the end of the
> nineteenth century, but was encoded in a network of personal
> contacts and informal understandings beyond and behind that
> state (Colls 1986: 50).

At the same time, the emergence of mass democracy 'did not
lead to a wholesale transformation in its system of government'
because successive governments 'worked to sustain the pre-existing
structures of power and authority, as well as the ideological norms,
values, and practices embedded within the British political system'.
The institutional framework was also dominated by those who not
only accepted but ensured readily that 'the primacy of executive
independence in determining and implementing those policies
deemed best suited to further the 'national interest' remained firmly
intact' (Kettell 2006: 15).

Government domination of a political world

How was this primacy embedded? The growth in the size of the civil service during the nineteenth century reflected the rise in the volume and range of governmental activity and led to government demands for an increasing share of parliamentary time to process government policy. This was at first an uphill struggle because of the 'conventions and procedures of the House of Commons. So far from being designed to facilitate public business, the lower house still bore the characteristics of a body whose historical function was to criticise government and obtain redress for grievances rather than to assist ministers of the crown to govern the country ... not until after the second Reform Act of 1867 did it begin to recognise that if government now was in reality an organ of the legislature, it must have the right to control the business of the legislature' (Gash 1979: 50; see also Lenman 1992).

Thereafter governments increasingly forced the pace of change. The obstructionist tactics of Parnell's Irish Party during the 1880s prompted several crucial government-inspired reforms that included the closure vote, which could curtail debate, and the guillotine, to speed the passage of legislation. Such reforms lay with whoever commanded the most votes in the House. Contemporary critics of the reforms were well aware of the powers this gave to governments but were unable to halt the changes introduced in the early twentieth century. These ensured governments exercised almost total control over the amount of time for both opposition and parliamentary criticism and scrutiny of government action (and in 1911 destroyed any residual possibility of internal challenge by negating the independent 'referend' role the House of Lords tried to introduce for itself).

The battle effectively left Britain at the start of the twentieth century claiming to be parliamentary democracy but in fact it had seen the consolidation of Executive control and power. Internally, the key to the strength of government from the end of the nineteenth century was the assumption of ministerial collective responsibility, a convention by which all members of the government supported its actions and decisions before Parliament and the public. Along with the parallel convention of individual ministerial responsibility (by which ministers were held accountable for all *official* actions and decisions of themselves and their officials, and ensured the latter had no independent status in terms of accountability) such conventions provided a constitutional wall around the activities of government.

The experiences of the Boer War at the turn of the twentieth century and the First World War taught governments that the Victorian experience of leisurely Cabinets (involving all its members), and lengthy parliamentary discussions were not satisfactory means for handling crises like war. These 'put a premium on decisive leadership, swift action, considerable secrecy, and a certain disregard of traditional scruples about the means used' (Kennedy 1981: 171), with an emphasis on prime ministerial leadership.

The emerging dominance of the contemporary Executive was paralleled by the management of information provided to the press and others as to its business and reputation (see Box 21). The relationship was symbiotic: 'as the makers of news: politicians fired the imaginations and captured the loyalties of journalists. As the purveyors of news to the general public, journalists were equally indispensable to politicians ... That left the press as the best available index to popular opinion as well as the single most convenient mechanism for guiding it' (Koss 1984: 9). Closeness to the press was matched by a growing predilection for the control of the flow of official information: 'without special intercourse it was impossible,' said Joseph Chamberlain, 'to secure in the press an adequate defence of the decisions and policy of Government' (quoted in Cockerell *et al.* 1984: 32).

The special intercourse was achieved through the development from 1884 of the lobby system, by which journalists took their stories directly and unattributably from political sources in part because of shared understandings and values and in part through interlocking relations between commercial and political interests. These ensured privileged access and partisan publications that suited both sides as well as maintained journalists' privileged access to the corridors of Westminster (see Box 22).

The relationship was to be fundamentally determined after the First World War when Chamberlain introduced a press office that focused press searches for stories and controlled access to and information from all areas of government (see Cockett 1989).

The converse – leaking or obtaining official information unofficially – was dealt with firmly with the first Official Secrets Act in 1889, intended to 'provide sterner measures against civil servants who disobeyed instructions and betrayed the trust placed in them by the government' (Hooper 1987: 22). It was not particularly effective and superseded by the 1911 Act which ensured that for almost 80 years what the public largely learned about governments was what governments wanted to tell them; 'the art of government was a

---

Box 21: Manipulating opinion

Roger Casement was a Foreign Office official who wrote a damning report on conditions in the Congo Free State, which was being systematically plundered by the Belgian king; for this he received a knighthood and public acclaim, but disillusioned at the slowness and lack of commitment for reform from the authorities he retired from public service and became increasingly involved in the issue of Irish Home Rule. Spurred on by a belief that Germany would support the nationalist cause during the First World War he went to Germany to win support for the cause. On his return to Ireland in a German submarine, he was arrested and sentenced to death for treason.

His appeal was rejected, and any pressure for a reprieve, whether on humanitarian grounds or the wish to avoid another martyr for the Irish cause, was swiftly diluted by the official making public of Casement's diaries, which graphically described his enthusiasm for homosexuality. As A. J. P. Taylor wrote later, 'the loathsome story has no interest except as illustrating the desperate measures that an Imperial Government will resort to when cornered' (Taylor 1976: 217). In the hands of the CID, the Home Office, the Chief of Naval Intelligence, and the Foreign Office, the diaries were skilfully leaked, with government approval in Britain and America, to politicians, churchmen and journalists in order to discredit Casement: 'the Cabinet was advised on the nature and use of the diaries by the Home Office Legal Adviser, Sir Ernley Blackwell, who counselled more succinctly and explicitly, "so far as I can judge, it would be far wiser from every point of view to allow the law to take its course, and by judicious means to use these diaries to prevent Casement attaining martyrdom"' (Campbell 1983: 419; see also Inglis 1974).

Box 22: Letter from Zinoviev

In January 1924 the first minority Labour government was elected. By October it had lost Liberal support and decided to call another General Election. Two days after Parliament was dissolved on 8 October the Foreign Office received the 'Zinoviev letter', named after its author, the president of the Communist International (the Third International). Addressed to the British Communist Party, it appeared to urge the Party to support the ratification of a treaty and the loan agreed between the Labour government and Russia, as well as implying that the government was susceptible to left-wing pressure and this was a necessary step on the path to revolution.

Authenticated by the Foreign Office, the letter and a draft protest note called for by the Prime Minister, Ramsay MacDonald, were released, without his authority, shortly before the election, by the head of the Foreign Office to the *Daily Mail*. Labour lost the election (although not necessarily because of the publication). The letter was a forgery, either by a British secret agent or by Russian exiles in Berlin on the instigation of the Polish government; it was sent to a former UK secret service agent and on to the head of MI16 (later MI6). It was then passed to the Conservative Party and the *Daily Mail* (in the latter case through Sir Reginald Hall, another former intelligence chief, Tory MP and friend of both the Party chairman and the editor of the newspaper (see Bruce Lockhart 1967; Kettle 1983; Chester *et al*. 1967; Andrew 1985).

The official Foreign Office explanation of the letter's release, together with the protest note, without political authorisation and so quickly, was that it wished to save the government embarrassment from appearing to withhold it while the press had it. This was, if not a degree of disingenuous collusion with press, political and secret service figures, then an incompetent handling of the matter by senior civil servants. Either way, its publication was inevitable; once 'a small, but powerful group of threatened men had convinced themselves that the letter was genuine, their incipient institutional paranoia made it almost inevitable that they should become equally convinced that Ramsay MacDonald was secretly plotting to prevent the letter's publication. It is entirely logical that they should have put the freemasonry of intelligence and ex-intelligence men to work' (Chester *et al*. 1967: 108; see also http://www.fco.gov.uk; yourarchives.nationalarchives.gov.uk).

mystery whose secrets were best understood by experts and that its smooth processes were not matters suitable for discussion and debate in newspapers' (Morris 1984: 371).

Embedding the Executive within the Establishment

At the centre of the consolidation of the Executive within the democratising state was a steady but irreversible process that sidelined the formal relationship between the legislature and the Executive, confirming the continuing decline of the House of Commons as an agency of effective criticism and accountability; 'few front benchers bothered to sit and listen to Members' views and ministers were chosen for their administrative capacity or for their political weight, but debating skill now mattered less ... Around the complex of decision-taking bodies, the Cabinet receded in prominence and the Prime Minister had added to his authority' (Macintosh 1977: 407).

For some commentators the dominance of the Executive had a considerable number of adverse consequences, especially in the failure of Parliament as the counterbalance to, and scrutineer of, the growth of Executive power. The sheer size, number and complexity of departments, together with secrecy and collective and individual ministerial responsibility, were severe constraints on the capabilities of Parliament to supervise and monitor their activities.

With an ineffectual Parliament, and an electorate with a declining participation or interest in politics (reflected in low turn-outs at meetings, low active party memberships and parties' support depending on brand name loyalty), and with 'strong' government, the 'effective power to make or prevent changes' appeared to pass to those institutions such as 'the Cabinet, the Civil Service departments, the professions and the City' (Inglis 1964: 132).

There was an increasing sense of the Executive continuing the tradition of representing a ruling elite or elite grouping within a loose-knit network of institutions – often colloquially termed the 'establishment' – recruiting its members from public schools, socialising them within its large complex institutions and its social and recreational networks of clubs, enmeshing them within secure, financial, comfortable, privileged occupations in the City and the Civil Service, and ensuring a lifelong support of existing government structures, processes and interests.

The centre of this was 'the supremacy of the government in and through parliament as a law-making and law-enforcing body. Because of this the political elite occupies a special position among the elites. Collectively it can, in the last resort, give orders to those who occupy the commanding heights in the economic and social sphere, and it enjoys this power because its organisation is even more comprehensive than that of the largest body outside the political field and because it has the means of enforcing its policy' (Guttsman 1963: 370).

This does not mean that the Executive is inherently monolithic: 'the rulers are not at all close-knit or united. They are not so much in the centre of a solar system, as in a cluster of interlocking circles

... they are not a single establishment but a ring of Establishments, with slender connections' (Sampson 1962: 624). Nevertheless, the rings may be linked by shared interests and backgrounds, ready to coalesce where mutual support and unspoken agreement for reciprocity underwrites the cluster:

> much more in England is done by subconscious influence than by conscious decision, much more by ambient feeling than by identifiable conspirators such as the word 'establishment' suggests. The power of the Establishment, such as it is, comes not from the fact that a dozen people impose their will on the rest of us but from the fact that there is in all of us a degree of establishment-mindedness – that we feel it right that the opinions of such persons should have attention paid to them. (Hollis 1959: 168; see Box 23)

Box 23: Networks and the establishment

The setting up of the 1957 Bank Rate Tribunal, which investigated whether the news of a bank rate rise had been leaked, was implicitly, if not explicitly, the result of Labour MPs' suspicions, as outsiders, that the government, Bank of England and Tory businessmen comprised three mutually dependent groups looking after each other's interests. The subsequent Tribunal report dismissed many of the allegations as gossip and argued that the Bank's non-executive directors acted entirely honourably in giving briefings on potential adverse proposals in the forthcoming Budget. The briefings were designed to forewarn and explain, with the intention of ensuring the maximum support for the government's measures.

The effect of the report was to prompt the study of the existence of informal relationships among top decision-makers, through marriage, social life, work and background. As Richard Chapman pointed out, there was a degree of similarity among those who knew of the impending rise that suggests 'they were drawn from a distinctive group in society, and this gives them certain advantages from the standpoint of common attitudes and makes communication between them easy' (Chapman 1968: 91–2). Linked by education, business, marriage, clubs and, later, peerages, they were part of a 'relatively small, tightly-organised, closely-knit community' where 'much of the business is done "on trust"' (Chapman 1968: 94).

Lupton and Wilson (1969) took the analysis a stage further to explore their argument that 'the basis of informality in social relationships is often a shared social background, which promotes shared beliefs and confidence in customary procedures. It was this evidence of informality and custom which led us to look for common social background, and links between persons other than those arising from formal needs of business life' (1969: 8). Taking the background of ministers, senior civil servants, the directors of the Bank of England, and the clearing banks, City firms and insurance companies, they noted that a majority had received major (and shared) public school and university education, shared club memberships, with a noticeable degree of interconnections through business and family links. One of the questions they raised – and one that had been raised by the Tribunal – was whether being part of such a group could lead to role conflict or conflict of interest. The Governor of the Bank of England had thought not, because 'an honest man must often divorce one set of interests from another' and because 'the national interest' could transcend all other interests.

The paradox of the modern state

How do such developments fit with the perceptions of the modern state? The contemporary British political system of government is seen, as discussed above, as a variant of the democratic state – the liberal democratic or representative democracy model. Like other western liberal democracies, the UK's democratic principles and values are taken as the norm:

advanced, complex economies, industrial and post-industrial, with considerable mixed-economy elements; urbanised societies with relatively high living standards; extensive social services and educational provisions; liberal-democratic political values; parliamentary institutions; free elections and competitive party systems; extensive interest-group participation in policy-making; sophisticated administrative systems, diversified functionally and geographically, subject to the rule of law and other controls; large professional bureaucracies headed by elected politicians. In a world perspective they form an obvious cluster. (Ridley 1984: 8)

The predominant contemporary ideology is assumed to inform and infuse the purpose and focus of all institutions and decision-making processes – making sense of what they do and offering a generally acceptable perspective as to why they do what they do. The paradox of this perspective is that, as Birch (1967) argued, the British political system 'cannot be justified in terms of the ideals of the radical reformers of the nineteenth century', but 'is a well-liked and appropriate system of government for Britain because it embodies and exemplifies many of the values which govern British people in their daily lives' (Birch 1967: 278–9).

In practice the contemporary system is more a constitutional figleaf over a traditional political system that has continuously aggregated power and authority from the top down:

> ... as a realistic description of the policy-making process the liberal democratic model is shot full of so many gaping holes that it is unnecessary to spend much time in criticism ... the democratic sovereignty model finds it hard, if not impossible, to come to terms with most of the political developments in Britain since 1880, namely: the rise of well-disciplined parties; the increasing influence of the bureaucracy; the growth of government; the tendency toward delegated legislation; the mushrooming of interest groups; and the increasing technical expertise necessary for government. These are factors which affect all Western democracies but it could be argued that Britain has fewer opportunities for the exercise of democratic rights than most. (Greenaway et al. 1992: 48–9)

The process has been continuing in institutional and political terms: 'the rise of disciplined parties has in many countries changed the nature of legislative-executive relations. An important function of representatives in most democracies is ... retaining their party in governmental power by upholding its majority in the legislature ... democratic legislatures have declined in all roles except that of supporting executives. Policies are often made by party conferences and transformed into legislation by executives' (Bealey 1988: 40, 41).

Within the Executive, during the twentieth century, the role of dominant prime ministers – Churchill, Attlee, and so on – took on the roles of both the public face of party and government and a central position within the management of government business. The civil service continued to share with governments the importance of maintaining the constitutional façade, avoiding the possibility of exposing the government to criticism, and having a common understanding as to the primacy of state interest, their consequential role and relationship to ministries, and the need for both sides to trust each other to make the departmental structure work and to present a united front publicly (see Helco and Wildavsky 1986). The keys to the organisational dynamics have been caution, incrementalism and reliability, underpinned by 'soundness' – 'a person in whom one can reliably place confidence and confidences' (Helco and Wildavsky 1986: 9), and 'a homogeneity, longevity, cohesiveness and network of contacts and information' that underpins the organisational culture and prime ministerial leadership at the top (Doig 1986: 64; and see Theakston and Fry 1989) (see Box 24).

Box 24: Suez – state crime or political necessity?

In 1955 the nationalist Egyptian government nationalised the Suez Canal Company, the French–Egyptian company that operated the canal. Simple repossession of the canal by force was considered illegal by the Cabinet because the Canal Company was an Egyptian company and Nasser had promised to compensate the shareholders. On the other hand there were few in the Cabinet who did not believe that the canal was an international asset (especially in terms of access to the UK Far East colonies) which Egypt could neither run effectively nor be allowed to use for 'a purely internal purpose'. At the same time, the UK armed forces' Chiefs of Staff warned the Cabinet that troop deployment, already under way, would be a lengthy operation, while the Cabinet itself was anxious not to risk upsetting other pro-British Arab states by any act of aggression.

Various scenarios were proposed in the following few months, with the intention of taking the canal outside the scope of internal Egyptian politics by putting it in the hands of an international agency. An international conference in mid-August sent the Australian Prime Minister to talk to Nasser. A US-inspired Suez Canal Users' Association (SCUA) was endorsed by the Cabinet – and then adopted by a second international conference in London – in September. At the same time, France and Britain called on the United Nations Security Council to push for a solution. In the next month, there was an agreement in New York between the British, French and Egyptian Foreign Ministers on 'Six Principles' for a negotiated settlement. This would ensure that the canal would be insulated from the 'politics of any country' even if there was no clear agreement on how this was to be policed.

The slowness of moving from diplomatic negotiation to implementation – the US was clear that force to ensure the success of the negotiations was not on the agenda – was broken by Israel's invasion of Egypt in October 1956. Following Egypt's failure to respond to Anglo-French demands that the security of the canal zone be guaranteed by its withdrawal from the area, Anglo-French military force landed to safeguard the canal. The official line, as told to the United Nations, was that Britain was 'compelled to carry through' its police action because of the state of chaos that reigned in the canal area.

Prime Minister Anthony Eden had warned the Cabinet some days earlier that military action by Israel against Egypt was likely and could precipitate a crisis. He said that if the Israelis did invade an ultimatum would be issued to both sides to withdraw from the canal area. If Nasser obeyed, his prestige would be 'fatally undermined'; if he did not then there was 'ample justification for Anglo French intervention to protect the Canal'. Of course, Eden added, 'we must face the risk that we should be accused of collusion with Israel' in arranging and then precipitating the circumstances of the ultimatum.

Questions in Parliament about conspiracy, collusion and cover-up began from the moment of the Israeli invasion. The official line was announced by the Foreign Secretary whose reply was unambiguous: 'it is quite wrong to state that Israel was incited to this action by Her Majesty's Government. There was no prior agreement between us about it. It is, of course, true that the Israeli mobilisation gave some advance warning and we urged restraint upon the Israeli Government ... What we are carrying out is the necessary police action' (HCP, 1955–56, 5th series, vol. 558, cols 1569–70). It was agreed in the Cabinet shortly after that this statement was to be the basis of responses to further questions (one minister told his parliamentary critics: 'I think that the honour of our country is safely in the keeping of the Government'). One month later, Gaitskell asked Eden directly in Parliament about collusion and was told that there was no 'prior agreement with Israel or foreknowledge ... to have a shrewd idea of what is likely to happen is quite a different thing from "collusion" ... most certainly we had discussions about plans with the French ... there were no plans got together to attack Egypt'. Denying any conspiracy, Eden finished with one final untruth: 'I want to say on this question of foreknowledge, and to say it bluntly to the House, that there was not foreknowledge that Israel would attack Egypt – there was not' (HCP, 1955–56, 5th series, vol. 562, cols 1492, 1493, 1518).

The Prime Minister's comments about there being no conspiracy were simply untrue; his denial of UK involvement was also untrue. The French had begun serious contingency planning immediately after the seizure of the canal. This soon evolved into joint planning with Israel after (depending on the French or Israeli versions) each asked the other what they would do if either Israelis invaded Sinai or the French invaded the canal area. Coordinated planning appeared to accelerate after the French decided military action was preferable to the SCUA proposals. The Israelis kept up the pressure on the French resolve with repeated warnings about the Soviet build-up in the Middle East and the threat of Egyptian nationalism being exported to French colonies (especially Algeria).

Despite their mistrust of British motives and dislike of British attitudes towards Israel, the Israelis also wanted British involvement on two grounds. First, Britain had an airbase on Cyprus from which it could launch bombers to attack the Egyptian airforce on the ground. Second, Britain's involvement with Israel could ensure that Iraq and Jordan, two Arab countries under British influence, were unlikely to attack Israel's east flank while the Israeli army was in Egypt. The French proposed a plan involving an initial Israeli invasion, followed by a Franco-British intervention to 'separate the warring parties' and seize the canal (Bar-On 1990: 201).

Despite Israeli reservations about offering a plan to the British 'designed primarily to satisfy British political requirements' (and described by them as 'the acme of British hypocrisy'), the French government flew its acting Foreign Minister and a Deputy Air Force Chief of Staff to London in October 1956 to put the plan to Eden and Anthony Nutting, the junior Foreign Office minister. Eden reacted, according to Nutting, with glee and excitement (Eden made no secret of his wish for Nasser's assassination, plans for which were pursued by MI6 (Scott Lucas 2000: 193; see also Dutton 1997: 395)).

The Israelis were still concerned over what they perceived as British duplicity and the possibility of delay before the planned Franco-British intervention. They were keen that the three countries should be equally committed partners and only agreed to carry out the plan after two extraordinary meetings between the three countries, held in Sèvres in France. The first, involving the British Foreign Secretary, agreed the context for the intervention, to give a veneer of legitimacy in terms of international law to UK involvement. The second meeting, attended only by two senior British civil servants (one of whom was the Chair of the Joint Intelligence Committee), concerned a formal written timetable for invasion, ultimatum and intervention (the Israelis wanted evidence of a 'joint' operation). Called by some a Protocol and by others a Treaty, it was signed by those involved; thus, 'secretly, without the knowledge of their Parliaments, their publics and most of their civil servants, and, in Britain's case, her military commanders, Britain, France and Israel had declared war upon Egypt' (Scott Lucas 1991: 247). Although Eden destroyed his copy of the document (he also tried to get the French to destroy their copy[3]) he was later to confirm agreement with the plan.

Ministers and officials were involved not only in the decisions that led to the action but also in those actions to address the consequences, usually through informal and unrecorded decision-making processes. Eden used a small Cabinet committee, the 'Egypt' Committee, which comprised himself and a chosen handful of ministers, meeting frequently but without any formal record of its deliberations, or formal reporting to either Cabinet or Parliament, during the run-up to the intervention (although it could hardly be argued that the Cabinet were not aware of what was going on in their name; see Carlton 1988: 59). This was reinforced by Eden's influence over his ministerial colleagues – the consequence of his long governmental experience, his style of leadership and political loyalty. There had been ministers who were unhappy at the use of military force, such as the Attorney General, Sir Reginald Manningham Buller, who voiced concern over the intervention, but their protests were late and low-key.

The Attorney-General later complained of not being consulted, and argued: 'it is just not true to say that we are entitled under the [UN] charter to take any measures open to us to "stop the fighting"'. He lamely told Eden 'I feel I must frankly say that I think the position of the law officers would become impossible' if a similar situation happened again' (see *Guardian*, 2 January 1987). Eden's line on legal advice from the Foreign Office legal adviser was blunt: 'that's the last person I want consulted. The lawyers are always against our doing anything. For God's sake, keep them out of it. This is a political affair' (quoted in Scott Lucas 1991: 238; see also Dutton 1997: 384).

Eden kept his tactics outside the formal decision-making processes, relying on 'the Suez "insiders" [who] blocked or simply ignored any advice that did not suit their purposes and utilised entirely inappropriate means to justify their actions' (Kelly and Gorst 2000: 5). The government also sought to protect itself through undermining its critics, destroying or concealing documentation and threatening potential sources of adverse comment – including the BBC, although its chair was one of those whose 'perception of the national interest' predisposed them to act in 'ways that could potentially damage the institutions over which they had charge' (Young 2000: 224). As Eden's Press adviser later wrote: "Parliament, the public and the bureaucracy were not only unconsulted, not only surprised, they were deceived ... This is not just moral judgement about deception; it is based on the knowledge that the power of Government to deceive is so immense that fooling all of the people some of the time can successfully and easily lead to fooling them all of the time' (quoted in Margach 1979: 109).

Former ministers like Selwyn Lloyd would defend both the collusion and the deception of Parliament as an 'act of state', justifiable in the 'national interest' (see Thorpe 1980; James 1986; Lloyd 1978). The possibility of an official inquiry was either blocked or manipulated by both parties. Prime Minister Harold Macmillan disingenuously avoided setting one up, while the incoming Labour government of 1964 refused either to release the Anglo-French agreement on grounds of constitutional convention or to accept a Bill in 1966 to set up an inquiry. Labour Prime Minister Harold Wilson was more than willing to shield his predecessor from public scrutiny, accepting like many others in the political world that Suez was done 'in the national interest ... and the swiftly aborted venture in 1966 to re-open the Suez case is good evidence of this' (James 1986: 622; see also Lamb 1987).

The strength of the Executive has also been its capacity to seek accommodation with those it wished to have as allies, who in turn have been able to exploit other facets of democracy – such as lobbying and pressure groups, and the employment of MPs as lobbyists or representatives of interests – to sustain the closeness between the state, and especially the civil service, and corporate interests. In some areas, this was formalised by legislation; thus the 1947 Agriculture Act – intended to promote a 'stable and efficient agricultural industry capable of producing such part of the nation's food and other agricultural produce as in the national interest' – formally required the involvement of the National Farmers' Union in the annual price agreements. Indeed, from the 1954 resignation of Tom Dugdale, the Conservative Minister of Agriculture, for the administrative failings of his staff (over land that was not returned to the heirs of the owners from whom it was compulsorily purchased during the war) to the resignation of another Conservative (junior) minister, Edwina Currie, in 1988 when she said that 'most' eggs were infected with salmonella, the combination of agricultural pressure groups and Conservative MPs ensured that governments were keen to placate and protect the industry.

In part this reflected governmental policy-making and decision-taking need for a continuing bilateral relationship of information, cooperation and mutual understanding that favoured those with continuing access; for example 'in the oil industry, it's not a case that we have a choice, the politics of energy and oil draw us into very close relationships with government' (Grant with Sargent 1987: 100). In part the relationship was based on protecting and supporting British commercial interests and jobs (thus the UK has a taxpayer-funded department – the Export Credit Guarantee Department – that provides insurance cover to exporters when no commercial insurance is available).

Corporate interests, ranging from multinationals to representative associations, established offices and staff to monitor, liaise with, feed information into and report back on the decision-making processes of Whitehall and Westminster. Those without a permanent governmental relations office hired professional lobbyists or MPs to press the industry's message on the policy-makers and the legislators (see Ellis 1988; Rush 1990; Jordan 1991). It was in this space that the negotiations for levels of regulatory control, favourable treatment and financial support took place, where citizen interests had limited access or representation.

The culture extended outwards, where pressure groups, business and representative associations shared the same values and perspectives and an awareness of discretion and mutual support. The culture was supported by a shared world of appointments, discreet access and the traffic of civil servants into business (with a lesser traffic the other way) which reinforced an inner circle of interests which had a continuous involvement in the negotiation of policies and the functioning of the machinery of government (see Jordan and Richardson 1979, 1987; Richardson and Jordan 1979). Those new to the relationship between the state and corporate interests were often to be amazed by the mirror images they saw; animal rights activists noted that it was 'often impossible to distinguish between the industrialists and MAFF officials' (Druce 1986: 53), while those opposed to the road lobby argued that the Department of Transport's bias towards the lobby was because both sides 'came from the same backgrounds, and maybe even the same school. Both are overwhelmingly male and middle class. At the top end of the scale they may frequent the same clubs. And almost without exception they share the seemingly trivial details of social conditioning ... that are so important in prejudicing attitudes to transport policy' (Hamer 1987: 112). As Self and Storing once said of the Ministry of Agriculture's almost symbiotic relationship with the agricultural interests, 'politicians and civil servants are likely to regard their tasks as completed when accommodation between the parties has been reached. They tend to lose sight of their broader obligation which is not only to accommodate the interests of conflicting parties but to search out and to promote the broader public interest' (Self and Storing 1971: 220).

As part of the process to promoting integration, governments have long used non-departmental public bodies (NDPB, colloquially termed 'quangos'), appointed bodies directly funded by and linked to central government departments which offer 'adaptability to the pressures of political expediency as well as administrative necessity in mitigating, supporting or fragmenting the continuous and pervasive expansion of the State machinery' (Doig 1979: 315) as well as allowing a widespread patronage state to develop:

> the 'appointed state' ranges far wider than the 'quango state'. Tens of thousands of appointed people are involved in many aspects of the governance of Britain – from the highest courts in the land to magistrates' courts, from central decisions in the NHS to local care trusts, from overseeing the BBC and independent television, the regulation of utilities and inspection of prisoners' conditions to the provision of social housing; post-16 education, tribunals, skills training, museums and local lottery grants. Crucial decisions affecting the health of communities, the preservation of the national heritage, the liberty of individuals and the prosperity of companies are taken by appointees. (House of Commons Public Administration Select Committee 2003: 7)

Despite efforts to bring a degree of transparency and merit-based criteria to appointments, particularly under the Conservative governments there was also a countervailing trend to not only 'remove areas of public policy from the direct political process but also provide ministers with the power to exercise patronage in the choice of board members. Thus they become a powerful instrument through which a government of a particular political disposition can extend and embed its ideological control over fields that are either politically salient or relatively difficult to control centrally' (Skelcher 1998: 50).

The rise of the management state

The inexorable growth of the modern state has had more general consequences. A particular feature of liberal democratic countries in the cluster has been the size and growth of the state. To deliver the liberal democratic agenda, particularly on low politics issues, the state itself has become a large and diverse aggregation of laws, agencies and procedures. A liberal democratic state focusing on low politics and the endless demands made on it could only expand, maintaining high tax rates to fund its activities and seeking to extend rather than restrain its spheres of influence.

It has also sought inclusion of organised interests, which have had as much involvement in the allocative and decision-making processes as governments, leading to a spiral of government overload, indebtedness and paralysis. To summarise Held's arguments: in order to secure maximum votes politicians too often promise more than they can deliver, and sometimes promise to deliver contradictory and therefore impossible sets of demands; competition between parties leads to a spiral of ever-greater promises, and appeasement strategies and the pursuit of self-interest by administrators lead to ever more state agencies (in health, education, industrial relations, prices and incomes, and so on) of increasingly unwieldy proportions (Held 1989: 119–20).

In essence, 'politicians will gain votes from the particular interest groups by spending. Officials will gain prestige and income by expanding programmes. The whole system of public spending and public services is therefore geared to expansion' (Flynn 1993: 12). This inexorable and ultimately bankrupting expansion (the UK had to go to the IMF for a loan in 1976) was the background to the significant and continuing reform begun by Conservative governments from 1979 onward:

insofar as in a general sense a specific developmental path that has been followed by developed countries has been identified, clearly those mechanisms of change that have propelled these states along this path continue to operate. In other words, developed states are not comfortably settled in a moment of rational-legal equilibrium. On the contrary, intensifying global competition has brought about a fiscal crisis in developed states necessitating public sector economies: privatisation, outsourcing, re-engineering and the like. (Doig and Theobald 1999: 17–18)

Reforms were introduced to drive down the costs of the state (through privatisation, performance measurement and the introduction of the contract culture), change the structures and procedures for the delivery of state functions and services, break the power of unions, and apply public choice theory (where the power to choose and spend was transferred to the public). Often generally (and retrospectively) labelled New Public Management (the term was first used in 1991 (Hood 1991)), the changes focused on the one hand on reducing the scope of public sector activity through privatisation, and on the other on increasing the role of competition, business practices and the market in the delivery of public services.

Hughes (1994: 69–73) identifies four changes which 'constitute the managerial programme': a focus on outputs; alterations to administrative inputs, such as hiring staff by contracts; changes to the scope of government, including privatisation and contracting-out; and finally, changing accountability relationships with politicians and the public, as managers become more responsible for results (which overlaps with the first change – focus on outputs). Similarly, Farnham and Horton identify three main 'managerial thrusts' throughout the public services during the 1980s, beginning with a tighter control of costs and control of inputs, shifting to an emphasis on 'outputs, quality and effectiveness of the services in meeting "customer", "consumer" and "client" demands and expectations before turning to a focus on "quality management"' (1996: 264). This also involved the break-up of government departments into policy departments and delivery agencies (initially termed Next Steps Agencies), linked by budget and performance indicators within which the latter could determine their delivery of public services or functions. In both cases, with broad budgetary and key performance indicators, and an emphasis on market forces and managerialism, agencies or bodies – many public, some private and some hybrid – were largely left to deliver public functions or services as they considered most suitable.

The rise of the management state has two implications. First, some academic commentators argue that the impact of structural and organisational reform turned the British political process into a 'differentiated polity' where policy became a zero-sum game between competing interests, accountability was diluted because there was no locus of responsibility through government – the centre's 'capacity to steer' – and the state became 'hollowed out' (see Rhodes 1997). Others have raised concerns about the effect of the continuous and comprehensive nature of the changes, involving organisational, cultural and managerial changes in creating varying organisational approaches across the public sector, not least to the balance between public service, competition, cost control and performance delivery, as well as public sector ethical environment, which may have led to 'misunderstanding among public servants about the quasi-private sector environment ... [and] ... inaccurate perceptions of private sector values and practices' (Harrow and Gillett 1994: 4, 5).

Development and change: maintaining the liberal democratic paradox and the primacy of the Executive

How far this means that there is still a definable Executive (and/ or Establishment) is debatable. Nevertheless, the connections and unwritten recognition of interests and backgrounds continue. Andrew Marr suggested that 'Britain is a small country where the top people in power, whether commercial power or political power, tend to become acquainted and lobby each other in a personal, private way that entirely bypasses the formal constitution' (Marr 1996: 251). At the same time, it should not be unexpected that maintaining political networks and the 'alliances, connections, sources of power and influence within the government system and between it and its constituencies outside' (Flynn 2002: 272), and co-opting like-minded people into the ambit of government should not continue, whatever the political nature of government. The 'interlocking network of influence is not unknown in other parts of the UK, nor is it confined to a period of Conservative government. It is the way in which a governing political party can exercise its power to ensure that its philosophy and policies are implemented' (Skelcher 1998: 88). Equally it would be 'naive to think that governments of whatever political colour will not want to place people sympathetic to their views and policies in organisations that are responsible for the delivery of government policies ... It is perhaps therefore not in the interest of either major party fundamentally to change a system that serves them well when in office' (Stott 1995: 161).

Contemporary commentators like Paxman see some of the sources of the elite system intact (see Ellis 1995 on the enduring role of Oxbridge), but the impact of reform is often changes to its coherence or influence, yet leaving what he terms an establishment 'bloody and bowed' but where 'no coherent new elite has yet supplanted it, but neither has a true meritocracy been forged' (Paxman 1991: 334). Others are explicit:

> Britain is ruled by a capitalist class whose economic dominance is sustained by the operations of the state and whose members are disproportionally represented in the power elite which rules the state apparatus ... as the dominant segment of the capitalist class in Britain, the inner circle plays a key role in articulating capitalist interests within the power elite. They are the planners and co-ordinators of the economy. Through their political participation, their informal contacts within the state, and their role in lobbying and party finance, they translate the City point of view into a dominant influence over state politics. (Scott 1991: 151)

Of course, it can be argued that 'there are two sets of difficulties involved in the attempt to analyse whether there is a power elite (with or without group consciousness, coherence or conspiracy) or a ruling class. The first is lack of information ... The second is that the interpretation of this evidence very much depends upon the general picture that one has of the workings of society as a whole' (Urry and Wakeford 1973: 8).

Nevertheless, others suggest that the format of the traditional binding of values and backgrounds is not necessary to ensure group adherence to the existing order. The acceptance to support actions and decisions of the state comes less from the values and backgrounds themselves than from the complexity and inter-relations of the various groupings who will work out their own relationships to reflect the circumstances of the time: 'political order is not achieved through common value systems, or general respect for the authority of the state, or legitimacy, or, by contrast, simple brute force; rather it is the outcome of a complex web of interdependencies between political, economic and social institutions and activities which divide power centres and which create multiple pressures to comply' (Held 1989: 151).

Certainly the roles of lobbyists, of MP lobbyists, of influence-peddling, and of the use of appointments to public bodies has continued to ensure access and integrate key interests in government processes. During the Thatcher era, 'the (inevitably) partial evidence available suggests that the Conservatives have also been far more ruthless than previous governments of both parties in ensuring that the 'one of us' principle dominates the distribution of patronage' in appointments to NDPBs (Weir and Hall 1994: 22). The post-1997 Labour governments not only continued the tradition but introduced the use of task forces which had the same advantages: 'the language of being "invited to the party", as senior civil servants describe the process of recruiting task force members, is very revealing. While it may suggest a certain openness to outsiders, it also implies that government is an essentially private function; that to participate in it is within the personal gift of the "party holders"; and that only a select group of potential party-goers will be chosen' (Barker *et al.* 1999: 38; see also Sullivan and Skelcher 2002; Commission on Public Private Partnerships 2001).

While governments have extended those who may advise them on policy, and fragmented the administrative structure through which policy is delivered, the central civil service has maintained its traditional relationship to governments. This was reflected in the 1985 Armstrong Memorandum which emphasised that civil servants were the servants of government (the current version talks of acting in a way that 'deserves and retains the confidence of ministers') and governed by political neutrality, impartiality, loyalty and confidentiality.

Secrecy still underpins 'the ethos of British central government. Ponting ... states that "Secrecy is at the heart of the way in which Whitehall works", Hennessy ... argues that it is the primary civil service value, "the bonding material which holds the rambling structure of central government together". Secrecy has consequences both for the exclusiveness of the system and for the manner in which business is conducted within it. It allows a clear distinction to be drawn between insiders and outsiders, and places strong restrictions on access to material' (Burch and Holliday 1996: 50). Further, Burnham and Pyper argue that the

'laws on secrecy are buttressed by a set of rules, codes and conventions designed to govern the behaviour of those working within government, and to place clear limits on the types of information they might disclose ... the 'unwritten' or uncodified nature of the British constitution makes it easier for governments and officials to mould it to enhance the retention rather than the disclosure of information, and to hamper public access to certain categories of information. (Burnham and Pyper 2008: 168; see also Robertson 1982)

Control over decisions and activities is still exercised by the use of the lobby system and the growth of the government information service. The Thatcher governments modernised and resourced a civil service-wide PR network, managed from the Prime Minister's Office that shifted the 'present and explain' role to the 'promote and proselytise' role, developing and combining the roles with that of spin doctor, or professional news manager. They also introduced a new Official Secrets Act in 1989. This restricted the catch-all approach of the existing legislation but particularly tightened up on those high politics areas that governments want to protect (defence, intelligence, international relations and security). The Act also removed the public interest defence, with the government arguing that there was no need for this because under the legislation 'the prosecution had in most cases to convince a jury that any leak of information had harmed the national interest' (Leapman 1992: 260–1).

The Blair governments consolidated their predecessors' approach, not only courting major newspaper proprietors but also developing the management and control of information into a 'new, interventionalist, activist, system of news dissemination that went out and aggressively made the government's case' (Oborne 2005: 150). It also included its critics; 'the ability to wound a political opponent is one of the great tests of an effective spin doctor because the timing and placing of an unattributable attack are as important as the choice of words which are used' (Jones 1996: 187).

Nevertheless the fiction of the liberal democratic model 'would scarcely seem to merit any consideration were it not for a paradox. Despite its empirical weakness, it retains an exceptionally potent hold upon the minds of the practitioners of politics. Politicians at whatever level almost invariably present themselves as the servants of the public charged with translating popular wishes into decision-making. Unelected officials, in public at any rate, also appear generally happy with this picture and it is one with which the media are most at home' (Greenaway et al. 1992: 49).

What this means in practice is that the state works, in relation to the multiplicity of functions and responsibilities, within the large but hierarchical system dominated by the Executive. Among that multiplicity may be a range of continuing state-focused interests which may or may not conflict with those wider democratic principles and policies which formally are supposed to shape the political process. That it can do so, and manage the conflict within that system, is a consequence of continuing to protect its inner workings and maintain inter-locking relationships with key agencies inside and outside the government. Its decision-making processes are, as Dunleavy notes,

> completely free of many of the restrictive or slowing conventions found in European legislatures with coalitional governments. No cross-party agreement is expected, still less the careful assembling of a pre-legislative consensus by government departments and parliamentary committees ... Although by convention governments are expected to consult before proposing legislation, they are thereafter free to ignore the results of the consultation, or to choose to take notice of only those responses which suit their purposes or come from political allies. (Dunleavy 1995: 60)

Further, within the paradox of the liberal democratic state, the development of the contemporary state 'has allowed the concentration of power in the hands of the executive (and the Prime Minister in particular) and the absence of any effective checks and balances. The position is perhaps all the more remarkable for the fact that power has concentrated in the hands of an executive branch which by accounts enjoys the support of less than half the voting public, and certainly much less than half the total adult population' (Ewing and Gearty 1990: 255–6).

Is there still a locus of the state?

The first point to note is the size and complexity of what is often labelled 'the state'. If the state intended to commit a state crime then the question must be asked as to where responsibility would lie within this complex and extensive decision-making system.

Governments and ministers are balancing (or exercising judgements on how to balance) competing issues, the attention to which or the resolution of which is clearly affected by time, urgency, the reactions of those affected and the impact on government performance, authority or credibility. The volume of government business has to be dealt with at a number of levels – departmental, interdepartmental, Cabinet committee and Cabinet – with often the Prime Minister, certain other ministers, key public officials playing disproportionate roles, and the government collectively through the Cabinet not necessarily seeing all business nor making key decisions (see Burch and Holliday 1996; Hogwood 1987).

In addition there are networks of departmental and inter-departmental committees paralleling the ministerial committee structure and crossing over the departmental structures 'to remove unnecessary dispute from the overloaded political tier' (see Jordon and Richardson 1987: 153–5). In terms of state crime, therefore, locating the centre of the modern state is not easy when it is argued that it is not 'a monolithic body ... in fact it is not a body at all', but 'a system of relationships which defines the territory and membership of a community, regulates its internal affairs, conducts relations with other states (by peaceful and by warlike means) and provides it with identity and cohesion. It consists of institutions and processes which are extremely various and complex, presiding over different spheres of the community which distribute different social goods according to different principles' (Jordan 1985: 1).

Does the multiplicity of intractable, cross-departmental issues, from the economy through employment to health and welfare, mean that the locus of the state *qua* state is no longer definable? Rhodes (1988) has argued that the government's shift from 'high politics' to 'low politics' has accelerated the decline of central autonomy through its interdependence with the sub-central government (quangos, nationalised industries, decentralised central departments, local government). The interdependence has resulted in a fragmented central policy-making structure (where individual ministers operate with a degree of autonomy and Whitehall business is conducted through multiple 'co-ordinating mechanisms and networks' (1988: 76). In other words, defining what is a state, and what is a state in terms of state crime, may have become more difficult given the size, complexity and range of functions now undertaken by the state but also by the continuing changes in terms of organisation autonomy and disaggregation where the changes in the past three decades have led to a smaller, fragmented governmental structure, leaving it less accountable, limited in its authority and increasingly interdependent on its interaction with other agencies (Rhodes 1997: 53–4).

Of course, passing responsibility for policy implementation means that state crime may be committed by public officials further down the hierarchy, where the links between the implementation and policy dimensions of the state are neither direct nor directed. While their acts or decisions may be unlawful, illegal, harmful or currently labelled a state crime, are these done on behalf of or with the approval of the state? Thus the key question remains: what is the state in terms of state crime in a liberal democratic context?

Much of the literature on state crime either ducks the issue of what is the state, or sees state crime as being committed by any state agency. In a modern state this could include any institution funded by public monies or whose staff or board members are appointed by politicians or public officials. If that was the case then the contemporary state within which state crime could occur could range from ministries to non-departmental bodies linked to them but also all the way down to those bodies, public or private, or a hybrid of the two, set up during the Conservative governments of the 1990s as 'a way of circumventing or even altogether replacing elected local authorities. Grant-maintained schools, self-governing colleges of further education, housing action trusts are examples of what we are here calling the "new state"' (Dynes and Walker 1995: 12). What is being described here, however, is the UK public sector (Massey 2005), rather than the state itself. Where the locus of the state may lie within such a structure needs to be identified in terms of *state* crime.

As Alder notes (2007), 'the Crown as the source of authority means that the UK has never found it necessary to create the notion of the "state" as a single legal entity' (2007: 113). In another case, judges thought 'the Crown' symbolised the powers of government and that the Crown was 'a fiction describing the executive' and 'that the expression "the Crown" symbolises the powers of government that were formerly wielded by the wearer of the crown' (2007: 322). In the Clive Ponting trial, Mr Justice McCowan's view was that 'we have general elections in this country. The majority party in the House of Commons forms the Government. If it loses majority support, it ceases to do so, but for the time being, it is the Government, and its policies are those of the State.' If there is to be a core to the complex and comprehensive public sector then it may lie in this concept of the Crown – or what it now represents. On the other hand, Alder argues that the Crown as a substitute for the state 'is an ambivalent concept. It includes the Queen as head of state and is also used as collective term for the central executive' (2007: 320).

Without a legal concept of the state, it has been the courts who have tended to define what is the state. A 2006 House of Lords case discussed this in relation to leadership and responsibility in the international context. It noted that under international law, individual responsibility can only be addressed once the question of whether or not the state initiated the crime. In this it turned to the International Law Commission's (ILC) *Draft Code of Crimes*, which noted that

> a State is an abstract entity which is incapable of acting on its own. A State can commit aggression only with the active participation of the individuals who have the necessary authority or power to plan, prepare, initiate or wage aggression ... Thus the violation by a State of the rule of international law prohibiting aggression gives rise to the criminal responsibility of the individuals who played a decisive role in planning, preparing, initiating or waging aggression. (R v. Jones 2006, House of Lords, para 64)

It is thus government that is the locus of the state – its directing or guiding mind – with a number of key departments and agencies that, in addition to the government, who could also have 'decisive roles' such as civil service departments, and their internal networks and relationships. These may be seen as the central or core executive:

> In brief, the 'core executive' is the heart of the machine, covering the complex web of institutions, networks and practices surrounding the prime minister, cabinet, cabinet committees and their official counterparts, less formalised ministerial 'clubs' or meetings, bilateral negotiations and interdepartmental committees. It also includes coordinating departments, chiefly the Cabinet Office, the Treasury, the Foreign Office, the law officers, and the security and intelligence services. (Rhodes 1995: 12)

Summary

In order to establish who may be responsible for *state* crime, the locus of the state has to be determined. Very much along the lines of how this question was addressed within the international relations discipline, for the *state* to commit a crime, we need to look at those who are the embodiment of the state and who determine its policies. Thus we are looking at (to paraphrase the quote on p. 59) *those exercising government authority or those of its officials or private individuals acting or performing at the government's command or with its authorisation*. Clearly this includes members of the government and/ or those with whom they work directly to develop and implement policy – the core executive. In addition to the core executive, which certainly has the capacity to commit state crime or commission state-corporate crime, and the traditions of doing so within a relatively specific historical context, the legislative, funding, performance and regulatory frameworks also allow the possibility of state-facilitated crime to be considered, along with state-commissioned crime through the corporate sector.

In this era of devolved and decentralised agencies and management, however, the question of those empowered to deliver policies within broad policy directives and objectives raises some interesting definitional issues about state crime which need to be addressed. The size, complexity and operational autonomy of public agencies, and the delivery of public services, raises the question of state crime occurring as a consequence of the interpretation or implementation of general policies.

Nevertheless, with continuing traditions of secrecy, ministerial collective responsibility and the integrated relationship between government and the higher levels of the civil service, it is hardly surprising that the UK system of national government has been described as 'an extreme example of closed government' (quoted in Burnham and Pyper 2008: 73). Within this, the national interest, or the interests of the state *qua* state, remains the primary driver. If there is one point that this chapter seeks to make, it is that the development of the state is a layered development, with a number of traditions and perspectives – where 'the ethos of the British political system' continues to be 'infused with important residues from earlier, pre-democratic times' (Burch and Holliday 1996: 10).

These 'deep historical antecedents' include: the 'unitary state, in which formal authority is concentrated at the centre'; centralised state decision-making involving a small, exclusive governing group of politicians and officials; the need to 'share power with a wider governing group', to maintain 'elite support and consent' and to be 'responsive to the power base which sustains it'; and a 'strong emphasis on the unity of the group ... expressed in the central convention of collective responsibility' (Burch and Holliday 1996: 11).

Such traditions have nurtured the capacity of government to act in the interests of the state, and to continue to do so within the context of democratic orthodoxy: 'the pragmatic development of British political and governmental institutions and practices has meant that alongside expectations about openness, democracy, public accountability and the like there have developed strong traditions and practices concerning the day-to-day doing of the nation's business which live very uneasily with those expectations' (Harden and Lewis 1986: 11).

In other words, democratic development may generally define the contemporary state and, indeed, be accepted as the prevailing orthodoxy. On the other hand, this does not necessarily mean that all policy is filtered through this orthodoxy and nor does it mean that there is not conflict between different parts or perspectives of the state as the state resorts to decisions and actions that maintain its existence as a state among other states or which takes a longer view that may or may not coincide with the expectations of the public or even all members of the core executive.

Notes

1 The state has been shown to be complicit in a number of plots and controversies, with those involving Roman Catholicism the most common (see, for example, Kenyon 1972).

2 It was publication of his memoirs that prompted MP John Ward to claim that 'it is not known, to me at any rate until today, that there are occasions when the Government of the day stoops to use even the spy and Secret Service Fund for the purpose of injuring political opponents. This is quite a new idea of British politics' (HC Debs (1910) 5th Series, Vol. XVI, col. 2413).

3 A copy is included in Tal (2001). It is explicit about the engineered collusion and proposed actions.

Chapter 5

State crime – what is a crime in the UK context?

Introduction

Much of the literature on state crime has concentrated on breaches of the criminal law:

> the idea of crime as a public crime does at least serve to focus our attention on a central issue about criminalization ... criminal convictions condemn the convicted person. Criminal punishments are not merely neutral techniques of prevention or deterrents; they express condemnation or censure ... to put it crudely and over-simply, civil law and non-criminal modes of regulation are primarily concerned with the prevention of harm and with compensation, as well as with spreading the costs of such harms and prevention, whereas criminal law is concerned with the definition and condemnation of wrongs. (Duff and Green 2005: 9)

In the UK context, criminal law not only reflects the wishes or needs of society but also 'must aim to lay down clear "rules of conduct" for them that will tell them precisely what they must or must not do, on pain of punishment if they break the rules ... It aims not merely to make clear what conduct is prohibited or permitted, but to declare to citizens what count as public wrongs that require a public condemnatory response' (Duff and Green 2005: 10, 13; see also Robinson 1997).

In other words, what is usually seen as a state crime is an offence against criminal law, not only for what it criminalises but also for its universal applicability: 'in Blackstone's Usage, torts are private wrongs because the impact of the wrong is limited to the interests of a private person. Crimes are public wrongs, for in addition to the particular victim the public as a whole is injured in its sense of security and wellbeing' (Fletcher 1998: 77).

Nevertheless, in terms of state crime, harm or loss through official actions or decisions is as relevant, and addressed as much through regulatory as criminal law. Chambliss uses the expression 'prohibited by law' to define the parameters – and if state crime is about acting in a way that is prohibited by law, then it must encompass action (or the absence of action) that harms or wrongs its citizens both by their conduct and by the results. If, however, state crime encompasses harm as well as wrongs, and private wrongs as well as public wrongs, then the legal framework should cover all formal forms of regulatory, civil and criminal law.

Thus state crime may involve 'activities that are regarded as *mala in se*, wrong in themselves, and those that are regarded as *mala prohibita*, subject to prohibition, where violations are often seen as "technical" rather than "criminal" offences' (Croall 2001: 13). Further, an activity or decision that offends against or breaches legislation may be described as unlawful. This includes the judicial review of the decisions of public officials to consider whether or not they have acted *ultra vires* – that is, where the official has acted beyond their legal powers and the action is thus 'illegal' (or unlawful). It is unlikely that such conduct would be usually described as criminal or a crime – a breach of criminal legislation – but, in terms of state crime, it does involve official policy or actions of the state being labelled 'unlawful'.

There is also the question of defining what is the offence – the *actus reus*, or conduct, part of a crime; the other part is the *mens rea* 'whether the defendant was to blame for his or her wrongful acts' (Herring 2004: 81). Here, as Herring notes, it is worth thinking about offences in two parts: 'conduct crimes require proof only that the defendant did an act. There is no need to demonstrate that the act produced a particular result. Possession of prohibited drugs would be an example. Results crime require proof not only that the defendant performed a particular act but that that act produced certain results' (2004: 82).

Both are relevant to the study of state crime. Indeed, conduct offences could be (and have been) as significant as results offences: 'first there are crimes whose sole or, at least, central manifestation is when the defendant succeeds in bringing about the relevant result as he or she intends (or tries to do this). In such crimes, the success (or the attempt to be successful) constitutes the underlying wrong. Secondly, there are crimes whose focal case is one in which, whether in the course of positive acts or through inactivity, the defendant *fails* (more or less culpably) *to prevent* a relevant result he or she was duty bound to avoid' (Duff and Green 2005: 22).

This then confirms the breadth of the focus of state crime; while criminal law may address the question of intent and motive, other legal perspectives allow acceptance of a state crime label as a consequence of conduct irrespective of intent and motive (which may be for the best possible intent and motives) but where a demonstrable hurt, harm or wrong has occurred. Here, too, the demonstration may be achieved through means other than a judicial process – although through some formal means that allows the evidence to be weighed, and representations to be made rather than simply informal censure.

This may move the application of the label of state crime beyond definable offences to normative assessments, but these have, depending on how they are undertaken, equal validity. Of course, the question is whether, in such circumstances, those involved may also be labelled state criminals when in many cases they are not. On the other hand there is no reason why their actions or decisions, taken while acting in an official capacity and acting on behalf of the state, and where harm, hurt or a private wrong occurs as a consequence, that those actions or decisions cannot be considered within the academic definitions of a state crime (although there may be a need to distinguish them from crimes committed by the Executive (see page 200). Indeed, the absence of formal adjudicatory processes that seek to address culpability and liability of individuals and organisations does not necessarily mean that the use of the term *state crime* to identify a range of wrongs or harm caused by the state is invalid or inapplicable.

It is important for any study of state crime to ensure that all unlawful activity is included. Even if the term 'state unlawfulness' or 'state illegality' does not have the same impact of 'state crime', consideration of state crime should recognise a matrix that reflects a full spectrum of criminal-regulatory law and conduct-results impact.

Whose UK laws?

The UK legislative framework[1] is neither straightforward nor necessarily comprehensive. The constitutional and legal environment operates in a matrix shaped by national, European and international frameworks.

Domestic law

UK public bodies and officials are subject to criminal, civil, regulatory and public (or administrative) law in regard to their official roles and responsibilities. The functions of public bodies are determined by legislation in terms of what they can do (and by definition what they cannot do). They are also governed by common law (law made by the courts in terms of interpretation of the legislation in specific instances – 'leading cases', which then extend the remit of the legislative intent).

Government has the power to amend or extend existing legislation (where the law contains provisions for government to promote and apply delegated legislation, of which Statutory Instruments (SI) are the most significant). SIs are also termed *delegated, subordinate* or *secondary* legislation and are powers granted, usually to a minister, to provide the detailed regulations which implement Acts of Parliament. They are reviewed by Parliament (see Office of Public Sector Information 2006).

Government also legislates under the Royal/Crown Prerogative which includes Orders-in-Council which may be both primary and secondary legislation within the UK. The Royal Prerogative is those common law powers vested in the Crown and exercised through the government. The powers are limited and normally relate to such actions as (in relation to foreign affairs) declaring war, diplomatic relations, making treaties and sending armed forces overseas, and (in relation to domestic matters) appointment of ministers, approving legislation and keeping the peace (see Alder 2007: 329–38). Parliament and the courts have limited control over their use, and then only if they are 'justiciable' – that is, if the activity, such as invasion or making a treaty, is seen as a matter for the court. As was suggested in the 2008 judgement on Diego Garcia (see p. 30), if the activity does not fall within the remit of the courts, the courts have made it clear that it is not their responsibility but that of Parliament to argue over their use: 'orders in council are made without the concurrence of Parliament or of any other representative legislature and so the political control is less direct. That lack of direct political control over them may well be considered undesirable in today's world. If so, the appropriate remedy is for Parliament, not the courts, to get involved in scrutinising the substance of such orders in council' (UKHL 61, Regina (Bancoult) v. Secretary of State for Foreign and Commonwealth Affairs (No. 2) in the House of Lords 2008: 43; see Box 25).

Box 25: Breaking its own orders?

Prime Minister Harold Wilson, who had come to power with the Labour government in 1964, had clear views on the possible break-up of the Central African Federation through Rhodesia's threatened departure from the Federation and the Commonwealth. He listed 'five principles' for independence, and had long negotiations with Rhodesia's Prime Minister, Ian Smith, who declared a unilateral declaration of independence (UDI) in November that year. Publicly, Wilson talked in uncompromising language, because, as Richard Crossman noted, Wilson saw the crisis as a 'test of his strength and statesmanship and power to survive a really difficult situation' (Crossman 1979: 141).

He quickly announced in Parliament that force would not be used against Rhodesia, privately calling the possibility of invading Rhodesia 'more window dressing than reality'. This left the Wilson government with no alternative but to invoke the 'economic war' with which Wilson had already threatened Smith, which was achieved through an Order-in-Council in December 1965. This made it illegal for a British registered company or British citizen directly or indirectly to supply Rhodesia with petrol.

What made the oil sanctions policy central to the future behaviour of the Wilson government was Wilson's use of it to deflect Commonwealth leaders in January 1966, when they called for a military invasion of Rhodesia. He persuaded them to agree to his strategy, 'partly achieved by my phrase "weeks not months", based on the advice we were receiving that the oil sanctions and the closure of the Beira pipeline would bring the Rhodesian economy to a halt' (Wilson 1971: 196). In fact intelligence assessments had already told Wilson that the Smith regime could survive economic sanctions indefinitely but there was no way he could, in policy terms, initiate a war he thought he could not win, nor could he damage the UK's status within the Commonwealth (nor his own in relation to his Party) by admitting the sanctions would not be effective.

Although the principal source of Rhodesia's oil – Beira – was blockaded and the pipeline closed, Rhodesia ran an oil-buying operation through GENTA, a government controlled oil buying company. It dealt with Shell and BP through its subsidiaries in Mozambique and South Africa whose government made it plain to the parent companies (which operated jointly there) that they should continue supplies to the subsidiaries. One of these – Shell Mozambique – was registered in London and therefore directly subject to the Order-in-Council.

The solution proposed by the South African subsidiaries was to take Shell Mozambique out of the oil route loop by agreeing with Total to supply Rhodesia while Shell South Africa was supplying the same amount of oil for Total in South Africa. Amounts and prices were negotiated between Shell/BP South Africa, Freight Services (a South African brokerage firm) and GENTA but, on paper, French oil was actually being shipped. The swap agreement was specifically designed to protect Shell Mozambique's *legal* position in terms of UK domestic law.

In 1967 the Portuguese and Zambian governments had complained that the British oil companies were breaking sanctions. The Zambian government's criticisms in February 1968 prompted Shell/BP to decide to tell the government about their swap arrangement. Shell/BP believed that the government was unwilling to prosecute anyone for sanctions breaking but thought that the government would welcome the news of a 'voluntary' gesture that disengaged Shell Mozambique from supplying oil and introduced a non-British firm into the supply route. Such action, Shell/BP believed, 'would be ineffective in curtailing supplies to Rhodesia, but this would be a subsidiary consideration to the political kudos which HMG believe they would gain in other quarters' (Bingham 1978: 254).

In February 1968 George Thomson, Minister of State at the Commonwealth Office (and author of a note to a Labour MP in June 1967 that claimed 'we are absolutely satisfied' that British oil companies were not supplying oil to Rhodesia), together with four senior civil servants from the Commonwealth Office, Foreign Office and Ministry of Power, met with two managing directors of Shell and BP. The latter explained the 'rearrangements in the *modus operandi*' that would prevent the 'diversion' of British oil and that would allow the government to state with 'complete' accuracy that no British company was supplying oil to Rhodesia.

If Thomson was unclear about the details of the swap arrangement in February, one of the civil servants present was put fully in the picture at a May meeting with Shell/BP representatives, and given agreement to pass the word around Whitehall so that 'if there were any further signs of Ministers wishing to sound off on this subject, the appropriate discouraging noises could be made' (Bingham 1978: 264).

The next meeting was scheduled for February 1969. A few days before, an internal Shell/BP memorandum noted, of the meeting the previous May, that 'this additional information has subsequently been, I understand, conveyed to Mr Thomson'. At this third meeting with the minister and senior civil servants the swap arrangements were spelt out in detail by the oil company representatives, one of whom noted that 'while this position was legally sound', the argument seemed pretty thin to him, while it was the Minister who agreed the position was 'quite defensible' and that it was a senior civil servant who suggested that 'the legal position was sound and could be defended'. The 1969 meeting was the last on oil sanctions.

There was little doubt that the government knew what was happening, although the Prime Minister took to relying on a small informal grouping of sympathetic ministers: 'the Prime Minister's arrangements for dealing with Rhodesia were becoming more and more obscure and the formal committee on Rhodesia seemed to have given way to an informal grouping of Ministers sympathetic to Harold Wilson's views' (Castle 1984: 545). Such informal activities were supported by civil servants who were sceptical from the outset about oil sanctions.

In turn Wilson himself claimed that neither he nor his colleagues knew of the swap agreement, and nor had his civil servants alerted him to what was going on. On the other hand, George Brown, Foreign Secretary from 1966 to 1968, admitted that 'none of us then in office could claim ignorance on the situation and so far as I am concerned that applies right up to the time that I left the Government in March 1968. I should be most surprised to learn – and I am choosing my words carefully – that the position changed in any material respect after that' (House of Lords debates, vol. 396, col. 460).

When the story broke in the UK media in 1976, the British government was categorically informing the UN in September 1976 that: 'the competent United Kingdom authorities have studied the report most carefully, and have discussed its contents with the British oil companies mentioned. These authorities are satisfied that the report contains no evidence of sanctions breaking by any British companies or individuals, and have accepted the assurances given by Shell and BP that neither they nor any company in which they have an interest have engaged either directly or with others in supplying crude oil or oil products to Rhodesia' (Bailey 1979: 43).

The Bingham inquiry was set up in 1977, by Wilson's successor James Callaghan to placate an increasingly irritated Zambia. It officially confirmed the swap arrangements and the political circumstances in which they took place. The report did not, because its terms of reference did not ask it to, report on who in the Wilson Cabinet knew and therefore colluded in the swap arrangements which effectively circumvented the government's own legal requirements (Brian Sedgemore, a Labour PPS at the time, alleged five ministers as knowing what was going on; see Sedgemore 1980: 18–24).

The inquiry gave a somewhat disingenuous interpretation of events, suggesting that the government saw the swap arrangements as 'a technical defence ... based on a narrow construction of the Sanctions Order' that allowed it to claim that no British oil was going to Rhodesia. This allowed the government to avoid a confrontation with South Africa, giving the companies a clear impression that 'compliance with the Sanctions Order was to be regarded as a matter of form rather than of substance, that it was the letter that mattered, not the spirit' (Bingham 1978: 221). The publication of the Report, and the inconsistencies in ministerial statements, together with arguments of civil service complicity, forced the Labour government to consider its response. The October 1978 Labour Party conference demanded a public inquiry, with all the relevant official papers being made available, because 'our reputation, our credibility as a party, as a Government, as a nation, is firmly on the line'.

Clearly the government was in a dilemma as to how to proceed, and considered various means of inquiry that would do them the least damage. It proposed in February 1979 a highly unusual joint Lords–Commons Committee of Inquiry to investigate whether Parliament or Ministers were 'misled, intentionally or otherwise'. The last time this particular form of inquiry was used was in 1916 to investigate the failure of the Mesopotamia and Dardanelles campaigns. Although they had quasi-judicial powers these types of inquiry met in private and as one commentator put it, 'as an experiment in procedure they were to be deplored' (Keeton 1960: 52; see also Public Administration Committee 2005, section 6). The Lords, calling the format for the inquiry a 'constitutional monstrosity' and 'constitutional enormity' for its implications in exposing to public scrutiny confidentiality of advice from civil servants and confidentiality of Cabinet discussions, rejected the proposal.

Before an alternative could be proposed, in May 1979 a Conservative government was elected. In December it announced that it did not intend to hold any inquiry nor would it consider prosecuting those involved in sanctions-breaking. Sir Michael Havers, the Attorney General, told the House that the 1968 and 1969 meetings gave the oil companies the impression of tacit, if not express, approval for the 'exchange' scheme. For any prosecution to be possible the Director of Public Prosecutions would have had to undertake detailed work to specify the offences and those responsible, and to collect the evidence. The crucial part of the argument was, as Havers said, that 'while the prosecution might confine criminal charges to the years 1971–77, the defence would investigate the entire history of events from 1966 onwards. Those events would cast their shadow over the whole case and this important factor would have a serious bearing on its outcome. Counsel were of the opinion that a jury might well be reluctant to convict if there appeared to be substance in the defence that those charged had acted in the belief that their conduct had the express or ostensible consent of the authorities' (HCD, 5th Series, vol. 976, col. 638).[2]

Decisions and actions of governments are also governed according to constitutional convention. These essentially govern how governments work; they are seen as binding on those to whose they apply but are not enforceable in, or by, the courts (if only because of the political issues that would arise if the courts sat in judgement on such matters):

A constitutional convention is a non-legal rule which imposes an obligation on those bound by the convention, breach or violation of which will give rise to legitimate criticism: and that criticism will generally take the form of an accusation of 'unconstitutional conduct'... Conventions comprise a set of binding rules, non-legal in nature, which supplement and inform the legal rules of the constitution, and which can adapt to meet changing circumstances (Burnett 2004: 30, 39).

An obvious convention is the Ministerial Code which 'binds' ministers to legal and normative requirements, including those that state:

- The Ministerial Code should be read against the background of the overarching duty on Ministers to comply with the law including international law and treaty obligations ... (1.2).

- It is of paramount importance that Ministers give accurate and truthful information to Parliament ... (1.2(c)).

Of course this mix of laws, custom and practice has implications for who judges and how one judges what, if any, breach has been committed:

large tracts of the constitution are subject only to these 'rules', such as, for example, the powers of the Sovereign, the existence of and relationships between the Prime Minister and the Cabinet, the relationships between the government and Parliament, between the two Houses (and the internal workings of each), and the appointment and disciplining of the judiciary. Whether to label these 'rules' as conventions, principles, doctrines, practices, understandings, maxims, or precepts; whether the courts recognise or declare them; which of them (if any) are binding (and if so why), and what consequence (if any) flows from the breach of any or all of them are issues that are well explored in numerous textbooks on democracy and on constitutional politics. (Brazier 1990: 3)

External law

States are also increasingly subject to external legal frameworks (including those states who are not signatories to the relevant laws, treaties or conventions) because, internationally, many states recognised the validity of joining together for mutual benefit – such as avoiding warfare or promoting human rights – which in turn also requires acceptance of external scrutiny: 'recognising the inherent limitations of a country's internal controls and procedures, however impartial and effective they may be ... some societies have progressed one step beyond these domestic mechanisms into the arena of collective international guarantees against state crime' (Hurwitz 2000: 283).

The UK state is subject to legislation initiated by the European Union (which primarily covers commercial activity and delivery of EU services). EU law covers those areas where the European Commission feels it has exclusive or partial responsibility as a consequence of the contents of various treaties that authorise it to act on behalf of, or for, the member states collectively.

The former means those areas where national governments cannot produce their own legislation but must follow EU requirements, and includes the Common Commercial Policy, the Common Agricultural Policy, fisheries policy, transport policy, competition rules, and those rules governing the free movement of goods, persons, services and capital. The latter covers a common market, economic and monetary union and implementing common policies or activities (such as equality between men and women, competitiveness, employment, consumer protection, the quality of the environment).

The UK 1972 European Communities Act defines the legal relationship between UK and EU law (which usually takes the form of treaties and laws, regulations or directives). It states that these are binding on the UK: 'for the purposes of all legal proceedings any question as to the meaning or effect of any of the Treaties, or as to the validity, meaning or effect of any Community instrument, shall be treated as a question of law (and, if not referred to the European Court, be for determination as such in accordance with the principles laid down by any relevant decision of the European Court or any court attached thereto)'. Essentially EU law overrides UK law and, where the two conflict, UK courts should refer to European courts those issues where there is a question of inconsistency.

As noted above, the UK is subject, by signature and membership, to international law, to conventions, and to customary international law. There is also the question of international or transnational conventions which, when signed and ratified by the government, commit the government or its successors to incorporating that convention – or the themes of that convention – in domestic legislation in due course. One example is the UK's ratification of the United Nations Convention Against Corruption which requires the UK to progressively realign its domestic law with the mandatory aspects of the Convention and also, more generally, to commit to the overall purpose of the Convention (signing up to the OECD Convention on Bribery of Overseas Public Officials has had similar requirements). Amendments were introduced in 2001. In 2010 the UK government introduced new bribery legislation.

Sometimes the international body concerned sets up a review process (such as GRECO for the Council of Europe) or a transnational process of adjudication (such as the European Court of Human Rights in relation to the European Convention on Human Rights ratified by the UK in 1951 and enacted in 1998). In both cases, the signing country makes itself subject to the adjudication or review process, whether or not it is binding. Thus the Rome Statute set up the International Criminal Court (ICC) to deal with 'the most serious crimes of concern to the international community as a whole'. These include genocide, crimes against humanity, war crimes and crimes of aggression.[3] The other offences were legislated for under the 2001 International Criminal Court Act (which gives effect to the Statute of the International Criminal Court and provides for offences under the law of England and Wales and Northern Ireland corresponding to offences within the jurisdiction of that Court) which allows them to be tried in the UK.

Who can commit what crime?

The scope of the UK legislative framework is extensive. It raises three questions: are public officials, individually and collectively, captured by the framework; is their conduct also covered by the definitions advanced by the state crime literature (and how far can their conduct be labelled as a state crime in terms of acting as agents of the state); and does that conduct in state crime terms relate to acting in pursuit of the state's (or, for those taking a state-corporate crime perspective, the corporate sector's) interests?

What types of state crime? Individuals

In addition to the wider legislative framework[4] which would apply to a public official in pursuit of his or her official duties, public officials are specifically subject to public law which governs their conduct – decisions and actions – in performance of their official duties and in relation to their dealings with citizens. Their conduct is governed by legality, procedural fairness, reasonableness and compliance with ECHR and EU requirements (see Box 26).

Public officials' actions and decisions can only be undertaken where their department or agency has the legal authority so to act or decide – to do otherwise is to act *ultra vires* and thus unlawfully. Public officials also have duty of care, and not to act negligently in the exercise of public law – their conduct should be 'fair, just and reasonable' – although the courts will shield public officials on the basis that 'there is a strong public interest in ensuring that public authorities are free to carry out their duties in the public interest, without the fear that they may be liable in damages if it is found that they could or should have exercised their discretion in a different way' (Treasury Solicitors/Government Legal Service 2006: 39).

Decisions and actions must not take into account 'irrelevant considerations', must take account of all 'relevant considerations' and must not come to a decision that 'is so wildly unreasonable or perverse that it cannot have been within his discretion to make it, and it was therefore unlawful'. In addition to the unlawfulness of any decision, public officials are also expected to ensure procedural fairness in reaching that decision as well as ensuring impartiality and independence in reaching that decision.

Thus, where there is discretion in decision-making it is bound by what legislation intends the public official to do, and whether or not what he or she then decides to do does not defy logic, moral standards, beyond the range of responses open to a reasonable decision-maker; has taken into account all relevant considerations (and ignored those that are not relevant); and not taken a decision which 'is so unreasonable that no reasonable person properly directing himself could have taken it' (these are known as the Wednesbury Principles; see Treasury Solicitors/Government Legal Service 2006: 14).

The 1998 Human Rights Act, which incorporates the ECHR into UK law, includes specific provisions, in that under Article 6, 'it is unlawful for a public authority to act in a way which is incompatible with a Convention right'. In particular, Article 8 of the Convention states that 'everyone has the right to respect for his private and family life, his home and his correspondence', and 'there shall be no interference by a public authority with the exercise of this right except such as is in accordance with the law and is necessary in a democratic society in the interests of national security, public safety or the economic well-being of the country, for the prevention of disorder or crime, for the protection of health or morals, or for the protection of the rights and freedoms of others' (see Box 26).

Would the actions described in Box 26 be labelled state crime? They overstep the boundary of delineated behaviour, and occur as a

---

Box 26: Over-stepping the official boundaries

Peacekeeping: In April 2004, two cousins of a soldier in the Kosovo Liberation Army who was shot dead by British peacekeepers in 1999 won a compensation claim against the MoD at the High Court. They were both injured in the operation that led to their cousin's death. The Kosovans won their case on the grounds that the soldiers had been negligent and committed trespass to the person by their actions. The judge stated that if the soldiers were on peacekeeping duties and not acting in self-defence then 'combat immunity' could not succeed. On duty of care, the judge said that the basic position was that soldiers owed the same duties as ordinary citizens.

Keeping the peace: In 1991 Paul Bennett, wanted in the UK for offences relating to the purchase of a helicopter, was in South Africa. Rather than seek his extradition, the UK police arranged for the South African police to deport him to New Zealand, via the UK, where he was arrested. The House of Lords argued that the judiciary should 'accept a responsibility for the maintenance of the rule of law that embraces a willingness to oversee executive action and to refuse to countenance behaviour that threatens either basic human rights or the rule of law'. On the basis that Bennett's return was an illegal abduction, involving UK police 'participating in violations of international law and of the laws of another state' and engaged in 'executive lawlessness beyond the frontiers of its own jurisdiction', the appeal was allowed.

---

consequence of the misinterpretation of what was permissible. They are committed on behalf of the state in pursuit of official policy, and done openly by those involved on their assumption that they are acting entirely in accordance with their interpretation of their legal position. Conversely, if in his or her official capacity a public official acts with malice, which does not have to be proved, and where the public official knew he or she was acting unlawfully and that this would cause injury to some person, or was recklessly indifferent to that result, 'a private law action for damages is possible for the tort of misfeasance in public office' (see Treasury Solicitors/Government Legal Service 2006: 39).[5]

Even if labelled unlawful, illegal (or criminal because of intent and motive) it would be difficult to see how such actions or decisions could fall with the academic definitions of state crime irrespective

of the types of law or harm. It would be difficult to argue that such conduct was undertaken with the approval of the state or with the intention of furthering the interests of the state.

The next issue is whether a public official could be accused of committing state crime while in pursuit of the interests of the state. In terms of preventing terrorism, following the July 2005 bombings in London, the ever-present possibility of further attacks put UK law enforcement in a position of being determined not to be responsible for failing to prevent a second attack. In the inquiry following the death of Jean Charles de Menezes, where police shot an innocent man wrongly identified as a potential bomber, the coroner sought to draw out the distinctions between lawful and unlawful killing by an agent of the state acting in an official capacity in terms both of intention and also a greater benefit when, as he pointed out, they were allowed to use up to and including lethal force in self defence:

1 unlawful killing: a finding beyond reasonable doubt that the firearm was not discharged in the belief that one of the officers was under imminent threat of being shot ...[6]

2 lawful killing: a finding on the balance of probabilities, that [the officer] believed, albeit mistakenly that he or [another officer] was under imminent threat of being shot ...

3 open verdict: a rejection of the proposition that [the officer] may have believed that he or [the other officer] was under imminent threat of being shot ... but an inability to conclude, beyond reasonable doubt, that such was not the case.

There is also, in terms of the definitional spectrum of the state crime literature, the possibility of state crime being committed by a public official in terms of types of state-corporate crime, and in terms of harm. Certainly the intertwining of MPs' official and private interests and the speed and complexity of legislative reform have allowed politicians to indicate that they could allegedly ensure legislative amendments that favoured the interests they would represent. Such possibilities continue to exist; whether such actions fall within the remit of state-corporate crime depends on the definition, what harm resulted, and what offences may have been committed[7].

In the case of harm as a consequence of the official conduct of public officials, the report on the case of Victoria Climbié (who died at the hands of her relative) by the Royal College of General Practitioners in 2003 noted that 'Victoria was known to no fewer

than four social services departments, three housing departments, and two specialist child protection teams of the Metropolitan Police. Furthermore, she was admitted to two different hospitals because of concerns that she was being deliberately harmed and was referred to a specialist children and families centre managed by the NSPCC. What transpired during this period can only be described as a catalogue of administrative, managerial and professional failure by the services charged with her safety' (RCGP 2003: 1; see Lord Laming 2003).

The Climbié report goes on to note that 'the front-line staff were all employees acting on behalf of the organisations which employed them', and 'those in senior positions carried the responsibility for the quality, efficiency and effectiveness of the services delivered and they must be accountable for what happened' in terms of ensuring 'that the services they provided to children such as Victoria were properly financed, staffed and able to deliver good quality services to children and families' (RCGP 2003: 1).

In terms of harm caused and the weaknesses of the regulatory framework, during the late 1980s and early 1990s a consultant anaesthetist at the Bristol Royal Infirmary in the UK expressed concern about how open-heart surgery on babies was conducted at the hospital and the higher than normal death rate for these operations. He raised his concerns with colleagues, fellow anaesthetists and hospital managers, then the Department of Health and the media[8]. Following a GMC inquiry in 1998, senior staff were found guilty of professional misconduct.

The later official inquiry noted that at the time the Chief Executive of the NHS Executive described the government-determined regulatory framework as 'one which relied on professional self-regulation based on a market mechanism, audit and a hierarchical relationship between various agencies', including the ministry. Apparently, 'even if these were all perfectly aligned ... there was no certainty that any of the parties would be in a position to identify or respond to issues of clinical performance' (Bristol Royal Infirmary Inquiry 2001: 82). The inquiry noted that it was not about people who did not care or who wilfully harmed patients, but was nevertheless more blunt about the 'light-touch' supervision and regulation:

> at national level there was confusion as to who was responsible for monitoring quality of care. The confusion was not, however, just some administrative game of 'pass the parcel'. What was at stake was the health, welfare, and indeed the lives of children. What was lacking was any real system whereby any

organisation took responsibility for what a lay person would describe as 'keeping an eye on things' (Bristol Royal Infirmary Inquiry 2001: 6).

Clearly, within the definitions proposed in the state crime literature, public officials could be involved in state crime, and some end up acting unlawfully on the direction of the Executive within the legal and other boundaries around their roles and responsibilities. Unlawful conduct as a consequence of the misapplication or misinterpretation of the wishes or intentions of the state is likely to be much more common, however. In order to ensure the widest context for the study of state crime, it is therefore necessary at least to address the totality of the legal framework in which the state works, and to include all acts and decisions that breach that framework, and are adjudged criminal, illegal or unlawful, particularly to encompass the range of official state law-breaking by individual public officials.

Whatever their motives, public officials may become involved in conduct which, even if it does not breach the legislative framework, causes harm or injury. Nevertheless, what distinguishes such actions is that although they may be undertaken with good intentions they are invariably *not* undertaken in pursuit of the interests of the state, even if they are undertaken (or not undertaken) within the context of state policy. Here the issue may be one of interpretation of, or failure to apply appropriately, that policy, but it is not necessarily one of committing state crime or state-corporate crime unless one takes a very broad approach or unless the definitional framework is revised to address this.

What types of state crime? Organisations

Most, if not all, of the issues and examples above relating to public officials relate not to an individual having sole or exclusive responsibility for initiating or delivering public policy, but to individuals working in an organisational context. There is substantial evidence that the various types of potential breaches of law, as well as causing harm, are a consequence of both organisational and individual conduct in terms of direct involvement and regulatory responsibility. In relation to harm, one of the reports on the death of Baby P in 2002 noted:

on reviewing the documentation, it is clear that communication between different health professionals was poor ... This was partly the result of inappropriate systems and partly due to staff not adhering to processes. At the same time, communication between the NHS, social services and the police was also poor, with a failure to ensure that these bodies were represented at multi-agency meetings. This had a negative impact both on the care that Baby P received and on the resultant actions taken by health professionals. (Care Quality Commission 2009: 15)

The report went on to note that part of this was a consequence of organizations self-certifying that their institutional arrangements to prevent harm were operational:

we are concerned that (with the exception of two specific standards in 2005/06) the boards of all four trusts declared themselves as complying with all of the core standards relating to safeguarding children, recruitment and training, mandatory training, professional development and public health partnerships, for each of the three years we looked at. In light of the shortcomings highlighted throughout this report, we are reviewing the declarations made by each of the trusts and making representations concerning the rigour of the standard, and the need for the regulator to have access to all relevant data from which it can determine the degree of risk to which children may be exposed. (Care Quality Commission 2009: 36)

Certainly, public bodies' interpretation of their legal and other responsibilities in relation to policy or state interests, especially in a centralised departmental policy environment, provides significant opportunity for state crime, state-facilitated crime or state-corporate crime, although more in terms of regulatory or private wrongs or harm than public or criminal wrongs.

Unsurprisingly, there has also been a growth in regulatory agencies that deal with both unlawful conduct and results offences (for example, behaving in a discriminatory way or causing harm by failing to ensure health and safety at work). Other agencies regulate the activities of other regulators (such as the Council of Tribunals), the legal activities of the state (such as surveillance), and the activities of the private sector delivering services or functions on behalf of the state. Public bodies are also regularly fined by regulators and others for organisational regulatory breaches:

- Britain's nuclear submarine base at Faslane has had so many safety breaches – including leaks of radioactive material – that they have become a 'recurring theme', according to a confidential government report. The worst breaches disclosed in the Ministry of Defence document, which was released under the Freedom of Information Act to *Channel 4 News*, include three instances when radioactive coolant leaked from submarines at the base into the Firth of Clyde in 2004, 2007 and 2008. The problem became so bad that the Scottish Environmental Protection Agency (SEPA) warned it would consider closing the base, which is on Gare Loch, north-west of Glasgow, if it had the power to do so. (*Daily Telegraph*, 27 April 2009)

- In 2010 the Royal Mail was fined £90,000 after admitting to health and safety breaches following the death of an employee who was crushed by a reversing HGV because it failed to adequately assess the risk to staff when employers have a legal duty to ensure that work can be done safely. In the same year Edinburgh Council was fined for failing to keep accurate records of the location and condition of asbestos and did not have suitable procedures in place to inform those working on or near the substance that it was there. (see www.hse.gov.uk)

In relation to possible offences, where these are committed by individuals in an organisational context, holding the organisation itself to account for the conduct of their officials, even where both are seeking to implement government policy, may be more problematic. Thus the UK government has a clear and continuing strategy (CONTEST) to address terrorism. The UK has always expressed support for the US efforts to maintain the flow of information and intelligence; this included involvement in the US kidnap and rendition programme (by allowing, for example, US planes to refuel in Diego Garcia) which was intended to allow the US to interrogate prisoners outside the restraints of the US legal processes.

In February 2010 a case involving a UK Guantánamo Bay detainee sought to allow publication of a document alleging MI5 complicity in his torture; one of the judges accused MI5 of failing to respect human rights, deliberately misleading Parliament, and having a 'culture of suppression' that undermined government assurances about its conduct. It later transpired that a lawyer acting for the Foreign Office asked for the comments to be removed from the court ruling; these were, although the letter and the paragraphs appeared in the media, raising questions about requests over the wording of appeal judgements.[9]

The accountability of an agency becomes even more difficult if and when its officials are required to act in ways that involve breaches of the legal framework – and such possibilities exist. For example, the trial of David Shayler, a former MI6 agent, ended with him repeating claims that he was 'gagged' from talking about 'a crime so heinous' that he had no choice but to go to the press with his story. The 'crime' was the alleged MI6 involvement in the plot to assassinate Colonel Gaddafi, hatched in late 1995 (*Observer*, 10 November 2002).

In relation to the death of Jean Charles de Menezes in 2005, the coroner ruled that on the basis of the evidence he had seen the jury could not bring a verdict of unlawful killing. The Brazilian was shot on an underground train one day after several attempted bombings, but also after a catalogue of police surveillance, tactical, operational and management errors. The coroner at the inquest in 2008 offered the jury two choices – lawful killing or an open verdict. He also insisted that no criminal or civil fault could be attached to individuals; nor could there be any decision that would be inconsistent with the outcome of the 2007 trial of the Metropolitan Police on health and safety charges following the shooting. At this trial the judge said that 'there was a serious failure of accurate communication which has not been explained', but he was deliberately not going to name any individual as having failed. This was 'a corporate failing with a number of failures contributing to the ultimate tragedy'. The coroner's jury rejected the option of lawful killing, but the coroner was quick to point out that an open verdict was not a mark of censure or disapproval, and that no verdict in any case would be framed in a way that implied criminal or civil liability, which would be more likely to rest with the organisation than the individuals directly involved.[10]

One area where the law has not until recently been able to run is that of criminality or criminal responsibility of an organisation or entity, particularly in the corporate sector. When organisations are held to account for any criminal or civil investigation, the key has been to identify the guiding or controlling mind – the individual or individuals acting or directing the organisation. Without that individualisation of intent or intention, addressing organisational responsibility has been a legal problem in terms of individual punishment:

it is difficult to penetrate the inner workings of the organization to know who did what in bringing about the criminal harm. Or sometimes it might be the case that one person possesses the relevant information, another makes a decision to act, and still another carries out the action. In this situation, the diffusion of function makes it impossible to hold a single individual responsible for the crime. These difficulties, plus the general sense that organized action has an increasing impact on the lives of ordinary individuals, have generated pressure towards the prosecution and appropriate punishment of 'legally created entities' that bring about criminally prescribed harms. (Fletcher 1998: 201)

There were increasing concerns over a number of high-profile cases[11] where death occurred as a consequence of (often indirect but causal) failings by management either because it did not ensure an appropriate management structure or culture, with fatal results. Most of these cases have been health and safety failings. Although the individuals directly involved could be prosecuted for the common law offence of manslaughter or under existing Health and Safety legislation, company management could not be punished for causing death or injury unless a 'guiding' or 'controlling' mind had first been found guilty of such offences.

For large organisations health and safety issues were rarely board or senior management issues (or at least those concerning non-compliance); fatalities may be the consequence of the overall way a company acted or performed, without any one individual acting in such a way that could be the basis of a prosecution. This prompted demands for some form of institutional responsibility where the guiding mind was absent, in that no one person was responsible for the outcome but the actions of several persons, with no intention to lead to an unlawful outcome, collectively contributed to that outcome. The result was the 2007 Corporate Manslaughter and Corporate Homicide Act which applies (unevenly) to both sectors.

The Act takes the existing ingredients of gross negligence manslaughter and lists four qualifying components (see www.cps.gov.uk/).

First, it requires that the institution is listed as eligible for prosecution. The Act removes Crown immunity (a legal status that protects Crown bodies, such as government departments, from prosecutions) and includes other central and local public bodies (private companies that carry out public functions are broadly in the same position as public bodies). The organisation must cause the death. The test for this follows guidance from a manslaughter case that requires that the negligence consist of an act or failure to act; the negligence must have caused the death in the sense that it more than minimally, negligibly or trivially contributed to the death; and the degree of negligence has to be such that it can be characterised as gross in the sense that it was of an order that merits criminal sanctions rather than a duty merely to compensate the victim.

Second, for a charge to be brought against the organisation rather than an individual, the prosecution will need to show that 'but for' the management failure (including the substantial element attributable to senior management), the death would not have occurred. The third component is that there is a 'relevant duty of care owed by the organisation to the deceased'; the fourth is that there is 'a gross breach' of that duty.

In relation to charging the institution, a substantial element of that breach has less to do with the guiding or controlling mind than about the 'reasonableness' of an organisation's approach to decision-making and the conduct of senior management in running the organisation:[12] 'those persons who play a significant role in the management of the whole or a substantial part of the organisation's activities. This covers both those in the direct chain of management as well as those in, for example, strategic or regulatory compliance roles.'

The Act applies to public sector bodies in certain circumstances, but on past experience, will require a strong level of proof. An outbreak of Legionnaire's disease in a leisure centre run by Barrow-in-Furness council in August 2002, caused the death of seven people. The council was charged with seven counts of manslaughter. A council architect and the council were found guilty of failing to take reasonable care under the Health and Safety at Work Act but the charge of manslaughter failed because the actions were not seen as deliberate, rather a consequence of a mix of a practical solution – saving money – and carelessness in not being aware of the consequences.

The wording of the 2007 Act, further, specifically excludes those areas where the state as an institution would get involved in accusations of causing death, including military activities involving 'potentially violent peacekeeping operations' and (along with the police) dealing with terrorism and violent disorder. The Act also excludes a breach of any duty of care owed in respect of things done in the exercise of 'exclusively public functions'. These relate to functions that have a statutory or prerogative basis (for example, conducting international diplomacy) or which the private sector could not do (such as invading Iraq, although military training could be considered as falling under the Act), and where there exists other means of control – for example, independent investigations, public inquiries and the accountability of ministers through Parliament.

In general, therefore, public bodies have the potential to commit a range of state crimes. On the other hand, many government departments and agencies are not under the direct control of the Executive and, in the implementation of policy, their offences are primarily in terms of civil action or regulatory law, and applying state crime concepts problematic.

What type of state crime? The Executive

While the core executive, in terms of individual departments and individual public officials, may be governed by the frameworks described above, the position of the government itself is less clear in terms of state crime. The actions or decisions of specific ministers may be ruled unlawful and government policies themselves, as in the case of Orders-in-Council, may be challenged in the courts by citizens and others. The government often appears in court on behalf of the actions or decisions of its departments, including at the European Court of Human Rights.

However, although governments can and do commit state crime, and self-evidently do so in pursuit of state interests, the capture of the government within the remit of at least the domestic legal framework is less evident. This is in part achieved by the government's capacity to legislate its own exemptions, to ignore the implications of its policies and, crucially, to be provided with significant discretionary space by the courts as a result of which they may be exempt from adjudication and accountability.

The 1947 Crown Proceedings Act stated that, for example:

> nothing done or omitted to be done by a member of the armed forces of the Crown while on duty as such shall subject either him or the Crown to liability in tort for causing the death of another person, or for causing personal injury to another person, in so far as the death or personal injury is due to anything suffered by that other person while he is a member of the armed forces of the Crown if at the time when that thing is suffered by that other person, he is either on duty as a member of the armed forces of the Crown or is, though not on duty as such, on any

land, premises, ship, aircraft, or vehicle for the time being used for the purposes of the armed forces of the Crown …'.

What that has meant in practice is that the Act effectively prevented 'any (nuclear) test veteran or any relative of a test veteran suing the Government for damages to compensate for injuries they believe were caused by the tests' (Blakeway and Lloyd-Roberts 1985: 194). It was argued that the continuing availability of the Act was in part a consequence of 'a degree of loyalty' by successive governments supporting a common policy (Smith 1985: 158). Further 'politicians on all sides are aware that the causes that appear attractive in opposition can prove expensive in Government. A single admission of negligence could open the floodgates to costly claims and stir up the simmering nuclear controversy in Britain' (Blakeway and Lloyd-Roberts 1985: 219).

Even where an adverse consequence is identified as a consequence of government policy-making and policy prioritisation, then often the only means of identifying if the government has caused harm are formal censure and sanction through civil courts, as in the case of tainted blood provided to haemophiliacs:[13]

> There is no doubt that the infection of so many patients, often with fatal results, is a horrific human tragedy. It was memorably described by Lord Winston as the worst treatment disaster in the history of the NHS, a view with which we agree. Subsequent events have done little to alleviate the hurt of the victims or their families. The haemophilia community feels that their plight has never been fully acknowledged or addressed … We are dismayed at the time taken by Governmental and scientific agencies to become fully alive to the dangers of Hepatitis C and HIV infections, and also by the lethargic progress towards self-sufficiency in blood products in England and Wales.
>
> From the promise of self-sufficiency to its attainment took five years in Ireland, but thirteen years in England and Wales. A prominent factor in this delay was the situation at BPL in Elstree. Not designed for production on the scale that was becoming necessary it also suffered from fragmented management and under-funding. Whether the lack of urgency over much of this period arose from over-hesitant scientific advice or from a sluggish response by Government is now difficult to assess. (Archer *et al.*, 2009: 103–4)

Indeed, the government responded, unlike in other countries where there were criminal prosecutions against those responsible or a judicial inquiry that identified 'wrongful acts', not only with a reluctance to disclose documents but also an unwillingness to establish an inquiry to see who might be responsible, thereby avoiding any adjudication on 'the tragedy of patients being infected with potentially fatal diseases through NHS prescribed treatment' and if state crime concepts could apply to the state's actions, not only in relation to the provision of tainted blood but also in trying to avoid an inquiry.

Governments are also protected by judicial caution and by the nature of public policy-making. A 2006 House of Lords case involving several defendants who had appealed against conviction for various trespass and damage offences in attempts to hinder preparations for the Iraqi war, on the grounds that they were legally justified to prevent the commission of the crime of aggression under customary international law, noted that the courts would be very cautious about wishing to sit in judgement on the 'culpability' of the UK state in terms of the international context: 'there are well-established rules that the courts will be very slow to review the exercise of prerogative powers in relation to the conduct of foreign affairs and the deployment of the armed services, and very slow to adjudicate upon rights arising out of transactions entered into between sovereign states on the plane of international law' (R v. Jones and others, 2006, House of Lords, para 30).

Indeed, the court stated clearly that 'the decision to go to war, whether one thinks it was right or wrong, fell squarely within the discretionary powers of the Crown to defend the realm and conduct its foreign affairs' (R v. Jones and others, 2006, House of Lords, para 66). In other words, the courts recognised the concept of the state in terms of crime but then exempted certain areas of state activity from the domestic legal framework, thus leaving only international law (and the vaguer concepts of customary international law and normative standards such as human rights), the application of which by the courts was limited (see below, p. 217).

What then determines the acceptability of state policy-making in, for example, the international arena, rests very much with the government. For example, Indonesia left what was to become East Timor in 1999, the year when 'almost the entire of East Timor was turned to ashes by the Indonesian military and their militia supporters. The destruction followed a United Nations organized referendum on August 30, 1999 in which 78.5% of East Timorese voted to break away from Indonesia. The effects of the destruction of East Timor are multi-dimensional, ranging from infrastructure breakdown and the collapse of government to heavy contraction of the economy (–35%), which is equivalent to $147 million according to IMF estimates' (Tiri and TIDS 2006: 3).

Gilby (2001) describes how two years earlier, in 1997, Labour had entered government, 'a few months after the Conservatives had licensed the sale of 16 Hawk 209s to Indonesia':

> In 1978, Robin Cook had described the Hawk sale as 'particularly disturbing', and in 1994 said Hawks had been 'observed on bombing runs in East Timor in most years since 1984'. The new Labour government had the option of revoking the licence for the 1996 sale ... It refused to, with Derek Fatchett claiming in Parliament in July 1997 that it was not 'realistic or practical'. Legally the government was entitled to revoke licences without fear of financial liability but, in the words of the Foreign Affairs Select Committee 'would be obliged to demonstrate that its policy towards that country had indeed changed in such a way as to require the revocation'. As government policy had not changed, the effect of which was to support a brutally repressive regime, the vital pillar of which was the military, the sales had to proceed. (Gilby 2001)

Acting outside the legal boundaries

Finally, any assessment of the application of the concepts of state crime needs to take account of those circumstances where a state not only finds ways to exempt itself from legal adjudication but provides a legal framework that allows illegal acts to take place on behalf of state interests.

The courts have made it very plain that the capacity of the state to operate outside any legal framework is limited (although there are areas of state activity – discussed below – where the courts accept no jurisdiction on whether or not any law is broken). At the end of the Operation Cotton trial in 2003 (see p. 23), Judge Bathurst-Norman made a scathing attack about who or which public agency could break the law. He talked of state-created crime, beginning from 'the fundamental premise that no member of the Executive is entitled to break the law and no matter how high his rank is, no member of the Executive may authorise another to break the law. By the same token, obedience to superior orders is no defence. Furthermore, it is not open to any court to authorise a person to break the law. Only Parliament in exercising its own law-making function is entitled to exclude a person, such as a police officer, from criminal liability under any of its Acts or in common law.'

Conversely, however, the courts have made it plain that within the UK the state cannot act unlawfully without there being a domestic law to breach. In the 2006 House of Lords case mentioned above, the defendants had argued their case based on customary international law, only for the Lords to reject their argument, stating that only the legislature could secure that recognition by amending criminal law; 'it is for those representing the people of the country in Parliament, not the executive and not the judges, to decide what conduct should be treated as lying so far outside the bounds of what is acceptable in our society as to attract criminal penalties' (R v. Jones and others, 2006, House of Lords, para 29). To reinforce this, the Lords argued that activities under the 1967 Criminal Law Act (using reasonable force to prevent a crime) could not rely on crimes proscribed by international law because the Act applied to domestically defined crime and not to 'crimes recognised in customary international law but not assimilated into our domestic law by any statute or judicial decisions' (R v. Jones and others, 2006, House of Lords, para 26).

So, if there is law, government can propose to Parliament exemption for official law-breaking; two examples can be noted. First, Article 5 of the 1994 Intelligence Services Act, which governs the Security Service, states that covert surveillance, including entering property, would be unlawful unless authorised by the minister. As to work overseas, the Act specifies under section 7 that their liability under UK criminal or civil law may be lifted with the agreement of the Secretary of State if he or she is satisfied that what they do would be 'necessary for the proper discharge of a function of the Intelligence Service' and that there are 'satisfactory arrangements' to ensure that they don't do anything beyond 'what is necessary for the proper discharge of a function of the Intelligence Service'. The authorisation or immunity applies to obtaining and providing information relating to the actions or intentions of persons outside the British Islands but it also allows MI6 to 'perform (sic) other tasks relating to the actions or intentions of such persons'.

Second, the 2010 Bribery Act allows as a defence for a person charged with any offence under the Act – including aiding, abetting, counselling, attempting, conspiring or inciting the commission of an offence – to prove that it was necessary for 'the proper exercise of any function of an intelligence service' and 'the proper exercise of any function of the armed forces when engaged on active service'.

Summary

The capability of individuals, public organisations and governments to commit what the state crime literature terms *state crime* is extensive, if patchy in terms of which type of law, and when. Nevertheless, a number of points need to be made. First, the closer one gets to stating that the government has committed state crime, so the more it is distanced from any legal responsibility in terms of domestic law. This is largely because the courts have accepted that there are activities of the state 'into the exercise of which the courts will not enquire'. For example, in relation to national security, the court in the 2006 House of Lords case stated that 'those who are responsible for national security must be the sole judges of what national security requires' (quoted in R v. Jones and others, 2006, House of Lords, 31). This does not mean that the courts have no jurisdiction; it means that if the courts decide the matter under consideration falls within the discretionary authority of the state, they will not proceed.

Second, and beyond this area (the state *qua* state), state agencies and individual public officials are subject to an extensive range of offences, from domestic criminal law to codified international law. Most of the offences that would involve a public agency or the state would fall outside the criminal law, and the development of a criminal offence of corporate manslaughter excludes many areas of state activity. While there may be some discussion on whether regulatory offences may be labelled a state crime, as would be an offence under criminal law, it is clear that in terms of legality any action of the state in pursuit of state interests that breaches a legal requirement is in theory a state crime. Whether this should also include customary international law, or even the concept of human rights, is more problematic because the process of adjudication would lie either with subjective assessments or with inquiries that are not focused on individual culpability or misconduct.

On the other hand, and in recognition of the breaches of criminal or regulatory law, or causing harm, which are not related to the interests of the state nor instigated or authorised by the government, consideration needs to be given to the labelling of offences that are breaches of the implementation of official policy by public officials acting in their official capacity but where not approved by the state.

In trying to determine the motives for state crime, the primary focus should be on those official decisions or actions in pursuit of state interests that break those domestic, regional and international laws to which the state and its agencies profess adherence and, in the UK context, would also be assumed to be fundamental democratic tenets. This does not exclude questions of customary international law or wider concepts of human rights and harm, although human rights is now extensively addressed under legislation. In terms of types of state crime and organisational deviance, and state-corporate crime, however, three questions remain: can a liberal democratic state commit state crime, why does a liberal democratic state commit state crime, and does it do so in terms of one type or several types of state crime identified in the literature?

Notes

1 For the purposes of this book, the primary focus is on legislation that is applicable generally within England, Scotland, Wales and Northern Ireland. It also primarily addresses central government. Most of the material will also focus on national government – the government, ministries and agencies.

2 Some years later, another Labour government attracted controversy over an Order-in-Council, this time banning the supply of army to 'any person connected with Sierra Leone'. In 1998, a deal to supply arms to the ousted President was being investigated by HM Customs and Excise (HMCE). The solicitors for the company involved wrote to the Foreign Secretary that its clients had been assured 'throughout that the operation had the full support' of the government. The subsequent inquiries noted that the contents of the Order were not widely known, that the Minister had not been briefed adequately or on time, that the FCO should ensure staff were aware both of the parameters of government policy and their responsibilities to ministers, and have guidance on dealing with PMCs, that the FCO should have liaised with HMCE sooner and more thoroughly, and that the government should cooperate more fully with subsequent parliamentary inquiries (see Foreign Affairs Committee 1992; Legg and Ibbs 1998).

3 In the 2006 R. v Jones case in the House of Lords (see above, p. 165), it was noted that the crime of aggression was the 'unlawful use of war as an instrument of national policy'.

4 Of course, in the modern state, it would be important to recognise that public officials are subject not only to criminal law but also to those laws that address the commission or involvement in crime (as well as those which govern the obstruction of the investigation of crime), such as the 1981 Criminal Attempts Act conspiracy to commit another offence, such as

deception, under section 12 of the 1987 Criminal Justice Act. The possibility of such offences was raised in the 2010 Police Ombudsman report into the role of a Roman Catholic priest in an IRA bombing, after which a Conservative government minister was involved in arrangements that agreed both the ending of the investigation and the transfer of the priest beyond UK jurisdiction; the report suggested that there was 'no criminal intent' by any government minister (Police Ombudsman 2010: 23).

5 There is a criminal office relating to the conduct of public officials. Misconduct in public office concerns circumstances where a public officer (someone who carries out 'their duties for the benefit of the public as a whole and, if they abuse their office, there is a breach of the public's trust') commits an offence when he or she 'wilfully neglects to perform his duty and/or wilfully misconducts himself to such a degree as to amount to an abuse of the public's trust in the office holder, without reasonable excuse or justification'.

In practice, however, the key ingredient is that of the intent (the *mens rea*), in that its use to date would suggest that using the offence to define many state crimes would be unlikely since the components of the offence include 'the existence of some improper, dishonest or oppressive motive in the exercise or refusal to exercise some public function' (see Maer 2009). Nevertheless, the offence without the motive, and particularly if it results in harm or injury, could fit with the academic concept of state crime.

6 Even when the public official never intended death to be a consequence, the law on manslaughter recognises that two criteria are: conduct that was grossly negligent given the risk of death, and resulted in death ('gross negligence manslaughter'); and an unlawful act involving a danger of some harm, that resulted in manslaughter ('unlawful and dangerous act manslaughter').

7 Members of the UK legislature are exempt from criminal law in relation to parliamentary proceedings. Their conduct is governed by internal rules, breaches of which are dealt with through internal processes.

8 The anaesthetist involved later stated that he and his family were 'living and working in Australia as a direct result of the treatment I received in Bristol after criticising the conduct of paediatric cardiac surgery at the Bristol Royal Infirmary. No medical or non-medical professional in the NHS should have to endure the threats and discrimination that I was subjected to in Bristol.'

9 In 2010, as a consequence of civil proceedings brought by twelve former Guantánamo detainees against the UK government, a range of documents were released, indicating UK engagement in the US's rendition and extra-jurisdiction interrogation policy. In July, the UK Prime Minister announced that there would be, once the court cases and two police inquiries had ended, an inquiry to assess allegations of complicity of UK agencies in torture and rendition since the al-Qaida attacks of September 2001 because 'the longer these questions remain unanswered, the bigger the stain on

our reputation as a country that believes in freedom, fairness and human rights grows'. In November 2010 a mediated settlement was reached with 16 Guantánamo detainees – with no admission of culpability and no withdrawal of the allegations – to avoid protracted and costly litigation that, it was argued, could compromise national security.

10 The Metropolitan Police paid compensation to the family in 2009. It had already paid £175,000 in fines and £385,000 costs in the health and safety case.

11 For example, reports on the 1987 Zeebrugge ferry sinking, the 1999 Paddington train crash and the 2000 Hatfield train crash alleged unlawful killing, 'incompetent management' and failures to manage and supervise working practices.

12 The new Bribery Bill (2010) also introduces an offence of corporate liability if the company does not have adequate procedures or if a 'responsible' person or persons consents or connives in the bribery; it does not cover the public sector for similar offences.

13 Up to the mid-1980s many UK haemophiliacs treated with blood and blood products subsequently contracted Hepatitis C and HIV; the infections caused over 1,700 deaths. By the mid-1970s it was known in medical and government circles that blood products, especially those imported from the USA, carried a danger of the hepatitis infection (and HIV by the mid-1980s), but the products continued to be imported and used.

Chapter 6

Not on the label? State crime and state crime variants: opportunities and motives in a liberal democratic state

Introduction

The previous chapter noted the complexity of the legal framework within which the UK state works. In looking at the state, it is clear that there is a core executive that makes up the state, and the focus of that core executive is the government. State crime therefore most directly applies to the government and, in its implementation of government policy, the core executive. The development of the state, or core executive, in the UK has led to a closed system of government that both espouses the tenets and practices of democracy and whose roles and responsibilities primarily focus on the delivering of services relating to the citizen in a domestic context.

However, the state has a long and continuing tradition of also accepting roles and responsibilities that focus on the state *qua* state. These primarily focus on the state, in a domestic context in exercising a range of monopoly functions – tax raising, policing, and so on – over its population and, in an external context protecting its sovereignty, geographic integrity, trading and diplomatic relations, and war.

A number of those areas are subject to domestic and international law, but not all; the courts recognise various state prerogatives in which it chooses not to interfere. This space, together with the continuing state functions relating to the interests of the state, often termed 'the national interest', provides both activity and motive that may fall within the general definitions of state crime. While many of those involved in such activities would not consider that their motives reflect those encompassed by the concept of organisational deviance, there is divergence between the actions of the state *qua* state, and the state as a democratic state. Similarly the state, in pursuit of the interests of the state, may favour economic interests, but how far that colours all relations with the corporate sector, and how far the latter control and direct the actions and decisions of the former, may be more debatable. At the same time, however, the possibility of state-facilitated crime, in terms of weak or limited regulatory oversight, does exist although, again, how far this is as a consequence of the dominance of the corporate sector over the state is also debatable.

On the other hand, the issues relating to the drivers for organisational deviance and corporate crime, as well as regulatory issues in the private sector, may, as a consequence of the promotion of business approaches and practices for the delivery of public services, lead to a type of state crime that is neither a direct consequence of government initiation or authorisation, nor in the national interest:

> It is obvious that rule and law breaking is a relevant subject, even in countries that are considered modern and democratic. The type of rule breaking varies considerably. On the one hand there are serious state crimes such as illegal arms trading, the misuse of power for private benefit and corruption. On the other hand, this study highlights the fact that the less serious examples of rule and law breaking must also be taken into account. The latter are widespread and may have serious consequences as they raise questions with respect to the effectiveness and integrity of government bodies and the state. (Huberts *et al.* 2006: 127)

This chapter argues that the continuing development of the modern state has created a number of locations for the opportunity for state crime, but the type of state crime may vary according to the location, and that motivation may vary accordingly.

State crime

Context

The reforms that took place in the Thatcher era were intended both to reduce the size of the state, and the range of activities in which the state was directly involved. They allowed the 'high' politics roles and responsibilities of the state to have a greater significance in the activities of the state. Thatcherism was not 'a break with the past, but a return to pre-war norms; it was the post-war era which represented an uncharacteristic "responsive" rather than "responsible" nature of British government. Mrs Thatcher's emphasis on strong, decisive leadership, her rejection of consultation, her preference for "Prime Ministerial" rather than cabinet government, along with a number of other features of her governmental style ... fit very well with the elitist, top-down view of democracy which underpins the traditional institutions and processes of British government' (Tant 1993: 216).

One of the major problems with the hollowed-out model proposed by some political scientists to describe state development in the UK, which argues that the reforms weakened the dominance of the Executive, is that its approach may have understood the changes that took place but may not always have been as successful in interpreting their implications.

Balancing the hollowed-out perspective, therefore, others would argue that the Thatcher governments 'sought to break with the dominant trend in post-war decades toward a regulated mixed economy, a welfare interventionist state', and their success was based 'in large part on the uncoupling or separation of the instrumental or performative dimension of the state, that is, the state as an instrument for the delivery of goods and services, from consideration of the state as a powerful, prestigious and enduring representative of the people or the nation' (Held 1989: 140).

The Thatcher era reflected an 'aversion to state intervention and control' and 'a belief that the state has neither the management capability nor the responsibility to ensure the general performance and effectiveness of the economy and its related institutions'. This was matched by the revival of 'the traditional symbols of the British nation state ... (precisely those symbols associated with Great Britain, the "glorious past", the empire and international prestige) ... There is good reason to think that this diffuse commitment has been – after some decades of relative dormancy – reactivated (at least in England) and brought once again to the foreground of British politics' (Held 1989: 140)[1].

Thus, rather than its hollowing-out, the divestment of accumulated responsibilities may have honed the state, where 'long-term "creeping centralisation of power in the core executive" looks set to continue' (Burnham and Pyper 2008: 244), in turn leaving it with clearer goals (or at least allowing the more traditional layers relating to the roles of the state to emerge), which in turn reinforces the role of the head of the government where:

The presence of a *de facto* presidency in the British system has been occasioned by British circumstances and traditions. Furthermore, it has been assisted and supported by some of the most central components of the British system. Parties, for example, have come not only to sponsor the issues of leadership in political competition, but also to project their leaders as individual summations of public hopes, anxieties and ideals. Cabinets ... underwrite prime ministerial prominence and leverage as the necessary instruments for remaining in office ... This amounts to collective peer group pressure to a prime minister to breach the collective ethos of the cabinet and to assume both a public persona and an individual pre-eminence for the sake of the cabinet and the party as a whole. (Foley 1993: 278)

This approach may thus reflect less the negative one of disengagement but more the positive one of doing so to concentrate on more traditional government interests, including those that reflect the reassertion of the dual polity and the focus on those issues seen as addressing the government's core business:

in many important respects Mrs Thatcher's government style, as well as her philosophical orientation, represented a reassertion of the British political tradition; rejecting consultation and 'responsiveness', stressing instead strong decisive leadership and the independent authority of 'responsible' initiatory government ... She was simply willing to utilise fully the opportunities presented within the basic framework of British government to achieve her policy goals ... Given that we have seen that official secrecy fits happily with the underlying assumptions and established conventions of British government, the analysis of 'Thatcherism' as the reassertion of the British political tradition therefore aids the understanding of its recent significant tightening. Similarly, Executive dominance has been shown to be a definitive feature of British government, and 'Thatcherism' saw this trend intensified in areas beyond that of official secrecy ... (Tant 1993: 250, 251)

Consequences

This context has reasserted the state, or the national interest, as a driver for decision-making in areas of traditional responsibility where government believes that it can not only be successful but

175

can operate relatively unfettered. The core functions – such as a monopoly of force, the economy, trade and an international role – also accords with those functions traditionally seen to be the continuing core responsibility of 'high politics', the preserve where government dominates policy formulation and implementation (see Hill 1997: 146). Furthermore, it can also be argued that the radicalism of the 1980s' Conservative governments was selective – 'limited to attacking aspects of the consensus on the priorities of domestic policy' – while also promoting traditional support among opposition parties and Parliament for the national interest in seeking 'to reinforce crucial aspects of the bipartisan consensus on external policy' (Gamble 1998: 204–5).

Such a framework, well exploited by Conservative governments, does not disappear with a change in government. Similar arguments have been advanced for the Blair government's participation in the Iraq war as facilitated by 'the underlying norms and values that are perpetuated by, and deeply entrenched within, its political structures. Conditioned by the principles of centralisation, hierarchy, and elitism, these ideational and institutional contours act to sustain a model of government on the virtues of a strong and decisive executive, a limited notion of representation, and a relative paucity of effective checks and balances' (Kettell 2006: 176).

Here it is entirely possible that the state – the government and the core executive – may choose between what it considers to be in the interests of the state and what may or may not be acceptable within a democratic state (and one of the main causes of the discussions, for example in relation to the invasion of Iraq, on the legality of the action and the presentation of the motives for the invasion to the population). The motive, however, may not be one of organisational deviance. It could be argued that the deviance relates to the principles and practices that are integral to a democratic state. On the other hand, the state itself needs to be recognised as having its own set of traditions, principles and practices, within which those decisions or actions it considers necessary, or even essential to protect, preserve or further the national interest, will take precedence over adherence to democratic tenets.

The drivers are therefore related to the sense of the interests of the nation-state that invariably focus on internal and external threats to, or interests of, the state and are linked to the core responsibilities of the state. Here the potential for state crime comes less from the consequences of deviant behaviour relating to the roles and responsibilities of the state than from the ability of governments, and those parts of the core executive responsible for the relevant implementation, to exploit pre-existing institutional and procedural approaches in pursuit of what is perceived as in the interest of the state or the national interest (see Box 28).

There is no doubt that the capacity of governments to have a propensity to commit state crime is deeply rooted in political traditions and practice. While the reassertion of the interests of the

---

Box 27: Political interests

The handover of Hong Kong to the Chinese after a century of leasehold was always controversial, given China's human rights and democratisation record. It posed a major problem for the UK government in terms of denying the wishes of the majority of the citizens in one of their dependencies when they had already, through a 1984 White Paper, promised a limited but developing track towards democratisation through a small number of directly elected representatives to the Legislative Council. The handing-back process was marked by increasingly clear differences of opinions and approaches between UK public officials and Chris Patten, the former Conservative minister and Hong Kong's last governor, as to whose interests were being better served.

The UK tilt toward China had long been accepted when UK and local negotiators bowed to an 'armlock' over democracy promises to allegedly influence the interpretation of the results of a 1987 'consultation' survey in which a significant majority indicated that they wished elections to happen. 'In a breathtaking sleight of hand, the Hong Kong Survey Office, which had the task of collating these responses, under instructions from Government House, and at the behest of the Foreign Office, contrived to suggest that the reverse was true.' It was known that pro-China groups were using certain forms to register their dissent; not only were these forms accepted, but skewed counting was used for the signatures on these forms, as opposed to those submitted by pro-democracy supporters, so that 'with an effrontery usually associated only with totalitarian states and banana republics, the Hong Kong government blithely announced that, on the basis of the submissions to the Survey Office, "more were against than in favour of the introduction of direct elections in 1988"' (Dimbleby 1997: 108).

---

state *qua* state were noticeable during the Thatcher era, the approach of New Labour in strengthening 'the role of the party leadership' and the re-establishment of 'its credibility as a governing force' to take advantage of the 'elitist configuration of Britain's political architecture ... subsequently conferred a largely untrammelled degree of freedom upon senior members of the party in office ... This has been reflected in the adoption of a political strategy designed to enhance New Labour in government to enhance Britain's position within the global political economy, and to augment the autonomy of the core executive itself' (Kettell 2006: 177).

Case study – in pursuit of the interests of the state?

The continual and inexorable role of violence in Northern Ireland in the 1970s and 1980s (see Moloney 2002) brought the question into sharp focus for both Labour and Conservative governments in terms of 'how a political system which claims to be democratic reacts to challenges to its democratic credentials by an armed attack on their legitimacy' (Miller 1994: 281). The focus on the need to confront the violence as the fundamental issue coloured the conduct of both the Provisional IRA (PIRA) and successive British governments during these decades.

PIRA's reliance on the role of violence was integral to its self-identified role as, said one alleged US-based gun runner, 'part of the anti-imperialist and anti-colonial struggle which is going on all over the world, as is the struggle against fascism, which is the offspring of imperialism' (quoted in Holland 1987: 111). As a consequence, 'violence is what gives the PIRA its importance. This realisation, combined with the PIRA's monochromic view of the world and its implacable and unappeasable nature, means that it is possible to predict with gloomy certainty that the troubles will continue for the foreseeable future. Even if the attitudes of the leadership were to change, it seems highly likely that a proportion of the rank and file would continue the tradition if only as a monotonous act of revenge' (Bishop and Mallie 1987: 449).

In such circumstances, the focus of both Labour and Conservative governments shifted to breaking the dependency of their supporters on the paramilitaries by concentrating on the latter, and from the 1970s on both sets of governments attempted rougher, more unorthodox means of seeking to end the violence.

In 1976, the European Commission of Human Rights ruled that the sensory deprivation techniques used by the RUC in interviewing suspects were considered to be 'torture, inhuman and degrading treatment'. Although there were official 'unqualified undertakings' to ensure no repetition, a 1977 Amnesty report alleged continuing ill treatment. To avoid the likely impact of any public inquiry into the allegations, the Labour government – publicly accepting, in Roy Mason's words, the need to strike 'a difficult balance between combating criminal activity and maintaining the civil liberties of a free society' – asked Amnesty to have its informants make formal complaints to the Northern Ireland DPP and set up an inquiry into general issues relating to interrogation rather than the specific complaints. The government's attempt to dampen down the issue was aided and abetted by the IBA pulling a Thames television programme on the report (see Taylor 1980). The inquiry report – the Bennett Report – went as close as it could to confirming the allegations and helped the Labour government lose the 1979 vote of no confidence.

The newly elected Conservative government, led by a Prime Minister whose response to the death of Lord Mountbatten and 18 soldiers at Warrenpoint in August 1979 was to reassert the need to meet violence with violence, enhanced the role of the armed forces and introduced both MI5 and MI6 (in the shape of Maurice Oldfield, its former head, as security coordinator) into the conflict (for details of the territorial battles and dirty tricks by MI5, MI6 and the armed forces see Foot 1990; Holroyd and Burbridge 1989).

This approach brought a number of agencies into play both to develop the intelligence capacity of the armed forces and to proactively strike at PIRA operatives; part of this involved unlawful interrogations (see Taylor 1980) and ambushes by the SAS (see Adams et al. 1988). The government also isolated the resolution of the conflict away from the democratic processes by treating it as a military issue, underpinned by an elaborate news management exercise to distance democratic principles from the activities of those engaged in the conflict on the ground (see Miller and Curtis 1984).

This in turn, as one commentator noted, created a number of rule of law and accountability issues:

Special Branch, military intelligence and the security services operate with a freedom which makes it virtually impossible for CID properly to investigate incidents involving personnel from any of their agencies. In reality CID has been neutered. The 'pitchfork killings'[2] episode illustrates how CID was unable to gain access to the information and people relevant to their inquiry. The RUC has no authority on army bases and is denied access to files relating to intelligence matters. This limiting of the central role of a police force is ... damaging to society and only serves to heighten suspicion of cover-ups and conspiracies. (Dillon 1990: 459–60)

Nevertheless, those concerns were brought home when a senior police officer did try and uncover evidence of criminal activity. In the last two months of 1982, six men in Northern Ireland were shot dead by RUC Special Branch officers, members of a proto-SAS counter-intelligence group known as the Special Support Unit. In two separate trials in 1984 before Diplock Court judges – judges sitting without juries – four of the officers were tried and acquitted of murder. In one of the trials the officer concerned claimed he had been persuaded by senior colleagues to conceal certain aspects of the operation in his later evidence; the judge acquitted the officer, stating it was not his responsibility to conduct 'an inquiry into why the officers who advised, instructed or constrained the accused acted as they did' (Taylor 1987: 89).

At the other trial the judge announced the acquittals 'without hesitation or reservation' because the three defendants were 'absolutely blameless' in 'bringing the three deceased men to justice, in this case, the final court of justice'. While this set of acquittals created a hostile political climate in which the Irish government was publicly announcing its concern that the judge's comments were 'entirely unacceptable and unworthy of decent judicial authority', the other acquittal prompted the Northern Ireland DPP to demand an investigation over whether RUC officers had lied and had committed criminal offences. Chief Constable John Hermon went outside the RUC for an investigation (see Taylor 1987).

John Stalker, then Deputy Chief Constable of the Greater Manchester police, was chosen for the task. Unfortunately for Stalker his decision to reinvestigate the shootings rather than review the RUC's own investigations meant prying into three sensitive areas of Northern Ireland policing: the use of moles and informers, the sophisticated electronic surveillance, and the joint RUC–MI5 activities that included cross-border activities. Such delicate and sensitive areas posed considerable problems for Stalker's inquiry which, although it found no evidence of a shoot-to-kill policy, was less than happy with procedures and tactics of the RUC Special Branch.

In early 1986, however, when Stalker had persuaded the DPP to have Hermon release key evidence about one of the shootings, Stalker suddenly found himself suspended from duty while his association with certain Manchester businessmen was investigated by the Chief Constable of West Yorkshire (see Stalker 1988; Taylor 1987). Ultimately cleared to return to work in August 1986 by the Manchester Police Authority, albeit with some comment about his choice of friends, Stalker felt sufficiently frozen-out to opt for retirement in March 1987.

The coincidence of Stalker being taken off the inquiry just as he was about to make a breakthrough in access to crucial information, and the subsequent failure of the government to have a satisfactory explanation ready, gave the media a field-day in pursuing various conspiracy theories to explain why. Stalker himself believed that he was hurriedly removed 'because I was on the threshold of causing a major police scandal and political row that would have resulted in several resignations and general mayhem' (Stalker 1987: 268). The escalating allegations dropped the issue firmly in the lap of the politicians who had to answer questions both on the shoot-to-kill accusations and on Stalker's suspension.

Stalker's successor, Colin Sampson, reacting to 'any suggestion that he'd been "nobbled", or a tool of the Conservative Government or had been brought in to whitewash or cover up' (Taylor 1987: 191), finished off the Stalker Report by recommending several prosecutions of RUC officers for obstructing and perverting the course of justice. Whether this involved political links was not pursued. The government's reaction was the announcement in January 1988, by Northern Ireland Minister Tom King, that there would be no prosecutions of the officers because it was not in the public interest to do so on the grounds of national security (the government issued public interest immunity certificates prohibiting the disclosure of sensitive security materials, including the Stalker and Sampson reports, which caused the inquest into some of the deaths to be abandoned in 1994).[3]

Three months after King's announcement, the Gibraltar shootings of three IRA operatives took place. The story first surfaced with media reports of the shooting of the IRA terrorists by British security forces as they left a car packed with 5,000lbs of explosives near the Governor's house. The car bomb, said reports, was loaded with bits of metal, shrapnel and so on, and timed to go off during a parade. A fierce gun battle was mentioned, as was the use of a robot to defuse the bomb. The official statement was less dramatic: the terrorists were on their way to the border after being seen near a parked car, where their presence and actions 'gave rise to strong suspicion that it contained a bomb, which appeared to be corroborated by a rapid technical examination of the car'. They were shot because they 'made movements' which led the security personnel to think their lives, and the lives of others, were in danger.

The revelations that the three were not armed, that there was no car bomb at that location, and that the shootings were carried out without warning by the SAS who were then whisked away by the Gibraltar police was the subject of a controversial Thames TV *This Week* programme. Since there were a number of issues – the responsibilities for arrest between the local police and the SAS, the authority to use legal force, and so on (see O'Brien 2005: 61), there were immediate calls for an inquiry and government explanations.

The Conservative response was a strong play on patriotism and the avoidance of a major terrorist attack while severely criticising the media for investigating the circumstances of the shootings – 'trial by television with partial witnesses,' said one minister.

Until the inquest, however, the government had refused to give the information the opposition demanded – the rules of engagement for the SAS and the process for authorisation – and insisted they wait for the inquest. After the inquest returned a verdict of lawful killing, the government still refused to comment and kept up a barrage of pressure on Thames, finally forcing it to hold its own independent inquiry into the programme. The inquiry conducted by a former Tory Minister and a leading barrister, found that the programme was made 'in good faith and without ulterior motives' (Windlesham and Rampton 1989: 144). The government reacted with hostility to the report. Indeed, Mrs Thatcher's anger over the programme, and its vindication by the report, was said to be a major factor in the break-up of the structure of independent television.

In 1995, in a case before the Strasbourg court, the families sought to argue that the killings violated Article 2 of the ECHR. The court declined to support this on the basis of the information the security forces had about the terrorists, but ruled that the absence of control led to force that was 'more than absolutely necessary'. Roger Bolton, the programme's producer, was later told by one of his contacts: 'it's none of your business. There are certain areas of British national interest that you shouldn't get involved in. *Death on the Rock* just wasn't necessary' (Bolton 1990: 305).

In 2003, there was a review of possible collusion in Northern Ireland between the various agencies and protestant terrorists[4] another Chief Constable, John Stevens, stated in his third and final report:

I conclude there was collusion in both murders[5] and the circumstances surrounding them. Collusion is evidenced in many ways. This ranges from the wilful failure to keep records, the absence of accountability, the withholding of intelligence and evidence, through to the extreme of agents being involved in murder.

The failure to keep records or the existence of contradictory accounts can often be perceived as evidence of concealment or malpractice. It limits the opportunity to rebut serious allegations. The absence of accountability allows the acts or omissions of individuals to go undetected. The withholding of information impedes the prevention of crime and the arrest of suspects. The unlawful involvement of agents in murder implies that the security forces sanction killings.

My three Enquiries have found all these elements of collusion to be present. The co-ordination, dissemination and sharing of intelligence were poor. Informants and agents were allowed to operate without effective control and to participate in terrorist crimes. Nationalists were known to be targeted but were not properly warned or protected. Crucial information was withheld from Senior Investigating Officers. Important evidence was neither exploited nor preserved (Stevens 2003: para 4.7–4.9).[6]

In relation to the murder of Finucane, Stevens also reported:

My Enquiry team also investigated an allegation that senior RUC officers briefed the Parliamentary Under Secretary of State for the Home Department, the Rt Hon Douglas Hogg QC, MP, that 'some solicitors were unduly sympathetic to the cause of the IRA'. Mr Hogg repeated this view during a debate on the Prevention of Terrorism legislation in the House of Commons. Within a few weeks Patrick Finucane was murdered. Mr Hogg's comments about solicitors' support for terrorism made on 17 January 1989 aroused controversy. To the extent that they were based on information passed by the RUC, they were not justifiable and the Enquiry concludes that the Minister was compromised. (Stevens 2003: para 2.17)

An inquiry into several of the deaths had been proposed in 2001 by both Irish and UK governments, as matters of grave public concern. Peter Cory, a retired Canadian judge, was appointed and issued his report in 2004 (Cory 2004). Using a broad definition of collusion – covering both inaction as well as actions, and patterns of behaviour as well as individual acts of collusion – Cory concluded through a desk review of existing documentation that there had been a number of concerns involving agents of the state:

- The FRU (Force Research Unit) appeared to countenance the commission of crimes by its agents, perhaps perceiving this to be a necessary evil in the fight against terrorism.

- The wilful concealment of pertinent evidence, and the failure to cooperate with the Stevens inquiry, can be seen as further evidence of the unfortunate attitude that then persisted within RUC SB and FRU. Namely, that they were not bound by the law and were above and beyond its reach. These documents reveal that government agencies (the Army and RUC) were prepared to participate jointly in collusive acts in order to protect their perceived interests.

- The documents either in themselves or taken cumulatively can be taken to indicate that FRU committed acts of collusion. Further, there is strong if in some instances conflicting documentary evidence that FRU committed collusive acts.

- The apparent failure of the Security Service to suggest to RUC SB that action should be taken on these threats (against Finucane) might, itself, be capable of constituting collusive action. At the very least, these matters add to the cumulative pattern of conduct demonstrated by the relevant government agencies.

Overall, Cory concluded that 'some of the acts summarized above are, in and of themselves, capable of constituting acts of collusion. Further, the documents and statements I have referred to in this review have a cumulative effect. Considered together, they clearly indicate to me that there is strong evidence that collusive acts were committed by the Army (FRU), the RUC SB and the Security Service' (2004: para 1.293). He then called for a public inquiry, which he had assumed would be under the 1921 legislation (see p. 227); in fact, new legislation in 2005 would hand control over the inquiry, the public nature of the evidence, and so on, to the government. Both Cory and the Finucane family protested the decision. This allowed the government to argue that it was 'no longer justifiable to continue to devote public money to preparations for an inquiry which the family would refuse to accept under the terms of the Inquiries Act'.

State-corporate crime

Context

There is little evidence of continuous and one-way subservience of governments to all corporate interests, in terms of an undifferentiated and unqualified pro-capitalism bias underpinning all state actions and decisions. On the other hand, there is evidence that governments *do* act in ways that support economic groupings, collectively or in relation to specific industries, when there is a convergence of policy or political interests.

The economic reforms following the election of a Conservative government in 1979 were not part of a single, pre-determined strategy but born out of half-formed and unsystematic ideological prejudices about the size and roles of the state, the restrictions on business, and the deadweight of corporatist consensualism pursued by the previous Heath, Wilson and Callaghan governments that ensured business and the unions sought to stalemate each other in the policy-making processes and elsewhere.

The main thrust of early Thatcher reforms was the jettisoning of state assets, and nationalised trading companies, more as a wish to hone the business of the state rather than reward the corporate sector. Its early approach to privatisation (see Feigenbaum *et al.* 1998) and a related regulatory framework precipitated but did fully anticipate the high profits and dividends, and even higher self-determined senior management remuneration packages, which provoked the 'fat cats' controversies that followed. The government's approach to the reform of business in general and the financial services in particular was also recognised as in part an enthusiasm for deregulation and a promotion of entrepreneurial activity. It was also born of a realisation of the need for the UK to compete internationally and to become a major international financial centre: 'the 1970s and 1980s in Britain witnessed significant changes in the business community as a result of developments in the markets of the global economy. New financial conglomerates arose and the ground rules were fundamentally altered as a Conservative government sponsored "deregulation" of financial markets to open them to international opportunities and to attract a much wider participation in share ownership' (Punch 1996: 177).

The ground rules were primarily posited on self-regulation, which the major financial institutions were quick to grasp. Lloyd's, the insurance market, had been hit by a wave of scandals involving the cosy insider world but had been reluctant to police itself in the face of alleged fraud (see Clarke 1986 for the scandals). This led to legislation that formalised more effective self-regulation and, more importantly, persuaded Lloyd's that this would be preferable to an agency along the lines of the US Securities and Exchange Commission. The Stock Exchange also managed to secure self-regulation as the 'Big Bang' (when the existing procedures on commissions, ownership and job differentiation were removed) took effect, as well as getting the government at that time to deflect a regulator, the Office of Fair Trading, that wanted to challenge its practices; 'in the late summer of 1983 Sir Nicholas Goodison, Chairman of the Stock Exchange, reached agreement with Cecil Parkinson, then Secretary of State for Trade and Industry, and the OFT were called off' (Clarke 1986: 96).

The Financial Services Act 1986, which sought to regulate financial services – from banks to independent financial advisers – had the role of self-regulation at its heart (albeit to be put on a statutory footing): 'external and statutory investor protection, though important, became less salient, and preserving (or creating) London's pre-eminence as an international financial trading centre became the central concern not only of financial entrepreneurs but also of a government faced with declining world markets and the possibility of creating new jobs' (Levi 1987: 89–90).

Consequences

The presence of a strong state and an ideological commitment combined to promote a wider range of entrepreneurial and managerial reforms beyond those which had appeared to work with the privatised industries, a self-regulating City and private sector companies:

> a free economy was also understood by some to mean a state strong enough to intervene actively in all institutions of civil society to impose, nurture and stimulate the business values, attitudes and practices necessary to relaunch Britain as a successful capitalist economy. This would make the Conservative party for the first time a bourgeois modernising party with no qualms about the radical restructuring of all institutions in state and civil society in the interests of increasing economic efficiency. (Gamble 1988: 232)

While the state of whatever political ideology has long had close relations with corporate interests and often favoured those which coincided with the interests of the state, the relationship between the Conservative governments and the City was not necessarily evidence either of indiscriminate favouring all interests all of the time, or of uncritical state subservience to corporate interests; rather it was the state creating supportive environments for such interests. On the other hand, the comfortable corporate-political nexus that was able to develop did so because of the flexible and somewhat forgiving impact of self-regulation that the state then introduced. Here the line between corporate self-interest, sharp practice and insider profitability became increasingly blurred – and tolerated so long as the intent was not so obviously and deliberately at the expense of the investor or the credibility of the self-regulatory institutions intended to protect them (and where government would on occasion step in to bail out those negative consequences that would threaten the credibility of the reforms and the confidence of those citizens encouraged to become part of the share-owning democracy) (see Box 29).

Indeed, it may be argued that the liberal democratic capitalist society promotes corporate and personal self-interest as part of the economic climate. With the removal of controls from commercial, economic and financial sectors, as well as the endorsement of financial gain and material status as a reward for and an indicator of worth and hard work, such reform may favour certain economic groupings, such as the City. Are, however, the manifestations of that entrepreneurialism – whether successive City scandals, the excessive salaries and perks secured by senior management (the 'fat cats' rows), or the significant profits made by companies, either in concert or individually, or the recent financial crisis among banks – simply capitalism at work? Or do they show a state-corporate context where what then becomes the dividing line between illegality, recklessness and negligence over other people's money, or the dividing line between using knowledge that benefits a client or a corporate entity or its senior management rather than investors, shareholders or customers, is evidence of state-facilitated corporate crime?

Thus it can be argued that the state does act to favour the interests of capitalism in general as a way to create employment or raise taxation, that sustains their *political* position, and that it seeks to minimise the regulatory and other controls environment in which the corporate sector works.

On the other hand, the state does not necessarily do this across the board, nor solely by obeying the wishes of the corporate sector. Indeed, there are countervailing pressures that require the state to take action on behalf of other interested parties and stakeholders, certainly in terms of the expectations in a democratic state. The state is aware of the asymmetrical relationship between the ordinary investor, client or customer (who are also voters) and the corporate sector, which requires some form of policing and monitoring (as the rise of the work of the Financial Services Authority and other regulatory agencies suggests).[7]

Box 28: Bailing out the cost of facilitating state-corporate crime?

Barlow Clowes was a Manchester-based company run by Peter Clowes. It moved from being an investment broker to managing its own investments through gilts – government-issued bonds – for which it was offering either capital growth or an income with a guaranteed return on the investment amount. Clowes' claims to be able to exploit varying rates – aired in the media – pushed up the levels of investment in the company. Clowes moved his business offshore (Jersey and then Gibraltar) and used new income to pay the fixed (and unrealistic) returns promised to existing customers. He spent much of the rest – nearly £100 million - on a lavish lifestyle.

The government regulator, the Licensing Unit, was a small section in the Financial Services Division of the DTI. It first wanted to close Barlow Clowes down, but with the Conservative government keen to promote business and loosen regulation, it then moved to license Clowes to trade (although one official noted that he 'had no concrete reason to worry although one naturally tends to look in askance at business controlled from Gibraltar and harbour unworthy thoughts about the real motives in moving there' (Lever 1992: 147).

The company was closed down in 1988, owing over £100 million. Clowes was sentenced to ten years for theft, making false statements for gain, and conspiracy to deceive. Under pressure from MPs, many of whom represented the small middle-class investor that put the Conservatives in power and had chosen to invest their pensions and life savings with Clowes, the government set up an inquiry – the Le Quesne Inquiry. The criticisms of the DTI contained in its report allowed MPs to call for the Parliamentary Ombudsman to investigate allegations of maladministration. This was duly proved and the government paid over £150 million in compensation.

Thus the state has to balance its duty to the electorate with its relations with the corporate sector, particularly in terms of the domestic market. The context changes, and such dynamics do not apply as strongly, however, where there is a complementarity of interests between the state and the corporate sector away from the domestic context and where the national interest and commercial interests may be mutually beneficial.

For example, exports and employment are strong imperatives for state engagement in behalf of corporate interests. During the post-1979 Conservative governments, the arms trade was promoted vigorously, accelerated by encouraging increasing closeness between government and the defence industry to work together, both in terms of MOD needs and the industry's capacity to satisfy both UK requirements and the export market, supported by the transfer and exchange of staff.

This created a community of interest that, to some, compromised the independence of government and the objectivity of its decision-making processes; a Treasury and Civil Service Committee report warned that 'at a time of increasing closeness and interdependence between government and the private sector', the 'traditional independence and impartiality of the Civil Service is in danger of becoming eroded or compromised' (Treasury and Civil Service Committee 1984; see also Defence Committee 1988). A significant number of those involved in arms manufacture and sales, as well as public officials and members of the armed forces, moved back and forth, often in circumstances which could, as the report into arms to Iraq later noted, be open to misinterpretation or be 'apt to give rise to precisely the suspicion which the rules were designed to avoid' (Scott 1996: D2.396).[8]

Case study – is it a state-corporate crime?

The Middle East has long been a favourite hunting ground for British business, particularly for arms manufacturers. Oil-rich countries with authoritarian regimes and a predilection for state-of-the-art hardware to maintain both internal control and the geo-political rivalries also had the wealth. This not only ensured that British governments did not have to worry too much about compromising the commercial relationship because of development aid, human rights or other issues, but also meant that they could be put under pressure to deal with specific issues if they did not want to lose contracts.[9]

Saudi Arabia was the largest single market for military sales in a part of the world that had the biggest share of UK arms exports (see Phythian and Little 1993; Phythian 1996, 2004). Saudi Arabia's oil wealth, and small decision-making elite directly involved in contract negotiations, made it a magnet for UK multinationals and arms manufacturers, involving multi-million pound contracts. In Thatcher's election as Prime Minister they found someone determined to use the government machinery to enhance the attractiveness of contracts with UK firms. Her efforts as she travelled around the Middle East culminated in the multi-billion pound Al-Yamamah arms deal, first signed in 1985.

After Saudi Arabia the next largest Middle East market was, until the invasion of Kuwait, Iraq, then undertaking a pointless war with Iran between 1980 and 1988 (see Al-Khalil 1991; Aburish 2000; Coughlin 2002; Darwish, and Alexander 1991; Sweeney 1993). As the war progressed the trade continued, in part because of 'a desire to support particular companies and a more general aim to improve the UK's share of the Iraqi market' (Miller 1996: 195).

Supporting the arms trade was core business for a number of government departments. The DTI was particularly enthusiastic about sales and trade but it also had responsibility for export control and licensing. These resulted from government requirements under either external conventions (for example, on nuclear non-proliferation), or domestic policy not to arm hostile or unstable countries.

Some controls were informal, in terms of countries on a UK government blacklist, such as North Korea; others were formal in terms of the 1939 Import, Export and Customs Powers (Defence) Act to protect strategic goods being bought by the wrong country. The 1939 Act provided governments with the legal power to demand that specific products apply for export licences for specific countries. The DTI dealt with the export licences as well as assessments to see if products might need a licence (known as 'rating' inquiries) through a licensing unit.

The MOD's interest was, like that of the DTI, two-fold, as promoter and regulator (with the inevitable conflicts between the roles). Thus the MOD was responsible for the technical expertise to advise on the suitability of exports and the promotion of sales. Successive governments' preference for supporting the UK defence industry while encouraging them to pursue overseas sales on the back of MOD sales helped reduce costs and protect jobs. The MOD's Defence Exports Services Organisation (DESO, formerly the Defence Sales Organisation) was effectively the arms sales promotions wing, with a head from the private sector and substantial, officially sanctioned, secondment of defence industry staff linked to the MOD through the Defence Export Sales Secretariat (DESS), which reflected 'MOD policy' within DESO.

The licensing of exports to Iraq and Iran was shaped by the introduction of guidelines in November 1984. The guidelines were, however, not intended to be either 'a palliative for domestic disquiet about the war, and the UK's role as a supplier of arms, or as a morally inspired set of constraints' (Miller 1996: 65; see also Friedman 1993; Sweeney 1993). They were primarily a set of criteria focused on defending the government 'against public and parliamentary criticism and criticism from the Americans and Saudis, whatever decisions we take on grounds of commercial and political interest. In following these concrete interests we have to make sure that our decisions are consistent with the guidelines but the war poses too many problems, and our interests are too finely balanced to allow mechanical application of the guidelines to dictate our policy' (Scott 1996: D3.132). Government ministers were reluctant to publicly discuss the guidelines, preferring a detailed confidential briefing for 'selected parliamentarians and trusted representatives of the media' (Scott 1996: D1.63). It was not surprising that a senior civil servant should note in 1984 in relation to the tilt towards Iraq (and to any reconciliation with a policy of neutrality and even-handedness) that 'there is no principle here, just expediency' (Scott 1996: D1.20).

In October 1985 Geoffrey Howe formally announced the existence of the guidelines in Parliament. These essentially summarised the purpose as not selling, or allowing the supply of 'any defence equipment which, in our view, would significantly enhance the capability of either side to prolong or exacerbate the conflict'. The announced guidelines were the only available record of government intent. Mr Justice Scott, chair of the later inquiry, argued that as such they had to be seen as 'policy'. For Geoffrey Howe to claim later that the guidelines were neither policy nor absolute but 'an aspect of the management of the policy' (Scott 1996: D1.81) was, Scott suggested, 'no more than a play on words'.

Further, under the legislation, the decision to grant or deny a licence lay with the government – or whatever administrative structure it set up – in terms of its regulations. Amending regulations and granting or denying a licence meant that 'the government can, at a stroke of the pen, change the export control law at will and by exercise of its discretion over the issue of licences can render legal or illegal any exports it chooses' (Scott 1996: G3.14).

One crucial aspect of this approach was an apparent unannounced change to the guidelines to suit government interests in favouring Iraq once its war with Iran was over. That it did so was clear within Whitehall. A note by a DTI official later reported: 'in December 1988 MOD, DTI and FCO ministers met to agree a revised but unpublished interpretation to the Iran/Iraqi guidelines which were becoming outdated'. Between the August 1988 ceasefire and the August 1990 invasion of Kuwait, government policy on non-lethal defence and dual-use[10] equipment was subject to alteration.

Manufacturers and the DTI were keen to take advantage of the Iraq market; both the UK and Iraq sent trade delegations to the other's country. That the government supported increasing sales, including defence equipment, to Iraq is clear from the participation of ministers in trade delegations to Iraq and how ministers and officials fought their departmental corners to extend ECGD (Export Credits Guarantee Department) cover to a greater proportion of defence sales (and to a greater proportion of such sales to Iraq). The outcome was a revised guideline in February 1989 amending the words in Guideline 3 ('defence equipment designed to prolong or exacerbate the conflict') to 'defence equipment which … would be of direct and significant assistance to either country in the conduct of offensive operations in breach of the cease-fire' (Scott 1996: G5.20).

Meanwhile, the overlap between the formal machinery of government decision-making, and sales, led to those departments involved in the arms trade cooperating in mutually convenient but less formal ways, with the encouragement of officials to help business on the one hand and the supply of information to officials from businessmen on the other.

Businessman Paul Henderson provided information for MI5 and the MOD while working for TI Machine Tools (Henderson 1994), a company later bought by the Iraqis (and renamed Matrix Churchill); he himself was to pass on information in 1988 to MI6 about the Space Research Corporation (SRC), 'an independent commercial concern controlling state-of-the-art ballistics research laboratories and workshops' (Lowther 1992: 97). Iraq was using SRC-designed guns – supplied by the Austrians and South Africans – and invited SRC in 1988 to pursue further work on both guns and projectiles. It also raised the possibility of a long-range 'Supergun' that could 'not only provide a surveillance capability but which would also circumvent an anti-ballistic missile shield' (Darwish and Alexander 1991: 183) and reach Israeli targets.

SRC then talked to two British metal-forging firms – Walter Somers and Sheffield Forgemasters – about casting pipes for what claimed to be a petro-chemical plant. In March 1990 SRC's owner was killed, with all the hallmarks of a professional assassination, shortly before HM Customs arrived at Teesport to inspect the pipes waiting to be exported. Within another two weeks, SRC's Chris Cowley (Cowley 1992) and Somers' Peter Mitchell were arrested on charges of the illegal exportation of goods under the 1939 Act.

At the end of 1990 the charges against both of those in the Supergun case were abruptly dropped, allegedly with Cabinet approval, because documents could be produced in court demonstrating that the government had known about the Supergun since 1988 and thus that the companies could not have misled the government. In December more damning revelations about the government's approach to exports to Iraq appeared in the *Sunday Times* with a report on an inter-departmental row over a £40 million machine-tool buying spree by the Iraqis which the FCO claimed were for military use.

Earlier, the Machine Tool Trades Association (MTTA) had asked for a meeting with Alan Clark, the DTI minister, which took place in January 1988. Clark advised them that 'the intended use of the machines should be couched in such a manner as to emphasise the peaceful aspect to which they will be put' and that applications should be made as soon as possible in case 'bureaucratic interference occurred during any departmental and ministerial discussions'.

One of the firms given, as one of those at the meeting noted, 'a nod and a wink', was Matrix Churchill, the Iraqi-owned machine-tool manufacturer whose directors had been arrested in October 1990 by HM Customs and Excise and had admitted knowledge that the machine tools exported in relation to one of their contracts could be 'for munitions production'.

Indeed, Matrix Churchill had already told the security services (and later the DTI) that they and other firms had signed contracts with the Iraqi government 'for the purchase of general purpose heavy machinery for the production of armaments in Iraq' (Scott 1996: D2.265). The secret services were critical of Whitehall's failure to listen to what it was being told; one of the service's officials described the handling of a visa application for an Iraqi procurement official connected to Matrix Churchill as a 'classic case of Whitehall wishing to have it both ways – preserve Matrix Churchill's trading relationship, and yet deny its military benefits to Iraq' (Scott 1996: D5.15). Indeed, it was Whitehall's lack of response to intelligence information that was to begin the road to the Scott Inquiry, when an SIS official decided to go to HM Customs and Excise to enforce exports controls on what he was convinced were the barrels of a Supergun.

From the outset HM Customs and Excise were aware of possible reservations in Whitehall over the Matrix Churchill case – Customs had noted in March 1990 that they had been 'warned off' pursuing Matrix's licences because the decision to grant them 'was made at ministerial level' (Scott 1996: G2.13) – but were prepared to continue. This prompted a prescient warning from a DTI official to one of his ministers about any public dissection of decisions on licences and possible worsening of trade relations with Iraq, noting that 'the dirty washing liable to emerge from the action proposed by HM Customs and Excise will add to the problems posed by the gun. For DTI the timing is extraordinarily embarrassing given recent correspondence between ourselves, MOD and FCO' (Scott 1996: G2.16).

Surprisingly, ministers agreed to Customs continuing the inquiries; a meeting of officials from the FCO, MOD and the DTI, on the other hand, determined that the official line was that both firms knew they were acting illegally and 'would be seen as the guilty parties' (Scott 1996: F4.20). Nevertheless the government prepared to present its previous actions in the best possible light by limiting access to sensitive personnel or material and doing the minimum required in assisting the investigators, to avoid being accused of obstruction or a cover-up. This tactic had already been used to disable a Trade and Industry Select Committee Supergun inquiry by denying the existence of accessible documentation, and limiting access to Customs and intelligence information, as well as to relevant witnesses. A similar approach was adopted prior to the forthcoming Matrix Churchill trial.

This was buttressed by steps taken to protect other material on the decision-making processes in Whitehall as a private matter, including documents felt too sensitive – such as those related to the security services, advice to ministers, and internal dealings of the Crown. A Public Interest Immunity (PII) certificate would be issued to indicate their unavailability. The grounds for issuing PII Certificates were that it would not be in the public interest to have such information in the public domain in relation either to specific documents or to all documents that fell within a given area or activity (a 'class').

Faced with the option to drop the prosecution rather than face disclosure, 'none of the departments regarded its PII class claims as of sufficient importance to justify an attempt to halt the prosecution rather than submit to disclosure' (Scott 1996: G14.30). When handed over, what they contained provided the defence with material on which to examine ministerial witnesses about the guidelines and licence applications. The first minister into the witness box was Alan Clark, who described what he said at the meeting with the MTTA in 1988 as being 'economical with the actualité', explaining that he was inviting companies to highlight a peaceful use for their machine tools even though it was, at least so long as the war lasted, very unlikely that they would be put to such use.

The impact of his evidence was compounded by his use of the term 'Whitehall cosmetics' to describe the need to keep the records ambiguous by avoiding the mention of any military use. It was on that revelation – that a company was being prosecuted for following what they interpreted as ministerial advice ('by implication', as Clark put it) – that the trial collapsed amid media and parliamentary uproar in November 1992. Said Scott, about another case going to court: 'the prospect of a jury being willing to convict ... for illegally exporting arms in a case in which the facts alleged to constitute the illegality had been known to Government and in which Government had deliberately decided to allow the export to proceed, was remote' (Scott 1996: H1.40).

As one commentator later noted: 'the collapse of the Matrix Churchill trial gave rise to two serious allegations against ministers. The first was that there was government complicity in exporting to Iraq lethal arms in violation of its guidelines. The second was that, in the pursuance of this policy, ministers were prepared to allow innocent men to be sentenced to prison and used Public Interest Immunity certificates to deny them materials which they needed for their defence' (Bogdanor 1996: 594; see also Leigh 1993). Indeed, media suggestions that the Cabinet may have endorsed 'a secret policy change' over arms sales to Iraq and thus possible complicity of current ministers in the controversy immediately prompted Prime Minister John Major in November 1992 to set up a non-statutory inquiry under a judge, Sir Richard Scott.

The Scott Report essentially showed that the 'policy' of Her Majesty's Government in relation to exports to Iraq was to be whatever Her Majesty's Government considered the most acceptable at a particular time. The government appeared to be balancing a number of issues: avoiding what it considered would be ill-informed criticism of the policy; protecting its public reputation; giving itself flexibility in terms of future policy as circumstances changed; as well as making unpublicised allowances for key constituencies (such as the defence industry or overseas governments).

The government therefore developed an approach of limited official pronouncements on policy and on any changes to the guidelines. Scott was emphatic that there was 'example after example ... of an apparent failure by Ministers to discharge' their obligations under *Questions of Procedures for Ministers* to 'give Parliament, including its Select Committees, and the public as full information as possible about the policies, decisions and actions of the Government, and not to deceive or mislead Parliament and the public' (Scott 1996: K8.1). On the other hand, the Scott Inquiry did not find that any government minister had acted insincerely or deceitfully in terms of the actions or decisions they had taken or approved.

Nevertheless, government ministers attacked Scott for his lack of 'any experience of international affairs or of parliamentary matters', and the inquiry as a 'fundamental mistake', Scott's 'tenacious enthusiasm for his own views' and the 'gap of non-comprehension between the solitary Scott and the real world'. When the report was published the government immediately launched an image management campaign to give the impression that it had been acquitted. Between publication of the report and the parliamentary debate, the Prime Minister let it be known that he was considering 'very seriously' reforms to the 'shortcomings' and 'mistakes' identified in the report. When the debate on the report took place at the end of February 1996, the government was less concerned with rebutting opposition criticism than with keeping its own party majority together, which it did by listing the 'reforms' that would take place, and survived the vote against it.

A decade later the contract signed by the Conservative government in 1985 (Al-Yamamah I) and 1988 (Al-Yamamah II) was due for extension. The new contract was worth at least £20 billion and its main focus was on the Tornado (a consortium-constructed jet involving BAE) and Hawk aircraft made by BAE. The original contract and all variations was with the government, which was to receive oil (the MOD was to receive management fees; BAE was appointed prime contractor to deliver the contract).

Since its inception, the contract had been subject to allegations of commissions and corruption. One issue was that the government, through the MOD, had responsibility for the integrity and audit of the contract, including possible commission payments and other arrangements. The National Audit Office (NAO) looked at the contract but only in relation to the MOD (the NAO had no automatic right to look at private sector contractors either working for the government or spending public money). Its work was constrained by the introduction of special accounting rules by the MOD for the contract 'to ensure Saudi confidentiality is preserved'. The NAO sent its reports, in confidence, to the chair of the Public Accounts Committee, who refused to issue them to his colleagues on grounds of Saudi sensitivities (a view also used by successive governments who also claimed that they were not responsible for the commercial activities of the prime contractor). The audit stated that there was no evidence of potentially illegal payments.

The government that had to address the allegations was one which, in 1997, had come to power proposing an ethical dimension to its foreign policy but had also made it plain that exports would be considered within the UK national interest. However, Labour's stance, certainly in relation to BAE, was complicated both by its arms manufacturing near monopoly and its continuing access to the government; its chairman was 'one of a very small group of outsiders whose requests to see Blair were always granted' (Kampfner 2003: 16). As Robin Cook, the Foreign Secretary, noted in 2002, 'in my time I came to learn that the Chairman of British Aerospace appeared to have the key to the garden door to Number 10. Certainly I never once knew Number 10 come up with any decision that would be incommoding to British Aerospace, even when they came bitterly to regret the public consequences' (Cook 2004: 73).

Nevertheless, this was the same Labour government that was undertaking commitments to international agreements on corruption. The Convention on Combating Bribery of Foreign Public Officials in International Business Transactions (the 'OECD Convention') came into force in 1999 and the UN Convention Against Corruption was signed in 2003. The former was translated into domestic legislation through the 2001 Anti-Terrorism, Crime and Security Act, which:

> made amendments to the Public Bodies Corrupt Practices Act 1889, the Prevention of Corruption Act 1906 and the Prevention of Corruption Act 1916 to ensure that the Acts cover the bribery and corruption of foreign public officials, as well as private sector persons, whether or not the offences are committed in the United Kingdom (UK). It also ensured that the common law offence of bribery extended to persons holding public office outside the UK. The Act gives the courts extra-territorial jurisdiction over bribery and corruption offences committed abroad by UK nationals and bodies incorporated under UK law. So where UK Nationals commit bribery abroad they can be prosecuted in the UK courts even though the corrupt act has no other connection to the United Kingdom. (Betts 2011)

In 2001 the solicitor of an employee of a travel firm retained by BAE had made allegations of corruption to the Serious Fraud Office. The SFO deputy director drafted a report which was sent to the MOD and to the head of the Ministry of Defence Police (MDP) fraud squad. The latter did some work on the allegations, despite the MOD's reluctance to pursue them. In 2003 the SFO letter was leaked to the press, at the same time as the SFO deputy became its head. It was decided to expand the inquiry with the MDP. This time political and ministry pressure on the investigation was matched by the publication of the main allegations being pursued by the investigation, in the *Guardian* in 2004.

The stories reported several million pounds of travel and hospitality, allegedly paid for by BAE, to key Saudi officials through the travel company. The investigations initially involved MOD officials but extended to BAE when some of the allegations fell under new anti-corruption legislation (a number of the other offences involved accounting and invoice activities). A few months later another travel agent working for BAE came forward with similar allegations; the investigation now covered other BAE contracts, including those in Romania, South Africa, Tanzania and Chile.

As the time approached to finalise the extension of the Al-Yamamah contract, and as the SFO had begun to ask for information from Swiss banks to follow the money trail, the Saudi government threatened to switch to a French-built fighter if the inquiry was not halted. In December 2006 the government's senior law officer, the Attorney-General, announced in the House of Commons that:

> The Director of the Serious Fraud Office has decided to discontinue the investigation into the affairs of BAE Systems plc as far as they relate to the Al-Yamamah defence contract. This decision has been taken following representations that have been made both to the Attorney-General and the Director concerning the need to safeguard national and international security. It has been necessary to balance the need to maintain the rule of law against the wider public interest. No weight has been given to commercial interests or to the national economic interest.

The grounds given (the careful references to commercial and economic interests were intended to pre-empt any OECD complaint that signing the Convention specifically meant that investigations could *not* be stopped on those grounds) related to the UK public interest in terms of intelligence cooperation with the Saudi government. He claimed that this was based on the views of the Prime Minister, two other ministers and the intelligence services. The Prime Minister was to add that 'our relationship with Saudi Arabia is vitally important for our country in terms of counter-terrorism, in terms of the broader Middle East, in terms of helping in respect of Israel and Palestine. That strategic interest comes first.'

After the inquiry into the Saudi part of the allegations was stalled, an NGO, the Campaign Against Arms Trade, decided to ask for a judicial review into whether or not the actions of the head of the SFO were lawful. The hearing in the High Court in 2008 decided that they were not. That decision was based on what the court termed 'the facts'. BAE had been fighting the Saudi investigations since 2005 as being 'seriously contradictory to the public interest' while the SFO, noting both commercial and security issues, had decided in January 2006 that it was 'in the public interest' to continue.

Pressure up to mid-2006 culminated in a specific warning made to the government: end the investigation or no contract renewal and no intelligence cooperation. What exercised the court (see [2008] EWHC 714 (Admin): Case No: CO/1567/2007) was that this threat related to the leading Saudi official responsible for the contract, but also subject to the allegations the SFO was investigating: 'the significant event which was soon to lead to the investigation being halted was a threat made by an official of a foreign state, allegedly complicit in the criminal conduct under investigation and, accordingly, with interests of his own in seeing that the investigation ceased' (para 24).

The court agreed that not only did acquiescence to the threat suit the objectives of the state but the threat itself was so blatant and so intended to achieve its objective that had such a threat been made by someone who was subject to the criminal law of this country, that person 'would risk being charged with an attempt to pervert the course of justice' (para 60[11]). As a consequence, and based on 'well-settled principles of public law', the director had, in giving in to the threat, 'ceased to exercise the power to make the independent judgement conferred on him by Parliament'.

Not only that, thought the court, the Attorney-General had no business to exert pressure on him, 'let alone make a decision in relation to an investigation which the Director wishes to pursue', and the government should appreciate the role of the courts in 'upholding and protecting the role of law' as well as for the courts to 'decide whether the reaction to a threat was a lawful response or an unlawful submission'. It decided that the actions of the director were unlawful.

The SFO appealed on three grounds:

- The discretion of the SFO director to investigate and prosecute crime.
- The role of the courts in reviewing the SFO's decisions.
- The SFO director not being bound by the OECD Anti-Bribery Convention on the grounds that it had not been incorporated into UK law.

The Lords ruled that the issue was not about the argument accepted by the other court. The director rightly took advice from those with knowledge he did not have, and lawfully took the public interest decision that the terrorist threat outweighed the continuation of the investigation. The Lords pointed out that this was not a question of whether the decision was right or wrong but whether the director had the authority to make such a decision. The appeal was allowed (House of Lords [2008] UKHL 60).[12]

In February 2010 BAE did a joint plea bargaining deal with the US Department of Justice and the SFO; a $400 million fine to the former for an acceptance that it was guilty of conspiring to make false statements to the government in connection with regulatory filings and undertakings, and £30 million fine to the latter for an accounting offence relating to the sale of a radar system to Tanzania. The SFO case involving BAE and South Africa was also dropped for 'lack of cooperation' from the South African government. The UK government's response to the deal was that 'it's right that these historical allegations have been addressed' (*Guardian*, 6 February 2010).

The need for a new variant – state agency crime

From these examples it is arguable that the academic perspectives of state crime and state-corporate crime are relevant, involving the government, as well as those agencies through whom the government wishes to implement its policy. On the other hand, while the nature of the latter is self-evident, the motives for state crime lie less in organisational deviance (presumably in terms of democratic principles or international standards) than in pursuit of the national interests, whether or not that conflicts with those principles and standards. In both, the circumstances containing the potential for state crime or state-corporate crime are relatively specific.

Beyond these types of state crime, there are those agencies whose relationship with state crime or state-corporate crime involves primarily their roles and responsibilities in implementing official policy, but without the direct involvement of government or the core executive. The UK context suggests that the study of state crime will need to address the fragmentation of the state where an increasing number of semi-independent agencies, often with large budgets and executive authority, deliver state functions and services within a general policy remit.

In the hollowed-out model, 'disaggregation, differentiation, interdependence and policy networks are central characteristics of the British polity which can be no more disregarded than the executive authority of the Prime Minister and the Cabinet or the role of Parliament' (Rhodes 1988: 412). Further, 'interdependence in intergovernmental relations and policy networks contradict the authority of parliamentary sovereignty and a strong executive. Institutional differentiation and disaggregation contradict command and control by bureaucracy' (Rhodes 1997: 199).

As a consequence, the UK becomes 'a "centreless society" with a segmented executive. The core executive may police the functional policy networks, but increasingly leadership is shackled by internal and external hollowing out' (Rhodes 1997: 195). From this perspective, the hollowing out is assumed to have led to a smaller, fragmented governmental structure that leaves it less accountable, limited in its authority and increasingly interdependent on its interaction with other agencies (see Rhodes 1997: 53–4), with 'policies being made (and administered) between a myriad of interconnecting, interpenetrating organisations' (Richardson and Jordan 1979: 74).

Two issues are identifiable. First, most state activity takes place in the public sector and away from the direct control and direction of the government. Many, within overall budgets and performance indicators, may be public institutions but they do not fall within the terms of the state or the core executive.

Second, and also in terms of state crime, the disaggregation of institutions and the devolution of budgets, authority and accountability may lead institutions to operate as they interpret their roles and responsibilities, but where the focus is on delivery, on economy and on performance measurement, this may lead to a propensity for regulatory or *mala prohibita* state crime (including both conduct and results types). If any such agency or their staff were to take a decision or action that fell within the criteria of a state crime, it would be extremely unlikely to be at the instigation of, or with the approval of, the state.

Nevertheless, the limited work on routine rule-breaking suggests that

apart from the more traditional examples of abuse of power or seeking financial gain, most of the cases appear to come from the failure to comply with or ensure the implementation of existing rules. The reasons for that usually lie less with the guilty mind, than with the other reasons, ranging from the competence of officials to the complexity of the functions and rules. The impact of New Public Management with its emphasis on performance and delivery, and the influence of private sector approaches, as well as the belief by a number of such bodies that they are not subject to the more general public rules or standards, is an added dimension. Finally there have been a number of examples where the rule breaking has occurred as a consequence of reforms introducing different or contradictory expectations of officials whose interpretation of the delivery of government intentions may lead to rule breaking. (Huberts *et al.* 2006: 100)

These changes have created circumstances in which public managers were not only taking on new functions but becoming increasingly closely involved with private sector attitudes, practices and organisations, particularly where these were providing expertise and techniques to improve services and delivery as part of public organisations' management or performance. The fragmentation of organisations and the primacy of the contract culture has increasingly affected how public managers perceive their roles, functions and future.

Throughout the public sector, the speed, purpose and complexity of the changes by and within organisations has thrown up a number of issues concerning job security and the sometimes conflicting objectives of speed of delivery, cost-cutting and performance by results, against those of due process, procedure and precedent – in other words, those issues of organisational development, and the consequences of a competitive and performance-driven culture, already identified in the concept of corporate crime (see above, p. 88).

The potential for applying a state crime perspective lies in the changed roles and responsibilities within which agencies now operate, and their capacity to work as autonomous entities for whom new public management has introduced quasi-private sector approaches and attitudes. Here the framework and language provided by the organisational deviance perspective has relevance for what could be termed *state agency crime*.

Slapper and Tombs (1999) noted that while it is difficult to pinpoint why an organisation at a point in time may opt for a deviant approach to business, or to understand why 'normal' rather than pathological organisations should act this way:

the prevailing ideology of any given society also affects the extent to which corporate crimes are produced and indeed are more or less acceptable. Certainly a value system which prioritises, indeed, valorises, the taking of risks, and even produces techniques whereby the taking of risks can be deemed to be acceptable, is likely to be one which accepts a level of corporate illegality as 'normal'. (Slapper and Tombs 1999, 142)

As the corporatisation of public services delivery continues within a contract, cost and competition public culture, so the development of a public corporate crime or state agency crime perspective may be academically useful – if not in terms of a legal framework, then certainly in terms of injury or harm (see Box 29).

With the changes to the public sector, it could be argued that such developments would also set the context for state agency crime, which could be explained by a number of issues raised by Croall in relation to organisational deviance (see p. 92 above) for the following reasons:

Rule breaking is encountered if (national) rules are not in alignment with the actual decentralised execution or when tasks are assigned to decentralised government organisations without ensuring that the required means are made available ...

Box 29: Health care – culture and consequences

1 The Urbani case

In February 2010 a non-English-speaking German doctor, Dr Urbani, with no experience of the NHS, was hired as an out-of-hours locum for a private sector care provider. During one call-out, he was responsible for the death of a patient. The coroner's verdict was 'unlawful killing', because his professional conduct was incompetent, not of an 'acceptable' standard; he had committed 'gross negligence manslaughter'. The subsequent House of Commons Health Committee Report returned to the question of the responsibility of the agencies, including oversight and regulatory roles, involved in the employment of out-of-hours doctors. The minister was explicit: 'I am making absolutely clear that PCTs should have been, by law, since 2004 looking at language skills. They had no discretion on this; it was a legal obligation. They should be doing it now. If they have not been doing it, and we know Cornwall was not doing it, then they were in breach of the law' (House of Commons Health Committee 2010: 9).

On the other hand, the committee was told that no action had been taken, against either staff or the agency itself. Indeed, it was suggested by another witness to the committee that the supervisory agency, the Strategic Health Authority, needed 'to take this seriously and make sure that the PCTs are doing their job properly. All SHAs should do that in England. There are enough checks and balances to make sure there is a safe system but it is not taken seriously and consistently from PCTs all the way through the system' (House of Commons Health Committee 2010: 9).

2 The Mid Staffordshire NHS Foundation Trust case

The 2010 inquiry (Francis 2010) was driven by public concern, specifically those of the patients and relatives, and reported on the organisation's culture:

> Clearly not all management and staff have adopted the attitudes and negative culture described in this chapter, but sufficient have, to lead me to conclude that such a culture has played a significant part in the development of the problems to be seen in this Trust. This culture is characterised by introspection, lack of insight or sufficient self-criticism, rejection of external criticism, reliance on external praise and, above all, fear. I found evidence of the negative impact of fear, particularly of losing a job, from top to bottom of this organisation. Regrettably, some of the causes of that fear have arrived at the door of the Trust from elsewhere in the NHS organisation in the form of financial pressures and fiercely promoted targets. Such a culture does not develop overnight but is a symptom of a long-standing lack of positive and effective direction at all levels. (Francis 2010: 184).

The consequences of this culture were less that good-intentioned staff made mistakes or errors under pressure or through conflicting demands, but rather that intentions became secondary to the potential consequences of failing to respond to the high priority placed on 'the achievement of targets, and in particular the Accident and Emergency waiting time target'. The pressure to meet the targets 'generated a fear, whether justified or not, that failure to meet targets could lead to the sack'.

The push for targets was matched by a continuing effort to drive down costs, particularly staff costs: 'the constant strain of financial difficulties, staff cuts and difficulties in delivering an acceptable standard of care took its toll on morale and was reflected by absence and sickness rates in particular areas'. The slump in staff morale was reflected in a 'lack of compassion and uncaring attitude exhibited by others towards vulnerable patients and the marked indifference ... to visitors, an atmosphere of fear of adverse repercussions', 'a forceful style of management (perceived by some as bullying)', conduct of Trust business 'in private' ('one particular incident concerning an attempt to persuade a consultant to alter an adverse report to the coroner'), and an 'acceptance of poor standards of conduct' (Francis 2010: 15–16).[13]

Some areas of rules are considered so complex or general that they create doubts concerning the intention of the legislator ...

In some situations rules are broken due to the fact that people disagree with the rule itself. This does not always imply breaking the rules; more often their implementation and enforcement do not occur consistently and wholeheartedly ...

The capacity can be insufficient; the necessary knowledge may be lacking; the administrative organisation and documentation (procedures) can be deficient. These conditions can easily cause problems in the area of rule and law enforcement, certainly when government organisations are subjected to high working pressures to achieve results ...

There is a limited chance of detection and sanctioning for rule-breaking conduct by a supervisor or a rule enforcer. This makes rule-breaking quite a risk-free thing to do. (Huberts *et al.* 2006: 117–8).

In other words, the drivers for organisational deviance lie more with corporate crime perspectives than with state crime perspectives and the study of rule-breaking in this context will require further development to provide an appropriate conceptual perspective.

Summary

The examples above suggest that the potential exists for the state crime or state-corporate crime concepts developed in the literature, but that the causes in relation to those suggested in the literature are not clear-cut. The state – the government and the core executive – is capable of seeking to achieve objectives by whatever means, although the areas or activities where this occurs may be limited to those that are seen to fall within the discretionary authority of the state (and one accepted by the courts – see above, p. 31, and below, p. 218).

Such motives have always been central to the high politics of the state, and continue to be so. While the behaviour and intentions associated with such areas may appear to be at variance with the tenets of a democratic state, it should not always be assumed that the conduct of the government or of government departments is the consequence of organisational deviance, or deviance from those tenets in that the state does not always operate as a single entity. Indeed, those involved would argue in terms of political necessity which is derived from the national interest as opposed to some wider deviance against ill-defined standards of democratic government.

Further, such variations within the state may also explain why the possibility of state-corporate crime may also occur alongside the possibility of state crime. Again, the complexity and multiple roles and responsibilities of the Executive would suggest that it is the relationship with specific corporate interests, rather than capitalism or the corporate sector as whole, that may be the basis of that possibility. There can be a degree of complementarity between the two perspectives – state crime and state-corporate crime – in particular in foreign policy and exports, especially military exports, where both serve to support the national interest.

Where both perspectives need review is in the disaggregation and devolution of the modern state. Here public officials become responsible for interpreting and implementing broad state policy. This may be done within government requirements that focus on financial and performance expectations, and also within a regulatory framework which shares, or even promotes, such expectations. When the law is broken or harm caused, however, it is not for the national interest or the interest of the state, and certainly not on behalf of or authorised by the government, but for reasons more analogous to those relating to corporate crime. The agencies and officials here cannot be originators or instigators of state crime, but in the continuing development of the state the interpretation of broad policy guidelines in increasingly autonomous agencies requires some framework within which to view state misconduct. Further, given the relationships between the Executive and the agencies, and the roles of the regulators established by the Executive, consideration should be given not only to the concept of state agency crime, but also to state-facilitated state agency crime.

Notes

1 It was Blair and not Thatcher who said, 'our history is our strength', just before the Iraqi invasion (see Kampfner 2004: 236).
2 A 1972 double killing in farm buildings, named after one of the murder weapons. One of those killed was a prominent Catholic civil rights campaigner. Soldiers were later convicted of the murder; they claimed they killed the two because of frustrations at their failure to answer the soldiers' questions (see Dillon 1990: 124–58).
3 The Northern Ireland Police Ombudsman was asked in 2007 to re-examine several deaths arising from so-called 'shoot to kill' incidents in the 1980s following a European Court of Human Rights ruling that the killings had not been properly investigated, violating the European Convention on Human Rights. The Committee of Ministers which supervises how states respond to the Court's judgements required that the British government 'take, without further delay, all necessary investigative steps'.
4 In 2003 the Irish government commissioned a report from a retired Supreme Court judge on the 1974 bombings, claimed by a Protestant terrorist group in Dublin and Monaghan. He concluded that without further evidence (including more than the limited information provided by the UK government) there was no evidence of complicity by UK officials.
5 These were Patrick Finucane and Brian Adam Lambert. The former was a solicitor whose death occurred shortly after a government minister commented adversely on solicitors whose defence of PIRA operatives appeared to be ideologically and not professionally based (see O'Brien 2005).
6 Similar allegations – of missing weapons and photographs, as well as the use of judicial reviews to stall proceedings – have been made about the MOD's response to the work of the Saville Inquiry (see Rolston and Scraton 2005: 561).
7 Thus, the increasing emphasis by government on personal responsibility for pension provision and the ending of final salary settlements in the private sector means that the state is aware of the need of some supervisory role to protect the integrity of the pensions marketplace and thus consumer trust, as well as provide cover when schemes collapse (the Maxwell theft from his company pension funds was a significant warning). This may explain why the government has proposed an industry-funded pensions protection fund and why the HMRC is taking

an increasing interest in a new fraud – pension liberation – that has grown significantly in recent years.

8 Responsibility for the rules governing the employment of civil servants within two years of resignation or retirement rests with the Advisory Committee on Business Appointments, an NDPB. It can advise, if requested to do so, on conditions that may be imposed on a civil servant before being employed by a commercial organisation which has or will have contractual dealings with their former department. It also currently gives advice to former ministers.

The Scott Report is a multi-volume report; the reference applies to the volume and paragraph.

9 In relation to Saudi Arabia, this has included a Conservative Cabinet Minister apologising for a critical UK TV drama. On another occasion, a Conservative government coincidentally offered aid money to a friendly country while requesting residence for a Saudi dissident; this occurred shortly after a major UK contractor warned about impending loss of contracts if the dissident was allowed to stay in the UK.

10 Equipment that could be used for civilian or military purposes.

11 In 2008 the House of Lords noted that 'the Divisional Court was right to hold that a person subject to the jurisdiction of the court who sought to impede an SFO investigation would be at risk of prosecution for attempting to pervert the course of justice, and also right to hold that the Saudis were not subject to the court's jurisdiction' (para 36).

12 The Lords also made a number of points why the courts were reluctant to interfere on a decision to prosecute. Firstly that power, broad and unprescriptive, lay with identified officials and, secondly, 'the polycentric character of official decision-making in such matters including policy and public interest considerations which are not susceptible of judicial review because it is within neither the constitutional function nor the practical competence of the courts to assess their merits' (para 31).

13 In June 2010 the government announced a further inquiry under the 2005 Act to 'examine the operation of the commissioning, supervisory and regulatory organisations and other agencies, including the culture and systems of those organisations in relation to their monitoring role at Mid Staffordshire NHS Foundation Trust between January 2005 and March 2009 and to examine why problems at the Trust were not identified sooner, and appropriate action taken'.

Chapter 7

Controlling state crime

Introduction

The question of the control of state crime will be very much bound up in perceptions of the nature of the state. Much of the state crime literature makes assumptions about the state's capacity to commit crime and avoid accountability by denial, by complicity or by control over the agencies of crime control.

Some might argue that state crime would never get as far as the area of crime control by its very nature – agencies of the state would not act against those at a senior level involved in state crime, and the media, controlled as it is by economic interests close to the state, could be persuaded to silence. For state crime, it could be argued that, like white collar crime, 'issues of criminalisation, law enforcement and sentencing are, therefore, political and ideological issues' (Croall 1992: 162).

On the other hand, it would be wrong to assume that how crime in general or state crime in particular is dealt with is shaped solely by the state either for its own interests or for those whose interests it represents. As Levi argues about white collar crime, its 'relative neglect by state agencies' is not 'explicable *satisfactorily* in terms of a power-elite thesis':

> First, it is an analytical leap of faith rather than a demonstration of fact to jump from showing that a particular policy serves the interests of particular groups to the view that this fact explains why the policy came about. And second, in liberal democracies,

sufficient conflicts of interest between powerful
even if one could identify a selection of people as
a ruling class, it would often be difficult for insiders
:rs alike to define what its 'average interests' were.
:m of identifying and enforcing 'common interest'
: more acute as modern capitalism breaks down the
commonality of background which has been an important feature
of the British commercial and political elite. (Levi 1987: 116)

If, therefore, the crime control responsibility is not monolithic, nor
fully encompassed within a specific ideological hegemony, then
there is also the question of who is responsible for investigating and
adjudicating on aspects of state crime. This includes a number of
agencies with sanctioning powers but there are a number of other
means of accountability.

The police, the courts and state crime

Criminal activities involving actions that could be classed as state
crime are the responsibility of the police, the Crown Prosecution
Service (CPS) and, occasionally, the Serious Fraud Office. There are
43 police forces in England and Wales. Few if any are ever involved
in state crime inquiries, although many are involved in investigating
crimes involving elected or appointed officials, ranging from alleged
unlawful party donations to procurement corruption.

As noted above, however, law enforcement agencies do on occasion
investigate potential state crimes – crimes in pursuit of the national
interest. Such investigations are fraught with difficulties at every
level, but not all agencies, as in the case of Supergun, are willing to
defer to political or civil service pressure or interference.

The courts will also address state crimes by state agencies, couching
their approach both in terms of human rights and in terms of the
abuse of executive power. In the 1993 case involving collusion by UK
and South African police to return an alleged fraudster (see above,
p. 154), the House of Lords made it plain that the latter role fell
within its remit:

In the present case there is no suggestion that the appellant
cannot have a fair trial, nor could it be suggested that it
would have been unfair to try him if he had been returned
to this country through extradition procedures. If the court

is to have the power to interfere with the prosecution in the present circumstances it must be because the judiciary accept a responsibility for the maintenance of the rule of law that embraces a willingness to oversee executive action and to refuse to countenance behaviour that threatens either basic human rights or the rule of law ... I have no doubt that the judiciary should accept this responsibility in the field of criminal law. The great growth of administrative law during the latter half of this century has occurred because of the recognition by the judiciary and Parliament alike that it is the function of the High Court to ensure that executive action is exercised responsibly and as Parliament intended. So also should it be in the field of criminal law and if it comes to the attention of the court that there has been a serious abuse of power it should, in my view, express its disapproval by refusing to act upon it. (See House of Lords, R v. Horseferry Road Magistrates Court, Ex Parte Bennett 1993)

In terms of individual hurt, as opposed to a public wrong, those harmed have the right to a civil case, which concerns disputes between individuals or corporate bodies (public and private), where the plaintiff or defendant would take their own case to either the county court or the High Court (with complexity or substance – such as the monetary value – determining which).

For example, in 2004, in relation to the case of the Kosovan shot dead by British peacekeepers in 1999 (see above, p. 154) and his two cousins injured, the judge stated that if the soldiers were on peacekeeping duties and not acting in self-defence then 'combat immunity' could not succeed and they owed the same duty of care as ordinary citizens. He compared the cases to soldiers in Northern Ireland who had faced negligence claims from incidents when they had to take aggressive action to keep the peace in the face of a disorderly and hostile crowd. He dismissed the argument that the Kosovan men were partly responsible for their own injuries by travelling in a vehicle with someone who was firing a gun in a 'potentially provocative' manner: 'in my judgment, it cannot sensibly be said that the claimants by their conduct shared in the responsibility for their injuries. Any imprudence on their part was dwarfed by the acts of the soldiers. The latter deliberately and without justification caused these injuries, and in my view it would not be just or equitable to reduce the damages on grounds of contributory fault' (*Independent*, 8 April 2004).

Beyond the UK, there are a number of judicial institutions to consider actions of the state. Such a dimension becomes important if, where states use crime to 'maintain the status quo, it is highly unlikely that states will adopt internal mechanisms that will control their criminality. Hence, external controls may be the only viable alternative in controlling state crime' (Yarnold 2000: 319). Some state crime commentators, however, argue that 'international state-sponsored organisations to control state crime – and, again, violations by the state of individual human rights *are* crimes – presents an extraterritorial jurisdiction and is slowly eroding national juridical self-sufficiency and sovereignty' (Hurwitz 2000: 284).

The European Court of Human Rights is concerned with allegations of violations of the Council of Europe's European Convention on Human Rights by any state who is a signatory to the Convention (and bound by its terms and conditions). Allegations may be made by citizens or other states (as Ireland did in the 1970s over the torture of internees; see p. 178) or individuals. The capacity of the court to follow up its recommendations with states, and the role of the UK joint parliamentary committee on human rights, also provides a useful means of scrutiny of state responses (even if the response is unhelpful – see the government's 2009 report (Lord Chancellor and Secretary of State for Justice 2009) on the Finucane and other cases involving deaths in Northern Ireland).

Second, the European Court of Justice cooperates with all the courts of the member states, which are the ordinary courts in matters of community law and which will refer to the court any issue concerning the interpretation of community law to see if their national legislation complies with that law in order to ensure the effective and uniform application of community legislation and to prevent divergent interpretations. The court's decision is binding. This process is intended to allow the court to determine whether a member state has fulfilled its obligations under community law. If not, then an action for infringement of community law may be brought before the court by the Commission or by another member state. If the court finds that an obligation has not been fulfilled, the state must bring the failure to an end without delay. Failure to act can also be held to be unlawful (although most of the cases involving the UK state relate to arcane issues such as European voting rights for Gibraltar citizens (2004) or assessment of Common Agriculture Policy financial irregularities (2010)).

Internationally, there are a number of international or *ad hoc* criminal tribunals, such as those for Rwanda and the former Yugoslavia, and the Special Court for Sierra Leone, set up for a specific purpose or inquiry. Of the permanent institutions two international courts are relevant to the UK. The role of the UN International Court of Justice is to settle, in accordance with international law, legal disputes submitted to it by those states who have signed up for the Statute, and to give advisory opinions on legal questions referred to it by authorised United Nations organs and specialised agencies. It does not deal with cases involving individuals. In 1999 the Federal Republic of Yugoslavia accused the UK and other countries of illegally violating 'its international obligation banning the use of force against another State, the obligation not to intervene in the internal affairs of another State, the obligation not to violate the sovereignty of another State ...' in participating in the NATO attacks (see above, p. 64). The charge was dismissed. In July 2010, the court ruled on Serbia's attempt to have the Kosovan state's declaration of independence made illegal; the court's judgement was in Kosovo's favour, saying that their declaration of independence did not violate 'general international law'.

Set up in 2002, the International Criminal Court is an independent, permanent court of last resort that tries persons accused of the most serious crimes of concern to the international community 'as a whole', namely genocide, crimes against humanity and war crimes. Its existence is based on a treaty. It will not act if a case is investigated or prosecuted by a national judicial system unless the national proceedings are inadequate or not genuine, for example if formal proceedings were undertaken solely to shield a person from criminal responsibility. Few cases have been brought before the court – currently including the Central African Republic and Uganda; the latest potential defendant is the President of Sudan. It has no jurisdiction over, nor can hear cases referred from, countries – or those countries' nationals – that have not ratified the treaty, unless referred by the UN Security Council (as in the case of Darfur).

Adjudicating and regulating the state

In the proposed area of state agency crime, and in terms of public or administrative law, and especially as a consequence of the rise of the rights-based legal framework, the activities and decisions of the agencies are increasingly subject to review and adjudication. There is an extensive tribunal and regulatory framework that addresses all aspects of state functions and services, including performance, expenditure, fairness and unlawfulness. They cover one or two areas: state agencies, or both public and private sectors.

In relation to administrative law, a number of tribunals, agencies and inspectors are accessible by citizens and/or established by the state to provide citizen redress. They offer citizens the right to challenge the legality and validity of a significant number of decisions that may impinge on citizens as individuals or as corporate bodies, from national to local level, from planning decisions to levels of state benefits (see Birkinshaw 1985).

In addition, a range of administrative tribunals exist, adjudicating over such areas as benefits, immigration and employment, whose remit in whole or in part includes the state's actions or decisions affecting a citizen. The current tribunal structure was set up by 2007 legislation after the Leggatt review, which concluded that 'the only way in which users can be satisfied that tribunals are truly independent is by developing clear separation between the ministers and other authorities whose policies and decisions are tested by tribunals, and the minister who appoints and supports them' (Leggatt 2001: para 2.23).

Other adjudicators include the Ombudsman system whose 'main functions are to consider whether matters have been properly and efficiently handled, or whether there has been maladministration' (Leggatt 2001: para 12.12), and the Audit Commission whose Audit Inspectorate can comment on the legality and propriety of officials' conduct and the legality of public expenditure.

Conversely, other agencies regulate how state agencies deal with the public during official activities, often as a consequence of the incorporation of human rights legislation into domestic law, with specific reference to interference by a public authority. In addition to laws that govern inquiries and investigations,[1] the Office of the Surveillance Commission was set up in 1999 to promote an effective and ethical process for the authorisation of covert surveillance in accordance with legislation, and provide public reassurance about the authorisation of covert surveillance.

The Surveillance Commissioner covers all covert surveillance carried out by public authorities in the United Kingdom, including police forces, under the 1997 Act, and about 950 public authorities (such as local authorities and health trusts) which are entitled to conduct covert surveillance under the provisions of the 2000 Regulation of Investigatory Powers Act (RIPA). This legislation is intended to govern the state's lawful use of surveillance methods, including the interception of communications (opening letters, reading emails, and so on), eavesdropping, use of informants (now known as covert human intelligence sources), and static and mobile surveillance. Complaints under RIPA are dealt with by another independent body, the Investigatory Powers Tribunal, set up by the Act.

Other rights-based regulators also cover both sectors. These include the former Commission for Racial Equality, which issued a 'non-discrimination notice' with sanctions for failure to act pursued through the civil courts (under amendments to the law it was now an offence for public authorities not to actively act to eliminate unlawful discrimination, or to promote equality of opportunity and good relations between persons of different racial groups); and the Equal Opportunities Commission, whose breaches involve civil sanctions.[2]

One significant regulator is the Office of the Data Protection Registrar/Information Commissioner, which oversees legislation relating to access to, the protection of, and the processing of data held on individuals in electronic and manual form. In 2002 the Freedom of Information Act established the right of citizens to access data held by public bodies; the responsibilities for implementing the Act being taken on by the existing agency dealing with data protection – the Office of the Data Protection Registrar – which is now entitled the Information Commission (IC). The IC produces guidance on data, its retention, access to the data, and so on and can issue an enforcement notice on any organisation failing to comply with its guidance. The IC also polices a number of aspects relating to the holding, use, access to, and withholding of information. The Commissioner may inquire into a failure to produce information, and why, as well as require compliance, including forbidding the offending institution from carrying out a particular function under that law until the regulator is happy that the institution is compliant with the legislation.

The role of the regulator has widened in the area of criminal justice, where inspectorates also now take on regulatory functions. In the case of the criminal law, there are two agencies responsible for overseeing the work of the police and prosecutors. Activities of the police are overseen by HM Inspector of Constabulary and breaches investigated by the Independent Police Complaints Commission (IPCC); activities of prosecutors are overseen by the CPS Inspectorate (CPSI). Finally, in relation to the provision of care, the Care Quality Commission regulates in relation to people's safety, dignity and rights provided by the NHS, local authorities, private companies and voluntary organisations (and taking over the work of the Healthcare Commission, the Commission for Social Care Inspection and the Mental Health Act Commission).

Many regulators and tribunals do not deal with state crime in terms of pursuit of the state interests, but with those offences and harm caused through the misapplication of policy by public officials at middle and junior level, most of whose conduct has been as a consequence of error, ignorance or incompetence rather than deliberate intent, although the potential for neglect and negligence exists.

In this area of state agency crime, the conduct of the state in terms of the regulatory, public law and administrative procedures is increasingly regulated; 'the overall scale of regulation inside government seems to be similar to the *entire* investment in regulation of private business in the UK' (Hood *et al.* 1998: 66; emphasis in the original).[3] Less policed, and less well policed, is the area of state crime.

The grey area: courts and the state

The point about the extensive regulatory and adjudicatory framework around the state, and the role of the courts in insisting that the state does not break the law, is that these relate primarily to the state agencies identified in the hollowed-out model. The possibilities of state agency crime – particularly in terms of regulatory, unlawful and 'harm' issues – are more likely to be monitored and regulated and there are a number of agencies responsible for breaches (although the question of their effectiveness, particularly in light of government expectations, may well suggest that state-facilitated state agency crime may be a new dimension also to be considered). The impact of human rights, public censure and public advocacy ensures that the potential for state agency crime, and some areas of state-corporate crime, may be more circumscribed than state crime.

The question of responsibility for oversight and regulation changes in relation to those agencies is identified in the honed model, primarily the government. Here the courts have traditionally stated that they do not have oversight responsibilities in relation to public policy decisions that have a statutory or prerogative basis – for example, conducting international diplomacy. They argue that responsibility for scrutiny and accountability, as the new legislation on corporate manslaughter indicates, be given to 'other forms of accountability such as independent investigations, public inquiries and the accountability of Ministers through Parliament'. However, in such areas, these forms of accountability have also tended to favour the interests of the state rather than the rights of citizens.

Similarly, where the courts are asked to sit in judgement, and where the courts see the balance between the interests of the state and those of the citizens, they have indicated their predilection to favour what they perceive as the state's view of its responsibilities towards the nation on behalf of citizens collectively; they see this as more important than the rights of citizens individually.

Feroz Ali Abbasi is a British national, captured by United States forces in Afghanistan and transported to Guantánamo Bay in Cuba in 2002. He was held captive there for eight months without access to a court or any other form of tribunal or even to a lawyer. His mother sought by judicial review to compel the Foreign Office to make representations to the US government on his behalf on the basis that one of his fundamental human rights, the right not to be arbitrarily detained, was being infringed.

This request for a judicial review was turned down, but the Court of Appeal then reviewed the original decision to see to what extent an English court could examine whether a foreign state is in breach of treaty obligations or public international law where fundamental human rights are engaged. It also wanted to consider whether a decision of the Executive in the field of foreign relations was justiciable in the English court. In particular it sought to consider if there were any circumstances in which the court could properly seek to influence the conduct of the state in a situation where this may impact on foreign relations.

The answer to the last issue, and influencing the answers to the others, was simple – no. The court decided that the Foreign and Commonwealth Office was in talks with the US, that US courts also shared the UK courts' concern to support human rights and that international bodies were involved in addressing the problem was all Abbasi could expect. Furthermore, the court was emphatic that it would not be appropriate 'to order the Secretary of State to make any specific representations to the United States, even in the face of what appears to be a clear breach of a fundamental human right, as it is obvious that this would have an impact on the conduct of foreign policy, and an impact on such policy at a particularly delicate time' (2002 EWCA Civil 1598, para 107).

In 2006 another similar appeals case involving complaints about the government's refusal to make representations to the US made plain the potential conflict between the role of the courts and the role of the state:

the courts have a special responsibility in the field of human rights. It arises in part from the impetus of the HRA, in part from the common law's jealousy in seeing that intrusive State power is always strictly justified. The elected government has a special responsibility in what may be called strategic fields of policy, such as the conduct of foreign relations and matters of national security ... In *Secretary of State for the Home Department v. Rehman* [2003] 1 AC 153 Lord Hoffmann said at paragraph 62: 'It is not only that the executive has access to special information and expertise in these matters. It is also that such decisions, with serious potential results for the community, require a legitimacy which can be conferred only by entrusting them to persons responsible to the community through the democratic process. If the people are to accept the consequences of such decisions, they must be made by persons whom the people have elected and whom they can remove.'

This case has involved issues touching both the government's conduct of foreign relations, and national security: pre-eminently the former. In those areas the common law assigns the duty of decision upon the merits to the elected arm of government; all the more so if they combine in the same case. This is the law for constitutional as well as pragmatic reasons, as Lord Hoffmann has explained. The court's role is to see that the government strictly complies with all formal requirements, and rationally considers the matters it has to confront. Here, because of the subject-matter, the law accords to the executive an especially broad margin of discretion. ([2006] EWCA Civ 1279, paras 147–8)

In other words, significant areas for adjudicating and sanctioning state crime are excluded from the formal criminal justice system,[4] with responsibility lying with the legislature.

Parliamentary accountability

In terms of adjudicating on many areas of potential state crime, therefore, the courts have long held that oversight and accountability lies with Parliament and not with the courts. As the sovereign law-making body and representative organ of the public it is in theory before Parliament that government are called to account. Further, the ordinary citizen would expect their concerns, if they cannot address them directly, to be addressed through representation and political representatives. Indeed, 'it is essential for the dynamic of democracy that the elected government, and those who act on its behalf, give to the electorate an account of what they have (and have not) done as well as of what they will (or will not) do. This enables the electorate to make, through its choice of those who govern, its choices of the policies and programmes which are to be carried through in its (the electorate's) name. Such is the theory' (Giddings 1995: 227).

In practice that accountability lies with the House of Commons: as a whole, with opposition parties, and with its select committee system. While MPs have a relatively homogenous profile, that homogeneity does not extend to why they want to be in the House or what they see as their core functions while they are there (see Mancuso 1995). This leaves the House rarely able to operate with a collective mind when trying to hold the government to account.

Any formal independence is further diluted through the party–government relationship and the fact that a significant part of Parliament is full of former ministers, current ministers and potential ministers, all of whom are well aware of the politics of pragmatism that runs through government decision-making. For example, one of the side issues relating to Diego Garcia (see p. 30 above) was its role in the story of the UK independent deterrent. Successive governments from 1945 onwards pursued the same strategy, irrespective of ideological or other commitments (one Conservative minister commented that his Labour successors 'albeit quietly' kept 'that work going after 1974'). At that time the planning was, for Labour, led by an informal group around the Prime Minister, although detailed planning was done by civil servants, and misleading information about the strategy given to Parliament. By claiming that it was a modification of the existing system, the 1970s Labour government was also able to fudge the escalating costs (some ten-fold in a decade, reaching over £1 billion at 1970s prices); 'the expenditure had been hidden in the annual Defence Estimates. Parliament had not been informed of this programme, and there had been no public debate, despite four changes of government during the life of the programme' (Greenaway et al. 1992: 188). There is thus a mutual awareness of political and policy imperatives that may lead to a number of countervailing influences to demands for effective scrutiny (see Box 30).

The traditional means of accountability – debate, parliamentary questions, and so on – are managed and controlled by both sides; Erskine May (the manual of parliamentary procedure and practice) abandons its usual even-handed blandness to be bluntly realistic about the limited range of activities available to 'Her Majesty's

Box 30: Called to account?

In 1983 GCHQ came up with a plan for its own British controlled spy satellite, the £500 million Zircon system. Under tight security the project was developed by Marconi and British Aerospace from funds hidden in the MOD defence procurement budget. Journalist Duncan Campbell, an indefatigable researcher, pieced together the details for an episode in the BBC *Secret Society* series, which the MOD sought to have banned from broadcasting. His analysis focused on the fact that Parliament, and in particular the Public Accounts Committee, had been kept in the dark about the project. Although 'the telling material in Campbell's piece, however, points more to the government's political embarrassment than to genuine security matters' (*Guardian*, 29 January 1987) that embarrassment was not exploited by the opposition. Labour leader Neil Kinnock, who was aware of the politics of unilateral disarmament and that it would 'never be tolerated by the British establishment', had a 75-minute briefing with Foreign Secretary Sir Geoffrey Howe. He announced that he accepted the government's arguments, on grounds of national security, for preventing the BBC programme being shown; indeed, the Conservative Attorney-General was to assure 'the High Court that the Opposition would back the government' in Parliament (see Heffernan and Marqusee 1992: 241–2).

Having thus avoided the possibility of the Prime Minister using patriotism as a basis for criticising him, neither Kinnock nor his colleagues tackled the more fundamental issue of parliamentary accountability, rather than the existence of the satellite, which was the basis of Campbell's inquiries. To some, Kinnock's approach to Zircon was 'well-judged, for patriotism has never been a vote loser' (Leapman 1987: 190) but as Duncan Campbell pointed out: 'the failure of the Opposition to establish a credible but critical position on national security issues opened the door, then and now, to an unprecedented wave of censorship and a diminution of parliamentary authority. In making the Zircon programme, we set out to show how Parliament has been deceived. But we omitted to note that the watchdogs were asleep' (*New Statesman*, 11 December 1987).

Opposition' in the House: 'since the strength of modern party discipline makes a Ministry largely invulnerable to direct attack in the House of Commons, the criticism of the Opposition is primarily directed towards the electorate with a view to the next election, or with the aim of influencing government policy through the pressure of public opinion' (Erskine May 1989: 200).

Indeed, in terms of procedure, standing orders control the allocation of time, the powers of closure, sending bills for their committee stage, and the guillotine, which invariably rely on the government's numerical majority; the government can order its business 'in any order it thinks fit' giving it 'virtually complete control over the time of the House' which 'can be further extended by the government, if the need arises' (Erskine May 1989: 259).

Ironically, one reason given for low attendances in the chamber during the working day (apart from the awkwardness of the hours and restrictions of procedure, which the House still refuses to fully reform) has been the development of the select committee system. These committees fall into three broad categories: general committees, of which the Public Accounts Committee (PAC) is the most prominent; the procedural or domestic committees that deal with the House's business (committee membership selection, accommodation and services, privileges and so on); and the departmental committees. The PAC has always had a high profile and is invariably described in the media as 'powerful'.

This is in part because it deals in newsworthy issues such as financial waste or mismanagement, and encompasses all government departments, but its real strength comes from the services of the Comptroller and Auditor General (CAG), an independent public appointment who heads the National Audit Office (NAO). The NAO's 600-strong qualified staff audits departmental accounts, and carries out value-for-money studies in a way not available to any other committees. The Act that established the NAO specifically refuses the CAG the right to 'question the merits of the policy objectives' of any organisation it audits; this means that it cannot question the political decision, only whether the money was spent correctly. In theory, therefore, the PAC should be the flagship of parliamentary accountability, but in practice it serves primarily as a news source for the media. This is for three reasons.

First, the PAC – by tradition and convention – takes its terms of reference literally: 'the examination of the accounts showing the appropriations of the sums granted by Parliament to meet the public expenditure'. This responsibility falls not on the government minister who determines how the money is to be spent but on the civil servant responsible for the actual expenditure, and it is the latter that is called to give evidence before the PAC. The second problem is that Parliament does not pay attention to PAC activities (although at least some parliamentary time is available to debate PAC reports and the government responses; the debates have not been noted for high turnout or enthusiastic debate).

Finally, the NAO and chairs of the PAC have both been known to bow to the wishes of the state, usually on grounds of the national interest or national security, to overlook concealed expenditure or decline to inquire into areas of legitimate public concern. For example, information about the £500 million Zircon spy satellite system in the 1980s was not passed to the PAC as a consequence of decisions that highly sensitive security information could be publicly withheld by the CAG from the Committee. A NAO report on Al-Yamamah was withheld from the PAC with its agreement by its chair on the grounds of national interest.

Departmental select committees were criticised by the Committee on Procedure in 1978 for their 'incomplete and unsystematic scrutiny' of the work of the Executive which had developed 'merely as a result of historical accident or sporadic pressures'. The consequence was a structure of departmentally based committees introduced in 1979 but whose proposed professional framework (such as paid chairs, powers of compulsion for witnesses including ministers, parliamentary debates, fixed periods for departmental responses and specific days for debates on reports) never materialised.

The departmental committee system may range over policy as well as administration, and produce a wealth of information, but the output has not been integrated into opposition or parliamentary activity, nor are the findings binding on governments. Procedural, coordination and cooperation and resourcing problems have not been addressed, particularly access to the NAO as the scrutiny agency (and governments have said that other committees may use a NAO report but cannot task it to undertake one). This has ensured that from the outset the committees did not have 'the effect that their proponents hoped or that their opponents feared … [and] for the most part, made little noticeable impact on government policy' (Adonis 1990: 108; Jogerst 1993).

Access to information, and officials, by all committees is controlled by the government, with ministers refusing to allow civil servants 'accountability to parliament separate from and overriding' their accountability to their ministers. This especially applies to policy information (and particularly in terms of information that may put a minister's judgement or rationale in dispute). The 'rules' (known as the Osmotherley Rules) state that governments decide which official may represent the minister before a committee, what the official may say, and so on, 'under their directions'. The rules indicate that 'information should only be withheld in the interests of "good government" – this is deemed to include all discussions of interdepartmental exchanges, civil service advice to ministers, the level at which decisions are taken and anything "in the field of political controversy". In other words, this means virtually all information that elected MPs would want to hear' (Dowding 1995: 111).[5]

In reality, therefore, the 'institutions of democratic representation remain crucial to the formal control of the state, but the disjuncture between the agencies which possess formal control and those with actual control, between power that is claimed for the people and their limited actual power, between promises of representative and their actual performance is likely to become more apparent' (Held 1989: 151). As the Public Administration Committee noted (2005), 'the Committee expresses its concern at the long-term diminution in Parliament's role in the process of public inquiries'. There are parliamentary committees that have identified loopholes for accountability of the state, but there is no Parliament to confirm their closure. Parliament remains unable or unwilling to hold the executive to account, while 'the Front Bench is generally loathe to seem "unpatriotic" in the defence export field while the mavericks behind them … generally lack the information necessary to pin ministers down' (Oliver 1996: 367).

Ministers answer questions by revealing as little information as possible or avoiding any answer at all on the grounds of cost or convention: but, as Scott pointed out in his report on Iraq arms sales, the issue of answers lies more in parliamentary questions as a game played 'for the benefit of and under unexpressed rules understood by Parliamentary players' (Scott 1996: D4.62). Nevertheless, it is symptomatic of the fact that 'the House of Commons has no real corporate spirit or sense of its own rights or independent functions and responsibilities as a body apart from government and opposition parties … It is difficult to escape the conclusion that our constitutional system entirely lacks effective mechanism for obtaining information about such matters, making authoritative findings of fact, measuring them against clear criteria, and responding by allocating responsibility and securing the making of amends where appropriate' (Oliver 1996: 367).

In terms of the discretionary areas of, for example, foreign policy, Parliament is even more reluctant than the courts to get involved in exercising oversight over potential state crime. For example, the case of the Pergau dam illustrated the gap between the courts' and the Commons' perceptions of state conduct, underlining the divergence from a strict legal interpretation of an unlawful act and the political interpretation of the act. Thus it could be argued that:

> the judiciary's concerns differ from those of Parliament: the courts are concerned with basic standards of legality, procedural fairness, and fundamental reasonableness, while Parliament is concerned with the broader merits of the decision. Although there is a lot in this distinction, an overlap remains. For instance, the courts' investigation of the Pergau Dam case required them to go in some detail into the merits of the case: was the Pergau scheme economically justifiable? And the values which the courts will enforce can and do conflict with those espoused by Parliament … (James 1996: 627)

Governments and the core executive, therefore, have the advantage in terms of accountability: 'decisions may be made quickly and perhaps secretly by political leaders, leaving the legislature to follow along behind, perhaps even inhibited by a view that it is damaging to the national interest to be critical' (Hill 1997: 146).

Non-judicial and citizen accountability

This leaves three extra-parliamentary means of accountability: citizens, independent investigations, and public inquiries.

The ordinary citizen, *pace* Green and Ward, does not normally have a role in the investigation of breaches of the criminal law, nor in preventing the occurrence of criminal activity, which the courts believe falls within the agencies of the state: 'in principle, therefore, the state entrusts the power to use force only to the armed forces, the police and other similarly trained and disciplined law enforcement officers. Ordinary citizens, who apprehend breaches of the law, whether affecting themselves, third parties or the community as a whole, are normally expected to call in the police and not to take the law into their own hands' (R v. Jones *et al.* 2006).

On the other hand, citizens' groups have been active in initiating judicial reviews into domestic policy decisions (see p. 198 above) and also in raising allegations of breaches of international law. One target was General Augusto Pinochet, the head of state of Chile between 1973 and 1990 when the military state committed various crimes against humanity (torture, hostage-taking and murder). On retirement he came to the UK for medical treatment in 1998; the judicial authorities in Spain issued international warrants for his arrest to enable his extradition to Spain to face trial. He was arrested in the UK but had his case dismissed on grounds of immunity as a head of state, but with permission for an appeal.

Relevant to the Pinochet case was that legislation on torture had been passed into UK law in 1988 providing a limited period after 1988 to be used as grounds for extradition. The House of Lords ruled that he could not claim immunity for any act that breached international law and agreed to extradition; until it was discovered that one of the judges had links to Amnesty International. A re-hearing still allowed for extradition but in 2000 the Labour Home Secretary ruled that he should be allowed to go home on medical grounds. This took place despite a judicial review by Amnesty International and others to check the validity of the medical evidence. One of the points about the case was the impact citizens can make as advocacy groups:

> there were the human rights organizations, whose efforts to apply and develop international criminal law were clearly in fulfilment of their own mandates, but who also benefited enormously – in terms of fundraising and membership – from their close involvement in such a high profile case. These organizations, with their transnational networks of activists and their connections with judicial authorities in different countries, were critical in bringing the various strands of the case together: of accused, of victims, of willing prosecutor, and of available jurisdiction. They had also been crucial in establishing some of the legal institutions that figured prominently in the case, most notably the Torture Convention. (Byers 2000: 439–40)

Such has been the success of this type of action that the previous Labour government decided in 2010 that its status in the eyes of international law would be enhanced if the government began tightening up on who can request arrest warrants and on what grounds, by restricting the right of prosecution for a limited number of crimes to the CPS. As the then Prime Minister put it:

> There is already growing reason to believe that some people are not prepared to travel to this country for fear that such a private arrest warrant – motivated purely by political gesture – might be sought against them. These are sometimes people representing countries and interests with which the UK must engage if we are not only to defend our national interest but maintain and extend an influence for good across the globe. Britain cannot afford to have its standing in the world compromised for the sake of tolerating such gestures. (*Daily Telegraph*, 3 March 2010)

A high level of concern can also lead to a public inquiry intended to explore that concern and determine whether or not that concern is worthy of censure. The 2010 inquiry into Mid Staffordshire NHS Foundation Trust was set up 'primarily to give those most affected by poor care an opportunity to tell their stories and to ensure that the lessons to be learned from those experiences were fully taken into account in the rebuilding of confidence in the Trust'.

Independent investigations and inquiries range from (now little used) Royal Commissions, *ad hoc* departmental committees and non-statutory official inquiries, through to official inquiries under specific legislation and more general formal inquiries with legal powers (see Wraith and Lamb 1971; Winetrobe 1997; Woodhouse 1995). There is little systematic basis for distinguishing between these forms of inquiry in terms of the subject matter they deal with, and there is considerable variation in their procedures, powers and outcomes. On the one hand they are highly flexible, and can be seen to be impartial and independent. On the other hand they are often lengthy (a Royal Commission used to take on average more than two years and a departmental committee over one year to report). Their membership lay in the hands of ministers who invariably rely on establishment figures (see Hennessy 1986) and their fate in the hands of government could 'range all the way from ... total disregard ... to wholesale acceptance and implementation of its recommendations' (Cartwright 1975: 204).

The primary use and outcome of most official non-statutory inquiries have been to provide evidence of governments' willingness to react positively to allegations of public concern, often focusing on the individualisation of the cause of the concern and of 'identifying it with the personal character and motivation of those individuals named. The explanation is seen to lie there, rather than in the institutions in the midst of which the offence took place, and which are and will be administered by the rest of the elite' (Clarke 1981: 151).

Such inquiries have also tended to reinforce the perception of the cases and circumstances as marginal, and proposals for reform as specific to the organisation or functions concerned without full consideration being given to underlying causes and the general applicability of reforms. Thus, while official inquiries may appear to fulfil a public interest function as a response to political or public concern, they inevitably end up as fire-fighting exercises – *ad hoc* attempts to confront, resolve and close a particular incident or set of circumstances.

Most public inquiries lack any statutory powers, which could be essential if the investigation required access to people and papers that might not otherwise be forthcoming (although there are examples where such means of inquiry have worked in potentially controversial areas and received the required assistance without recourse to powers of compulsion).

Those with statutory powers were set up under the Tribunals of Inquiry Act. The Act was quickly passed in 1921 to deal with allegations of corruption over armaments contracts in the Ministry of Munitions. The need for this legislation was based on the susceptibility to political influence of pre-existing methods of inquiry, and a dearth of statutory measures at the time to deal with problems in particular policy areas. The 1921 Act placed greater reliance than before on quasi-judicial processes. It allowed for a Tribunal to be established on the order of both Houses of Parliament to investigate 'a definite matter of urgent public importance', with the powers of a High Court that included taking evidence on oath, and compelling the availability of witnesses and documents. Despite the primary criterion of being a definite matter of urgent public importance, there has been no discernible pattern to the use of Tribunals. The costs and delays associated with the Saville Inquiry into the Bloody Sunday shootings made it the last of the Tribunals under the 1921 legislation.

In 2005 the Act was superseded by the Inquiries Act, which allows ministers to set up 'formal, independent inquiries relating to particular events which have caused or have potential to cause public concern, or where there is public concern that particular events may have occurred'. Such inquiries have powers to call for witnesses and documentation, although ministers determine the terms of reference and appoint their memberships. The legislation makes it clear that any such inquiry has 'no power to determine civil or criminal liability and must not purport to do so. There is often a strong feeling, particularly following high profile, controversial events, that an inquiry should determine who is to blame for what has occurred. However, inquiries are not courts and their findings cannot and do not have legal effect.

The aim of inquiries is to help to restore public confidence in systems or services by investigating the facts and making recommendations to prevent recurrence, not to establish liability or to punish anyone'[6] (www.opsi.gov.uk/Acts/acts2005).

This raises the question of who then uses the information to hold the government to account and seek appropriate sanctions? Bogdanor (1996) writes that the Scott Report into the arms sales to Iraq raised the 'crucial question about ministerial accountability' and how it can be enforced in a House of Commons dominated by party politics and an adversarial political system'.

> In theory, the House of Commons can enforce the resignation of a minister who has breached the code, but, under modern conditions of strict party discipline, that will hardly ever occur. In the Commons debate on the Scott report, after all, only one MP from a major party defied his Party's whip. *Questions of Procedure for Ministers* (Cabinet Office 1992) and other codes regulating ministerial behaviour, lay down admirable sets of principles to which ministers are supposed to adhere. In the absence of any means of making these principles effective, however, they seem doomed to remain little more than pious aspirations. Ministerial accountability is, after all, an obligation owed to Parliament. How can Parliament make it effective? (Bogdanor 1996: 603–4)

This then leaves the role of the citizen who may approach the courts (the High Court under the Civil Procedure Rules, Part 54) when he or she considers that the state has acted outside its powers, in terms of a judicial review:

> Judicial review is a legal mechanism by which the decision of a public authority may be challenged in the courts on the grounds that it is illegal, unreasonable or unfair. In the 1940s and 1950s such challenges were infrequent and rarely succeeded. But in the past twenty-five years the position has changed dramatically ... Judges often emphasize that judicial review is not an appellate jurisdiction but a supervisory one. By this they mean that it is not an all-purpose appeals procedure for citizens to challenge decisions they dislike; the courts only establish certain broad parameters of legality outside which decision-makers should not stray.

An application for judicial review must be based on one of the three grounds summarized by Lord Diplock in the GCHQ case: illegality – in other words, the decision-maker acted outside the power conferred on him or her; irrationality – that no reasonable person could have reached the decision complained of; procedural impropriety – for example, because a prescribed procedure was not followed, or because the authority making the decision failed to observe the rules of natural justice, or because the procedure was unfair towards a party affected by the decision. (James 1996: 614, 615)

Any citizen (as individuals or an organisation) with 'sufficient interest' – including advocacy for a particular public interest where they represent the interests of those directly affected – may ask for a judicial review. The courts will interpret 'interest' widely: 'If the person challenging the decision can say that he is affected by it and there is no more appropriate challenger, and there is substance in his challenge, the court will not usually let technical rules on whether he has sufficient interest stand in its way' (Treasury Solicitors/Government Legal Service 2006: 28).[7]

Citizens have a further advantage. The use of the Freedom of Information Act can now provide much more information about reasons for decisions; and decisions made by ministers personally (carrying his or her signature although actually dealt with by officials) will require ministers to attend the courts:

it is a mistake to think that the Minister who made the decision need not personally get involved in defending it at Judicial Review, or that his reasoning or documents recording it are immune from disclosure under some principle of confidentiality. Whether the Minister, or one of his officials, sign the witness statement, it is imperative that the Minister be thoroughly acquainted with all the information in the case and approve what is being said in evidence by him or on his behalf – and that that evidence is supported by the documents in the case. (Treasury Solicitors/Government Legal Service 2006: 34)

Summary

The adjudicatory framework in terms of the actions and decisions of the state is extensively if unevenly developed. Certainly a public official can be subject to the full legal framework, whether acting unlawfully or illegally in pursuit of state interests or involved in the misapplication, maladministration or misinterpretation of the law in pursuit of their official duties. The applicability of the law to public organisations, however, is more focused on the regulatory dimension of the legal framework and the attempts to bring the organisations within the ambit of the criminal law have been diluted in the recent corporate manslaughter legislation.

Indeed, once actions or decisions that may be subject to adjudication fall within the 'exclusively public functions' which are primarily the responsibility of government and the core executive, then the adjudicatory responsibility moves largely away from a legal context to a context involving Parliament, public inquiries or the public. As the reform to the 2005 Inquiries Act points out, however, none of these has the formal capacity to apportion blame or sanction offenders.

In some areas the courts have responsibility to adjudicate but where the courts and the criminal justice system have declined to operate, then the means to require governments to explain their conduct are heavily influenced by the unwritten traditions. These permeate the political world – a tradition where there is 'the general agreement that it is better not to probe too deeply when things go wrong ... these are rarely followed by any kind of official enquiry or even by a public or Parliamentary demand for an enquiry' (Birch 1964: 243).

Much of the focus of formal or informal means of accountability also relates to state agency crime rather than state crime. The closer agencies are to the actions, decisions and policies of the government, particularly in relation to the interests of the state, then adjudicating on the interests of the state, and whether or not they have been achieved lawfully or otherwise, is weighed in favour of the state.

In part accountability thus lies within the contemporary political system where the national interest as a motivator for certain types of government behaviour is hidden within subsequent political developments: because 'we live in a society whose basic political culture has never been radically up-ended by revolution or war, these secretive components are heaped one on top of the other ... Because of Britain's historical continuity, in which institutions are superimposed or grafted on to existing ones, and because of the habit of secrecy about their own powers and limits within these institutions, the real mechanisms of government are hard to see' (Leigh 1980: 2).

Notes

1 One area where some form of regulatory framework has been called for has been the state's right of entry: 'there are on the statute books in Britain today no fewer than 266 different laws allowing public authorities the right to enter private homes. Some require a warrant to be issued, some not; some require notice to be given, some not; some state the permissible hours of entry, some not; some carefully define the discretion of the entering person; some not. The overall picture is a mess of confused and intrusive regulation' (Snook 2007: vi).

2 The 2006 Equality Act merged the Commission for Racial Equality, the Equal Opportunities Commission and the Disability Commission; the new Equality and Human Rights Commission began work in 2007.

3 Regulation of the private sector has not been as extensive or as great, although parts of the corporate sector – primarily financial services – have come under a more prescriptive regulatory framework led by the Financial Services Authority as it has been currently configured (FSA). The FSA itself made it plain from the onset of its establishment that it saw its role to be an active regulator because the previous approaches to 'London's markets were no longer fit for purpose' and that 'the new civil regime, combined with a clear code of market conduct describing acceptable and unacceptable behaviours, will be a significant complement to the criminal law, which of course remains in force'. Further, it was argued that 'it was right for regulators in future to pin clear responsibilities on the senior management in regulated firms for compliance with regulatory obligations. It is simply not satisfactory that, in the past, senior management have been able to walk away from major breaches and financial collapses without any adverse consequences for themselves' (Davies 2001).

4 Similar demarcation applied in the US when civil actions were taken against private companies working in Iraq. The latter's defence – and the dismissal of the actions by the courts – was 'based on the principle that the judiciary could not second-guess the executive branch when it came to decisions of war. The Bush administration had absolved the contractors precisely by binding them so closely to the war effort. The Pentagon had, in essence, created a special class: the contractors were bound by neither the military justice that applied to soldiers nor the civilian legal system' (Miller 2007: 299–300).

5 In 1985, after the Ponting case (see p. 73 above), the Treasury and Civil Service Committee generally endorsed the view (held by the civil service and the government) that civil servants' first responsibility was to ministers and it was ministers who determined policy and therefore decided who could and should be told what, how much and when (it also suggested that civil servants should never leak information ministers wanted to hold back because that decision was the ministers' prerogative).

6 Thus the continuing inquiry into the death of Baha Mousa at the hands of UK soldiers in Iraq has stated that, under the Act, none of those involved – all of whom, apart from one, was acquitted of abusing civilian detainees by a court-martial – could have their innocence or any other criminal or civil liability challenged. The MOD has already made substantial payments for what it terms substantive breaches of the ECHR. The sole conviction was for an offence of 'inhumanely treating' a civilian detainee under the 2001 International Criminal Court Act (see page 152).

7 Judicial review is used, for example, for staying extradition proceedings from the UK, to reverse refusals for leave to stay in the UK, and planning decisions. Thus, for example, the Campaign to Protect Rural England and Environmental Law Foundation (CPRE/ELF 2001) advises campaigners on the use of judicial review, reminding them that it applies to: decisions by public authorities; decisions by domestic tribunals and certain courts (e.g. the magistrates' court); decisions by Parliament if contradictory to European Union Law or Convention (e.g. the European Convention on Human Rights); and the legality of subordinate regulations and rules, which includes statutory instruments. It warns that judicial review cannot be used for decisions made by the Crown Court (in most circumstances), the High Court, the Court of Appeal or the House of Lords. It notes that 'in judicial review proceedings the court will intervene as a matter of discretion to: (a) either quash, prevent, or require a decision; (b) clarify the law; or (c) to compensate the applicant …' (p. 2). The court cannot rule on the policy merits of a decision, only in order to right a recognisable public wrong.

Chapter 8

Conclusion: themes in state crime

Introduction

This book has sought to explore six key themes: what is state crime according to the literature, what is the state, what is a crime, what are the drivers for the state to commit a crime, what are the roles of the various institutions of the state in being involved in state crime, and what, in terms of monitoring or investigating state crime or unethical conduct, are the roles of those institutions, from the police through to Parliament, responsible for holding governments and state institutions to account? While it argues for the development of a perspective on state agency crime to address those breaches of law or harms caused by public officials acting in an official capacity, this argument has emerged from using the literature on state crime within which to study a developed democratic state. As such the book has noted a number of issues relating to those themes.

What is state crime?

The majority of authors consider state crime as committed variously by state or public officials, states or governments, although there is less agreement on where criminality takes place (from government, to deviant organisations, to individuals), why it takes place (from official policy to individual self-interest), what it involves (from torture to tax evasion), the processes through which it happens (from initiated to facilitated, from commission to omission), and finally the consequences of it (from a formal breach of criminal law to causing harm). Green and Ward, and Chambliss, for example, restrict state crime to the achievement of organisational or state goals, rather than individual gain.

State-corporate crime theory also has a valid perspective in terms of state crime, links state crime specifically to ruling elite theories, and does so in a number of cases where the state is also seeking to reflect the principles and practices of developed democratisation. Thus, where the state is a creature of dominant economic interests and either actively pursues crime through those interests or acts in ways that advantage those interests, it does so by balancing the demands of state interests, capitalism and democracy:

> capitalism relies on the state to create the conditions of accumulation and enforcement that capital cannot create for itself. The US idea of democracy, for all its undoubted benefits, especially in the constitutional protection of civil liberties, is designed to make politics subordinate to class inequality and differences of economic interest. Up to now, US democracy has served capital well by preserving the balance between 'formal' democracy and capitalist class rule, both outside and inside the state. (Wood 2006: 18–19)

This perspective raises a valid issue about democratic states balancing a number of potentially contradictory demands both made of the state, and the state's own internal imperatives, is a valid one. On the other hand, this perspective also assumes an undifferentiated subservience to capitalism both as ideology and the operating of business and interests. In the UK context this assumption is less well evidenced than that of periodic coalescing of, or communities of interests around, common or mutually beneficial objectives. It is also less evidenced than that of the state sharing common goals with specific sectors or businesses, or the state relying on business as an arm of state policy or pursuit of national interests.

Unfortunately the variety of approaches very much reflects not only an absence of agreed terminology but also preconceived assumptions about what state crime or state-corporate crime should be about, and who may be involved. In terms of contemporary approaches, and recognising a number of the issues noted above, Green and Ward have sought to provide a synthesised assessment of this discipline, and develop organisational deviance as the underpinning rationale by which to consider state crime:

> State crime is one category of *organisational* deviance, along with corporate crime, organised crime, and the neglected area of crime by charities, churches and other non-profit bodies ... Organisations make decisions and implement them, set goals and pursue them, follow rules and break them ... The central concepts of criminology, such as deviance, motivation, opportunity structures, control and labelling, can be applied to organisations just as well as to individuals. Clearly the state does not always or even in the majority of cases act as a unitary force. The state comprises an ensemble of institutions which do not necessarily share a single set of interests and goals. The same will often be true of large-scale institutional structures within the state ... Nevertheless, there are instances where the entire coercive apparatus of the state acts in a coordinated way (even if this conceals internal conflicts ...) (Green and Ward 2004: 5)

Although this perspective addresses the issue of the complexities of the state, it is too narrow in assuming that state organisations can only commit state crime – that is, in terms of organisational deviance – or that state crime, when the state acts in the interests of the state, may only involve the 'coercive apparatus'. It is also not specific as to where the locus of the state lies.

At the same time, the use of a generic term such as *state* implies a common motive – organisational deviance – across both government and government agencies. It also assumes that the actions of the state may be driven only by deviance from, presumably, international normative standards, such as human rights, or international and domestic legal standards or democratic principles. It is in turn based on the assumption that the state is the same as the democratic state, and thus all actions of the state that breach those standards, rights or principles are both deviant and seen by those involved as such. The important point here, particularly in terms of state development, is to recognise the state *qua* state and to understand that there are various layers of responsibilities, roles and perspectives embedded within the modern state, not all of which are infused or shaped by contemporary standards, rights and principles, particularly when it comes to the state's core functions, and the maintenance of those domestically and internationally. It is within this context that the issue of state crime should be focused.

What is the state?

The second issue, for contemporary states, is to recognise the coherence, complexity and connectivity of the state; only a few authors recognise both the scale and complexity of the modern state and the changes that have followed the new public management reforms. For the purposes of state crime, the state is the government and the core executive, and it is from there that state crime is initiated, authorised, approved or condoned, and against whose actions and decisions can be assessed in terms of state crime. Other agencies, either officially or unofficially, may interpret what they think the state wants them to do but unless this follows specifically on from actions or decisions of the state – i.e. the government and core executive – and is intended to further the interests of the state, this is not state crime, rather state agency crime.

The need for a state agency crime perspective, where state agencies and agents breach standards, rights and principles during the performance of official services or responsibilities, but not undertaken at the behest of the state in pursuit of state interests, reflects the convergence between public and private sectors. There are also thus grounds for arguing that organisational deviance may apply equally to both. Certainly in terms of a contract culture, performance measurement and overall financial demands, harm done to citizens by hospitals and by local government social services departments may be as great if not greater than that visited on workers as a consequence of the health and safety regulatory framework. As Huberts *et al.* (2006) note, this should be a new but distinct area of study.

What is a crime?

Third, the traditional assumption that crime is solely the preserve of the criminal law is recognised by most authors as outdated and restrictive. States are subject to, and in many cases are signatories to, international laws and conventions specifically developed to prevent and manage inter-state (and increasingly intra-state) conflict. Contemporary states are also subject to a complex and extensive domestic legal framework where criminality, illegality and unlawfulness may all be labels applied to state conduct.

In the UK context, this includes formal legislation together with a range of other legal forms and conventions that are recognised, within the political world at least, as binding on those involved. Further, the development of legislation means that law itself, in terms of either the legislation or the sanctions, may contain both criminal and regulatory dimensions; trying to maintain a distinction between criminal law and regulatory law is increasingly artificial. Overall, and including harm or injury caused by official state actions or policies, the potential for crime by the state is significant.

Further, the use of normative standards, such as harm, should not be discounted, not least in relation to the time-lag between more formal restrictions and regulation, and areas where harm and private wrongs occur, such as state agency crime. As noted above, however, there will be a distinction between the types of standards, rights and principles against which different types of state crime, state-corporate crime and state agency crime are assessed, and attention needs to be given to ensuring a degree of commonality and comparability when considering the different types.

What are the drivers?

One of the key themes in relation to state crime, state-corporate crime and state agency crime is one of motives. In relation to the second, it is assumed that such crime may exist in a modern state in that the state is subordinate to the dominant economic culture, capitalism. Even in a democratic state, that dominance, as suggested above, continues but has to be managed by the state in a way that also balances the development of citizen expectations of the state.

In practice the relationship between capital and the state is not as clear-cut, all-encompassing nor as uni-directional as some authors have suggested. Governments have a number of interests to address within a democratic system and the evidence would suggest a favouring of specific industries for political reasons – and where state-corporate crime may occur – rather than the overall influence of capitalism on the decisions and policies of the state. Certainly in terms of international relations, favouring their domestic corporate interests is about geo-political influence, and not simply about the interests of business itself. Since the end of the Cold War the US view, for example, is about compliant competitors, non-compliant competitors and renegade adversaries while the UK's view may be as a result of both the preparedness of the military and arms exports in terms of the importance of the UK's 'national interests' (see Curtis 1998: 42, 55).

The dominant approach of most state crime authors is to assess breaches of the legislative framework, or the causing of harm or injury, as the consequence of organisational deviance. This approach has the advantage of being applicable to both public and private sector institutions; in the UK the convergence of procedures and practices between the two following new public management makes such an approach particularly useful. On the other hand, as argued above, many of the concerns revolve around reasons other than the pursuit of state interests. While this area, as Huberts *et al.* (2006) have argued, requires further study, it also requires another label – state agency crime – to distinguish it from state crime and state-corporate crime.

In relation to state crime, most commentators' adherence to the organisational deviance approach makes the question 'deviant from what' interesting. State crime would appear to occur where the state considers the interests of the state as a state are best served or protected, whether or not this conflicts with international and domestic law, democratic principles or, on occasion, corporate interests. The development of the UK state has long identified those interests and the need to attend to them remains, albeit with less visibility than that given to welfare-distributive issues that normally dominate the political agendas. Nevertheless, the culture and tradition that seek to preserve the UK state within the geo-political context, as well as the capacity of political leaders to devote time to such matters when they come to the fore, have been increasingly evident in the past half-century.

On the other hand, what appears to be the core driver for state crime – the national interest – is hard to pin down: 'it is usual, for example, to discuss foreign affairs in terms of interests; and to say of this or that policy that it serves British interests has a fine conclusive ring. But in fact the phrase is little more than shorthand for whatever course has seemed important to our political leaders at a particular time' (Cradock 1997: 210). This comprises two strands.

First is the awareness of state history – Thatcher had Suez and Blair had Bosnia as reminders of 'bad' policy. They were also aware of the need to manage the demands and expectations of the other actors and audiences which may inhibit or accelerate the decisions or actions the state may wish to pursue, how they may wish to pursue them (often away from the normal and formal decision-making processes) and what may be the consequences for the state's interests as opposed to either the public interest or the expected compliance with international and other standards. In particular, 'defence is the one area of external relations in which policy is almost invariably guided by considerations of *realpolitik*. What matters is not good intentions and the mutual benefits of economic intercourse, but the balance of military capabilities and the convergence or divergence of security interests' (Sanders 1990: 252–3).

Certainly in the case of the US-led invasion of Iraq, the wider geo-political influence was something that Bush sought and Blair wanted to support:

> It was not really about WMD ... WMD was only used as the excuse because that was the only issue on which the bureaucracies in Washington could agree and on which there was also some degree of allied agreement. The real objectives were much broader, even revolutionary. The first was simply to demonstrate American power and the willingness to use it. It had become an axiom of the neoconservatives that bad things were happening in the world because America was perceived as a paper tiger unwilling or unable to respond to attacks ... Demonstrating that this was not true and that America had to be respected, it was believed, would chill hostile activity all by itself. Such a demonstration needed a target, and Saddam was perfect. (Prestowitz 2004: 288).

Second is the question of how the state then pursues that interest within a modern state. The difficulty for many state crime authors is to appreciate such a driver for state crime. It would not be conceptually easy (and would also reflect a misunderstanding of the development of the modern UK state) to try and argue that the state is 'organisationally deviant' in terms of international relations because its actions or decisions deviate from international standards or democratic principles unless one assumes the state *qua* state is only infused by those principles and is solely committed to compliance with these standards. Further, those in government would not argue that their conduct was deviant. Indeed, they would argue that the sustainability of the democratic state is in part predicated on decisions and actions that ensure the sovereignty and integrity of the state as a state, particularly in geo-political and longer-term perspectives. They would suggest that, rather than deviance from democratic standards, the choices and necessity required of government come from contexts where such standards do not operate, and a degree of pragmatism is necessary to exploit opportunities or mitigate reversals in order to enhance the UK's status and the national interest.

On the other hand, this approach should be qualified, given the development of international law and normative standards, and thus the adherence of a liberal democratic state to those standards, to democratic principles and to rights, could provide the benchmark for such behaviour. In practice, however, it is a limited and partial framework. Indeed, the courts have made it plain that they cannot adjudicate on such conduct in terms of domestic law – although they can on occasion sit in judgement on public officials involved in implementing such a policy – because public policy in certain areas is solely the responsibility of the state.

What are the roles of those involved?

State crime can occur because the 'British political and administrative system' allows it to happen, in terms of the authority of the political leadership and the roles of the public officials to support the requirements of the leadership; the core executive follows the intentions of the government while the nature of the UK state both encourages and protects this from scrutiny and effective accountability.

Often the need for a decision or action occurs over a short time-scale. Instigating or initiating action can be done quickly; the capacity of the state machinery to then respond can also be achieved outside the normal procedures. This ability or capacity to do this points 'to an elite preoccupation with speedy policy-making giving inadequate scope for legislative scrutiny; to a strong form of political hyperactivism induced by the UK's particular system of party competition; to the over-confidence of a talented but inexpert administrative elite; and to the periodic failure of internal checks and balances inside the core executive' (Dunleavy 1995: 68).

Interestingly, an assessment of the Bush administration's progress to the invasion of Iraq followed the same pattern:

under normal conditions, new policy initiatives undergo months, if not years, of study and deliberation, in the government's national security apparatus. Cabinet departments and other agencies, often with very different institutional interests, get to have their say on how to shape new proposals, and interagency meetings are held to hash out differences. Congressional leaders often have input, as do lobbyists for major industries, and sometimes even ambassadors from foreign countries that might be affected. In the process, compromises are made and sharp edges are smoothed. If things go well, by the time a proposal gets to the president and his most senior advisors, it tends to represent something close to a consensus, and policy gets forced toward the center ... this creaking process does serve one purpose: it tends to weed out really stupid and dangerous ideas, unethical and even immoral ideas, ideas that could get people killed or could even start wars. (Risen 2007: 64–5)

Government and its leadership has both the tradition and the capacity to engage in state crime, and will often do so outside the normal decision-making processes that seek the centre ground. The core executive is as steeped in the need to protect and pursue state interests as it is in the democratic principles, but is also capable of supporting the actions and decisions of the state in such circumstances. While the formal legal system can and does adjudicate on occasion on some of those involved, much of the responsibilities of the other institutions are caught up in the need to support the government as well as providing a means of oversight. On balance, the machinery of the state, including Parliament, favours the state in key areas, and particularly those 'high politics' areas that are concerned with the national interest or the interests of the state.

Monitoring state crime

This leaves few institutions particularly focused on adjudicating on state crime undertaken in terms of the state's interests. The ability to act in ways that are unlawful or illegal results in part because acting outside the normal processes also means acting outside the normal checks and balances built into the parliamentary and administrative process; invariably responsibility and accountability are retrospective. The reasons behind state illegality are often claimed necessary for more important purposes. As a result of the US-inspired war on terror, the

Bush administration has eavesdropped without warrants; data-mined the phone and bank records of millions of Americans; launched domestic intelligence-gathering operations by the US military; surveilled antiwar demonstrators; and indefinitely incarcerated American citizens without trials. Overseas, there has been widespread use of harsh interrogation techniques, allegations of torture and massacres of civilians, the creation of secret CIA prisons and the clandestine practice of 'rendition' – the kidnapping of suspects who are transported to other countries for anonymous imprisonment. (Risen 2007: 225–6)

Governments clearly allow or carry out decisions or actions that are illegal or unlawful. In nearly all cases where the illegality or unlawfulness does not relate to the pursuit of state interests there are judicial and regulatory frameworks. In terms of state crime, however, how do governments or officials respond to being held accountable? Outside the formal legal framework, the main means in a democratic context is the ballot, the public inquiry or Parliament: 'when a public official is held responsible for an unpopular policy, he or she almost inevitably responds with an "account" in order to mitigate citizens' anger, to deflect subsequent blame and to bolster faltering evaluations', with the intention to achieve 'an acceptable justification or excuse' (McGraw 1990: 120).

McGraw goes on to suggest that the political excuses range from denial of partial or full responsibility through to mitigating circumstances, ignorance, or horizontal or vertical diffusion of responsibility. Political justifications include present or future benefits, and reframing of standards 'used to evaluate undesirability of decision consequences' (1990: 121). In so doing, both the inquiry system as currently developed through the 2005 Inquiry Act, existing *ad hoc* public inquiries, and the work of the parliamentary committee system are susceptible to such justifications (which in any case may relate to past decisions and events that, like the consequences, are frequently not reversible). As noted above, they are often tolerant of the necessity of government to circumvent or override legal frameworks and democratic standards to act in pursuit of the national interest.

In other words, the state will act in the interests of the state and seek to mitigate, justify or in other ways seek to fit their actions or decisions within democratic tenets, or, by evading, ignoring or overriding them, argue a national interest imperative. Here foreign affairs forms an example of what this means in practice:

> the moral and legal predilections that shape decision-making about war derive more from the decision-maker's own community than from a sense of universal obligation. Moreover, the primary responsibility owed by political leaders is to their own citizens. Leaders have a duty to protect the physical security, material wealth and common life of their citizens, and these obligations override other obligations to law and morality. (Bellamy 2006: 118)

If citizens cannot see how such obligations will benefit them, as the government and core executive perceives them, or cannot make the connection between the national interest and the benefit to them, or if the actions and decisions cannot be justified with reference to democratic standards, then governments often step outside normal decision-making and accountability processes while seeking to pre-empt and manage both justification and reaction, as well as manage the consequences and later scrutiny.

This applies not just to the UK but many other liberal democratic states, and state crime is as possible today, and tomorrow, as it was in the past. Indeed, the propensity and capacity of the UK state – and other states – to act accordingly is an integral part of the nature of the state and the pursuit of the national interest. Some would argue in the UK context that 'the art of politics lies in concealing behind a façade of rigid adherence to immutable principle those deviations or reversals which events and responsibility so often force upon governments' (Blake 1966: 764). Others are less charitable:

British interests are sacred, and therefore take precedence over every moral code. The unquestioning acceptance of these principles is fundamental and indispensable to anyone wishing to hold any permanent place, however menial, in that powerful section of society known as the ruling class ... Once total allegiance is given to these principles, then every pursuit, however unethical, degrading and untruthful, is permissible. (Feehan 1984: 29)

References

Aburish, S. K. (2000) *Saddam Hussein: The Politics of Revenge.* London: Bloomsbury.

Adams, J., Morgan, R. and Bambridge, A. (1988) *An Ambush.* London: Pan Books.

Adonis, A. (1990) *Parliament Today.* Manchester: Manchester University Press.

Alder, J. (2007) *Constitutional and Administrative Law.* Basingstoke: Palgrave Macmillan.

Al-Khalil (1991) *Republic of Fear.* London: Hutchinson Radius.

Almond, G. A. and Verba, S. (1965) *The Civic Culture.* Boston: Little, Brown.

AMAN Coalition for Integrity and Accountability (2007a) *Reconstruction Survey.* London: TIRI.

AMAN Coalition for Integrity and Accountability (2007b) *Reconstruction National Integrity System Survey.* London: TIRI.

Andrew, C. (1985) *Secret Service: The Making of the British Intelligence Community.* London: Heinemann.

Archer, The Rt. Hon. Lord, Jones, N. and Willets, J. (2009) *Independent Public Inquiry Report on NHS Supplied Contaminated Blood and Blood Products.* www.archercbbp.com.

Audit Commission (2007) *Public Interest Report. City of Westminster.* London: Audit Commission.

Bailey, F. G. (1969) *Stratagems and Spoils: A Social Anthropology of Politics.* Oxford: Blackwell.

Bailey, F. G. (ed.) (1971) *Gifts and Poison: The Politics of Reputation.* Oxford: Blackwell.

Bailey, M. (1979) *Oilgate.* Sevenoaks: Coronet Books.

Baker, N. (2007) *The Strange Death of David Kelly.* London: Methuen.

Banks, J. A. (1981) *Victorian Values.* London: Routledge and Kegan Paul.

Barak, G. (1990) 'Crime, criminology and human rights: towards an understanding of state criminality', in D. O. Friedrichs (1998) *State Crime, Vol. 1: Defining, Delineating and Explaining State Crime*. Aldershot: Ashgate.

Barak, G. (ed.) (1991) *Crimes by the Capitalist State: An Introduction to State Criminality*. Albany: State University of New York Press.

Barker, A. (1994) 'Enriching democracy: public inquiry and the policy process', in I. Budge and D. McKay (eds) *Developing Democracy*. London: Sage.

Barker, T. with Byrne, I. and Veall, A. (1999) *Ruling by Task Force*. London: Politicos in Association with Democratic Audit.

Barnett, H. (2004) *Constitutional and Administrative Law*, 5th edn. London: Cavendish Publishing.

Bar-On, M. (1990) 'The influence of political considerations on operational planning in the Sinai campaign', in S. I. Troen and M. Shemesh (eds) *The Suez-Sinai Crisis 1956*. London: Frank Cass.

Bealey, F. W. (1988) *Democracy in the Contemporary State*. Oxford: Clarendon Press.

Bellamy, A. J. (2006) *Just Wars*. Cambridge: Polity Press.

Bethlehem, D. (2004) *International Law and the Use of Force: The Law as it is and as it Should Be*. Minutes of Evidence. House of Commons Foreign Affairs Committee, 8 June.

Betts, M. (2011) 'Corruption', in A. Doig and S. Greenhalgh (2011) *Handbook of Fraud Investigation and Prevention*. London: Gower.

Bingham, Lord (1978) *The Report on the Supply of Petroleum and Petroleum Products to Rhodesia*. London: HMSO.

Birch, A. H. (1964) *Representative and Responsible Government*. London: George Allen and Unwin.

Birch, A. H. (1967) *The British System of Government*. London: George Allen and Unwin.

Bishop, P. and Mallie, E. (1987) *The Provisional IRA*. London: Corgi.

Blackburn, R. (ed.) (1993) *Rights of Citizenship*. London: Mansell.

Blake, R. (1966) *Disraeli*. London: Eyre and Spottiswoode.

Blakeway, D. and Lloyd-Roberts, S. (1985) *Fields of Thunder: Testing Britain's Bomb*. London: Unwin.

Blix, H. (2004) *Disarming Iraq: The Search for Weapons of Mass Destruction*. London: Bloomsbury.

Bloody Sunday Inquiry (2010) *Report of the Bloody Sunday Inquiry*. http:// report.bloody-sunday-inquiry.org (accessed 20 June 2010).

Bogdanor, V. (1996) 'The Scott Report', *Public Administration*, 74: 593–611.

Bolton, R. (1990) *Death on the Rock and Other Stories*. London: W. H. Allen/ Optomen.

Bradlee, B. (1988) *Guts and Glory*. London: Grafton Books.

Brazier, R. (1990) *Constitutional Practice*. Oxford: Oxford University Press.

Brazier, R. (1997) *Ministers of the Crown 1997*. Oxford: Oxford University Press.

Bristol Royal Infirmary Inquiry (2001) *Learning from Bristol: The Report of the Public Inquiry into Children's Heart Surgery at the Bristol Royal Infirmary 1984–1995*, Command Paper 5207. www.bristol-inquiry.org.uk

Brownlie, I. (1963) *International Law and the Use of Force by States*. Oxford: Clarendon Press.

Bruce Lockhart, R. (1967) *Ace of Spies*. London: Hodder.

Bulpitt, J. (1983) *Territory and Power in the United Kingdom*. Manchester: Manchester University Press.

Burch, M. and Holliday, I. (1996) *The British Cabinet System*. Hemel Hempstead: Prentice Hall/Harvester Wheatsheaf.

Burch, M. and Wood, R. (1990) *Public Policy in Britain*, 2nd edn. Oxford: Blackwell.

Burnham, J. and Pyper, R. (2008) *Britain's Modernised Civil Service*. Basingstoke: Palgrave Macmillan.

Burns, J. (1987) *The Land that Lost its Heroes*. London: Bloomsbury.

Butler, Lord (2004) *Review of Intelligence on Weapons of Mass Destruction: Report of a Committee of Privy Councillors*, HC898. London: The Stationery Office.

Byers, M. (2000) 'The law and politics of the Pinochet case', *Duke Journal of Comparative and International Law*, Vol. 10: 415–41.

Campbell, J. (1983) *F. E. Smith: First Earl of Birkenhead*. London: Jonathan Cape.

Cardosoo, R. C., Kirschbaum, R. and van der Kooy, E. (1983) *Falklands: The Secret Plot*. East Moseley: Preston Editions.

Care Quality Commission (2009) *Review of the Involvement and Action taken by Health Bodies in Relation to the Case of Baby P*. London: Care Quality Commission.

Carlton, D. (1988) *Britain and the Suez Crisis*. Oxford: Basil Blackwell.

Cartwright, T. (1975) *Royal Commission and Departmental Committees in Britain*. London: Hodder and Stoughton.

Castle, B. (1984) *The Castle Diaries, 1964–1970*. London: Weidenfeld and Nicolson.

Chambliss, W. J. (1989) 'State-organized crime: American Society of Criminology 1988 Presidential Address', *Criminology*, 27: 183–208.

Chambliss, W. J., Michalowski, R. and Kramer, R. C. (eds) (2010) *State Crime in a Global Age*. Cullompton: Willan Publishing.

Chandler, D. (2000) *Bosnia: Faking Democracy after Dayton*. London: Pluto Press.

Chapman, R. (1968) *Decision Making*. London: Routledge and Kegan Paul.

Chester, L., Fay, S. and Young, H. (1967) *The Zinoviev Letter*. London: Heinemann.

Chilcot, Sir J. (2010) *The Iraq Inquiry*. www.iraqinquiry.org.uk.

Chilston, Viscount (1960) 'The Tories and Parnell', *Parliamentary Affairs*, 4: 55–71.

Clarke, M. (1981) *Fallen Idols*. London: Junction Books.

Clarke, M. (1986) *Regulating the City: Competition, Scandal and Reform*. Milton Keynes: Open University Press.

Cockburn, A. and Cockburn, P. (2002) *Saddam Hussein: An American Obsession*. London: Verso.

Cockerell, M., Hennessy, P. and Walker, D. (1984) *Sources Close to the Prime Minister*. London: Macmillan.

Cockett, R. (1989) *Twilight of the Truth: Chamberlain, Appeasement and the Manipulation of the Press*. New York: St Martin's Press.

Cole, J. A. (1984) *Prince of Spies*. London: Faber and Faber.

Coleman, R., Sim, J., Tombs, S. and Whyte, D. (eds) (2009) *State, Power, Crime*. London: Sage.

Colls, R. (1986) 'English and the Political Culture', in R. Colls and P. Dodd (eds) *Englishness: Politics and Culture 1880–1920*. London: Croom Helm.

Commission on Public Private Partnerships (2001) *Building Better Partnerships: Final Report*. London: Institute for Public Policy Research.

Committee of Public Accounts (1994) *17th Report: Pergau Dam Project*, HC155. London: HMSO.

Cook, R. (2004) *The Point of Departure*. London: Pocket Books.

Cornish, P. (2004) *The Conflict in Iraq*. Basingstoke: Palgrave Macmillan.

Cory, P. (2004) *Cory Collusion Inquiry Report into Patrick Finucane's death*. London: The Stationery Office.

Coughlin, C. (2002) *Saddam: The Secret Life*. London: Pan.

Cowley, C. (1992) *Guns, Lies and Spies*. London: Hamish Hamilton.

CPRE/ELF (Council for the Protection of Rural England/Environmental Law Foundation) (2001) *Judicial Review and Planning Decisions*. London: CPRE/ELF.

Cradock, P. (1997) *In Pursuit of British Interests*. London: John Murray.

Croall, H. (1992) *White Collar Crime*. Buckingham: Open University Press.

Croall, H. (2001) *Understanding White Collar Crime*. Buckingham: Open University Press.

Crossman, R. (1979) *The Crossman Diaries: 1964–1970*. London: Hamish Hamilton and Jonathan Cape.

Curtis, M. (1998) *The Great Deception: Anglo-American Power and World Order*. London: Pluto Press.

Darwish, A. and Alexander, G. (1991) *Unholy Babylon: The Secret History of Saddam's War*. London: Victor Gollancz.

Davies, H. (2001) 'N2 a starting point, not a destination', Foreign Banks and Securities Houses Association Conference, London.

Defence Committee (1988) *Second Report*, HC392. London: HMSO.

de Haven-Smith, L. (2006) 'When political crimes are inside jobs: detecting state crimes against democracy', *Administrative Theory & Praxis*, 28(3): 330–55.

Department of the Taoiseach (1997) *Bloody Sunday Report and the Report of the Widgery Tribunal*. www.taoiseach.gov.ie/eng/Department_of_

the_Taoiseach/Policy_Sections/Northern_Ireland/Northern_Ireland_
Publications/Bloody_Sunday_Report_and_the_Report_of_the_Widgery_
Tribunal.shortcut.html (accessed 10 February 2010).

Dillon, G. M. (1989) *The Falklands, Politics and the War*. London: Macmillan.

Dillon, M. (1990) *The Dirty War*. London: Hutchinson.

Dimbleby, J. (1997) *The Last Governor*. London: Little, Brown and Company.

Ditton, J. (1977) *Part-time Crime: An Ethnography of Fiddling and Pilferage*. Basingstoke: Macmillan.

Doig, A. (1979) 'The machinery of government and the growth of governmental bodies', *Public Administration*, 57, Autumn: 309–31.

Doig, A. (1986) 'A question of balance: business appointments of former senior civil servants', *Parliamentary Affairs*, 39(1): 63–78.

Doig, A. (2005) '45 minutes of infamy? Hutton, Blair and the 2002 invasion of Iraq', *Parliamentary Affairs*, 58(1): 109–23.

Doig, A. (2006) *Fraud*. Cullompton: Willan Publishing.

Doig, A. and Theobald, R. (1999) *Corruption and Development*. London: Cass.

Domagala, A. (2004) *Humanitarian Intervention: The Utopia of Just War? The NATO Intervention in Kosovo and the Restraints of Humanitarian Intervention*, SEI Working Paper 76. Brighton: Sussex European Institute.

Dovi, S. (2005) 'Guilt and the problem of dirty hands', *Constellations*, 12(1): 128–46.

Dowding, K. (1995) *The Civil Service*. London: Routledge.

Druce, C. (1989) *Chicken and Egg: Who Pays the Price?* London: Green Print.

Duff, R. A. and Green, S. P. (eds) (2005) *Defining Crimes*. Oxford: Oxford University Press.

Dumbrell, J. (2005) 'Bush's war', in A. Danchev and J. Macmillan (eds) *The Iraq War and Democratic Politics*. London: Routledge.

Dunleavy, P. (1995) 'Policy disasters: explaining the UK's record', *Public Policy and Administration*, 10(2): 52–70.

Dutton, D. (1997) *Anthony Eden: A Life and Reputation*. London: Arnold.

Dynes, M and Walker, D. (1995) *The Times Guide to The New British State*. London: Times Books.

Dyson, H. F. (1980) *The State Tradition in Western Europe*. Oxford: Martin Robertson.

Egremont, M. (1980) *Balfour*. London: Collins.

Ellis, N. (1988) *Parliamentary Lobbying*. London: Heinemann Professional Publishing.

Ellis, W. (1995) *The Oxbridge Conspiracy*. London: Penguin.

Ermann, M. D. and Lundman, R. J. (2001) *Corporate and Governmental Deviance: Problems of Organizational Behavior in Contemporary Society*. Oxford: Oxford University Press.

Erskine May, T. (1989) *Parliamentary Practice*, 21st edn. London: Butterworths.

Ewing, K. D. and Gearty, C. A. (1990) *Freedom under Thatcher*. Oxford: Oxford University Press.

Farnham, D. and Horton, S. (1996) 'Public service managerialism: a review and evaluation', in D. Farnham and S. Horton (eds) (1996) *Managing the New Public Services*. Basingstoke: Macmillan.

Feehan, J. M. (1984) *Operation Brogue*. Dublin: Mercier Press.

Feigenbaum, H. B., Henig, J. and Hamnett, C. (1998) *Shrinking the State: The Political Underpinnings of Privatisation*. Cambridge: Cambridge University Press.

Fletcher, G. P. (1998) *Basic Concepts of Criminal Law*. Oxford: Oxford University Press.

Flynn, N. (1993) *Public Sector Management*, 2nd edn. Hemel Hempstead: Harvester/Wheatsheaf.

Flynn, N. (2002) *Public Sector Management*, 4th edn. Harlow: Financial Times/ Prentice-Hall; Pearson Education)

Foley, C. (2010) *The Thin Blue Line*. London: Verso.

Foley, M. (1993) *The Rise of the British Presidency*. Manchester: Manchester University Press.

Foot, P. (1990) *Who Framed Colin Wallace?* London: Pan.

Foreign Affairs Committee (1985) *Events Surrounding the Weekend of 1–2 May 1982*. HCPII. London: HMSO.

Foreign Affairs Committee (1994) *Third Report*, HC271. London: HMSO.

Foreign Affairs Committee (1999) *Second Report: Sierra Leone*. HC116-1. London: TSO.

Foreign Affairs Committee (2003) *Ninth Report of Session 2002–3. The Decision to go to War in Iraq*, HC813-I. London: The Stationery Office.

Francis R. (2010) *Independent Inquiry into Care Provided by Mid Staffordshire NHS Foundation Trust January 2005–March 2009*, HC375. London: The Stationery Office.

Freedman, L. and Gamba-Stonehouse, V. (1990) *Signals of War*. London: Faber & Faber.

Friedman, A. (1993) *Spider's Web*. London: Faber & Faber.

Friedrichs, D. O. (1998) 'Introduction', in D. O. Friedrichs (ed.) *State Crime, Vol. 1: Defining, Delineating and Explaining State Crime*. Aldershot: Ashgate.

Friedrichs, D. (2000) 'State crime or governmental crime: making sense of the conceptual confusion', in J. I. Ross (ed.) *Controlling State Crime*. New Brunswick: Transaction Publishers.

Friedrichs, D. O. and Schwartz, M. D. (2007) 'Editors' introduction: on social harm and a twenty-first century criminology', *Crime, Law and Social Change*, 48 (1–2): 1–7.

Gamble, A. (1998) *The Free Economy and the Strong State*. London: Palgrave Macmillan.

Gash, N. (1979) *Aristocracy and People: Britain 1815–1865*. London: Edward Arnold.

Gavshon, A. and Rice, D. (1984) *The Sinking of the Belgrano*. Secker and Warburg.

Giddings, P. (1995) *Parliamentary Accountability*. London: Palgrave Macmillan.

Gilby, N. (2001) *Labour, Arms and Indonesia: Has Anything Changed?* London: CAAT.

Gordon, M. and Trainor, B. (2007) *Cobra II*. London: Atlantic Books.

Grant, W. with Sargent, J. (1987) *Business and Politics in Britain*. London: Macmillan.

Green, P. J. and Ward, T. (2000) 'State crime, human rights, and the limits of criminology', *Social Justice*, 27(1): 105–15.

Green, P. and Ward, T. (2004) *State Crime*. London: Pluto.

Green, P. and Ward, T. (2005) 'Introduction', *British Journal of Criminology*, 45(4): 431–33.

Greenaway, J., Smith, S. and Street, S. (1992) *Deciding Factors in British Politics*. London: Routledge.

Guttsman, W. L. (1963) *The British Political Elite*. London: MacGibbon and Kee.

Hamer, M. (1987) *Wheels Within Wheels: A Study of the Road Lobby*. London: Routledge and Kegan Paul.

Harden, I. J. and Lewis, N. (1986) *The Noble Lie: The Rule of Law and the British Constitution*. London: Hutchinson.

Harrow, J. and Gillett, R. (1994) 'The proper conduct of public business', *Public Money and Management*, 14(2): 4–6.

Healthcare Commission (2009) *Investigation into Mid Staffordshire NHS Foundation Trust*. London: Healthcare Commission.

Heffernan, R. and Marqusee, M. (1992) *Defeat from the Jaws of Victory: Inside Kinnock's Labour Party*. London: Verso.

Helco, H. and Wildavsky, A. (1986) *The Private Government of Public Money*. London: Macmillan.

Held, D. (1989) *Political Theory and the Modern State*. Cambridge: Polity Press.

Held, D. (1995) *Democracy and the Global Order*. Cambridge: Polity Press.

Henderson, P. (1994) *The Unlikely Spy*. London: Bloomsbury.

Hennessy, P. (1986) *The Great and the Good*. London: Policy Studies Institute.

Herring, J. (2004) *Criminal Law*. Oxford: Oxford University Press.

Hersh, S. M. (2005) *Chain of Command*. London: Penguin.

Hill, M. (1997) *The Policy Process in the Modern State*. Prentice Hall/Harvester Wheatsheaf.

Hillyard, P. and Tombs, S. (2007) 'From "crime" to social harm?', *Crime Law and Social Change*, 48 (1–2): 9–25.

Hobsbawm, E. and Ranger, T. (1983) *The Invention of Tradition*. Cambridge: Cambridge University Press.

Hogwood, B. (1987) *From Crisis to Complacency: Shaping Public Policy in Britain*. Oxford: Oxford University Press.

Holland, J. (1987) *The American Connection*. Dublin: Poolbeg.

Hollis, C. (1959) 'Parliament and the Establishment', in H. Thomas (ed.) *The Establishment*. NEL.

Holroyd, F. with Burbridge, N. (1989) *War without Honour*. Hull: Medium.

Hood, C. (1991) 'A public management for all seasons', *Public Administration*, 69 (1): 3–19.

Hood, C., James, O., Jones, G., Scott, C. and Travers, T. (1998) 'Regulation inside government: where new public management meets the audit explosion', *Public Money and Management*, 18(2): 61–8.

Hooper, D. (1987) *Official Secrets*. London: Secker and Warburg.

Horne, A. (1989) *Macmillan 1957–1986: Volume II*. Basingstoke: Macmillan.

Horsman, M. and Marshall, A. (1995) *After the Nation State*. London: Harper Collins.

Hosken, A. (2006) *Nothing Like a Dame: The Scandals of Shirley Porter*. London: Granta Books.

House of Commons Health Committee (2003) *Sixth Report 2002–03: The Victoria Climbié Inquiry Report*, HC570. London: The Stationery Office.

House of Commons Health Committee (2010) *The Use of Overseas Doctors in Providing Out-of-hours Services: Fifth Report of Session 2009–10*, HC441. London: TSO.

House of Commons Public Administration Select Committee (2003) *Government By Appointment: Opening Up The Patronage*. State Fourth Report of Session 2002–03. HC165. London: The Stationery Office.

Huberts, L., van Montfort, A. and Doig, A. (2006) *Is Government Setting a Good Example? Rule Breaking by Government in the Netherlands and the United Kingdom*. The Hague: Bju Publishers.

Hughes, O. E. (1994) *Public Management and Administration*. New York: St Martin's Press.

Human Rights Council (2009) *Human Rights in Palestine and Other Occupied Arab Territories: Report of the United Nations Fact Finding Mission on the Gaza Conflict* (Goldstone Report). Geneva: Office of the United Nations High Commissioner for Human Rights.

Hurwitz, L. (2000) 'International State-sponsored Organisations to Control State Crime', in J. I. Ross (ed.) *Controlling State Crime*. New Brunswick: Transaction Publishers.

Inglis, B. (1974) *Roger Casement*. London: Coronet Books.

Inglis, B. (1964) *Private Conscience: Public Morality*. London: Four Square Books.

International Development Committee (2000–01) *Fourth Report: Corruption*. Appendix 1.

Iraq: UN Documents of early March 2003 (2003) Cm 5785. London: The Stationery Office.

Isikoff, M. and Corn, D. (2007) *Hubris*. New York: Three Rivers Press.

James, R. R. (1986) *Anthony Eden*. London: Weidenfeld and Nicolson.

James, S. (1996) 'The political and administrative consequences of judicial review', *Public Administration*, 74: 627.

Jamieson, R. and McEvoy, K. (2005) 'State crime by proxy and juridical othering', *British Journal of Criminology*, 45 (April): 504–27.

Jogerst, M. (1993) *Reform of the House of Commons: The Select Committee System*. London: University of Kentucky Press.

Johnston, M. and Wood, D. (1985) 'Right and wrong in public and private life', in R. Jowell and S. Witherspoon (eds) *British Social Attitudes: The 1985 Report*. London: Gower/Social and Community Planning Research.

Jones, B. (2010) *Failing Intelligence*. London: Dialogue.

Jones, N. (1996) *Soundbites and Spin Doctors*. London: Indigo.

Jordan, A. G. (ed.) (1991) *The Commercial Lobbyists*. Aberdeen: Aberdeen University Press.

Jordan, A. G. and Richardson, J. J. (1979) 'Pantoflague: a civil service perk', *New Society*, 22 February.

Jordan, A. G. and Richardson, J. J. (1987) *British Politics and the Policy Process*. London: Allen and Unwin.

Jordan, B. (1985) *The State: Authority and Autonomy*. Oxford: Basil Blackwell.

Jorgensen, N. H. B. (2000) *The Responsibility of States for International Crimes*. Oxford: Oxford University Press.

Joyce, J. and Murtagh, P. (1986) *The Boss*. Dublin: Poolbeg Press.

Kampfner, J. (2004) *Blair's Wars*. London: Free Press.

Kauzlarich, D., Matthews, R. A. and Miller, W. J. (2001) 'Towards a victimology of state crime', *Critical Criminology*, 10 (3): 173–94.

Keeton, G. W. (1960) *Trial by Tribunal*. London: Museum Press.

Kelly, J. (1971) *Orders for the Captain*. Dublin: Kelly.

Kelly, S. and Gorst, A. (2000) *Whitehall and the Suez Crisis*. London: Frank Cass.

Kennedy, P. (1981) *The Realities Behind Diplomacy: Background Influences on British External Policy 1865–1980*. London: Fontana.

Kenyon, J. (1972) *The Popish Plot*. Harmondsworth: Penguin.

Kettell, S. (2006) *Dirty Politics? New Labour, British Democracy and the Invasion of Iraq*. London: Zed Books.

Kettle, M. (1983) *Sidney Reilly*. London: Corgi.

Kidwell, R. E. and Martin, C. L. (eds) (2005) *Managing Organisational Deviance*. London: Sage.

King, M. (1986) *Death of the Rainbow Warrior*. Harmondsworth: Penguin.

Klare, M. (2004) *Blood and Oil*. London: Hamish Hamilton.

Koss, S. (1984) *The Rise and Fall of the Political Press in Britain*, Vol. 2. London: Hamish Hamilton.

Kramer, R. C. and Michalowksi, R. J. (2005) 'War, aggression and state crime', *British Journal of Criminology*, 45 (4): 446–69.

Kramer, R. C. and Michalowski, R.J. (2006) 'The original formulation', in R. J. Michalowksi and R. C. Kramer (eds) *State-Corporate Crime*. New Brunswick: Rutgers University Press.

Kramer, R. C., Michalowski, R. J. and Kauzlarich, D. (2002) 'The origins and development of the concept and theory of state-corporate crime', *Crime and Delinquency*, 48(2): 214–43.

Lamb, R. (1987) *The Failure of the Eden Government*. London: Sidgwick and Jackson.

Laming, Lord (2003) *The Victoria Climbié Inquiry: Report of an Inquiry by Lord Laming*. London: HMSO.

Leapman, M. (1987) *Kinnock*. London: Unwin Hyman.

Leapman, M. (1992) *Treacherous Estate*. London: Hodder and Stoughton.

Legg, T. and Ibbs, R. (1998) *Report of the Sierra Leone Arms Investigation*. Cm 1016. London: TSO.

Leggatt, A. (2001) *Report of the Review of Tribunals: Tribunals for Users – One System, One Service*. London: Ministry of Justice.

Leigh, D. (1980) *The Frontiers of Secrecy: Closed Government in Britain*. London: Junction Books.

Leigh, D. (1993) *Betrayed*. London: Bloomsbury.

Lenman, B. P. (1992) *The Eclipse of Parliament*. London: Edward Arnold.

Lever, L. (1992) *The Barlow Clowes Affair*. London: Macmillan.

Levi, M. (1993) *The Investigation, Prosecution, and Trial of Serious Fraud*, Research Study 14. London: HMSO.

Levi, M. (1987) *Regulating Fraud*. London: Tavistock Publications.

Lloyd, S. (1978) *Suez 1956*. London: Book Club Associates.

Lord Chancellor and Secretary of State for Justice (2009) *Responding to Human Rights Judgements: Government Response to the Joint Committee on Human Rights' Thirty-first Report of Session 2007–08*, Cm 7524. London: Crown Copyright.

Lowther, W. (1992) *Iraq and the Supergun*. London: Pan.

Lupton, T. and Wilson, C. S. (1969) 'The social background and connections of "top decision makers"', in R. Rose (ed.) *Policy-Making in Britain*. London: Macmillan.

Macintosh, J. P. (1977) *The British Cabinet*, 3rd edn. London: Stevens and Sons.

Madeley, J. (1982) *Diego Garcia: Minority Rights Report 54*. London: Minority Rights Group.

Maer, L. (2009) *Misconduct in Public Office: Note*. London: House of Commons Library. SN/PC/04909.

Magill Magazine (1980) Dublin, June.

Mancuso, M. (1995) *The Ethical World of British MPs*. Canada: McGill-Queen's University Press.

Mangan, A. and Walvin, J. (eds) (1987) *Manliness and Morality*. Manchester: Manchester University Press.

Margach, J. (1979) *The Abuse of Power*. London: Star Books.

Marlow, J. (1970) *The Peterloo Massacre*. London: Rapp and Whiting.

Marr, A. (1996) *Ruling Britannia: The Failure and Future of British Democracy*. London: Penguin.

Mars, G. (1983) *Cheats at Work: An Anthropology of Workplace Crime*. London: Unwin.

Massey, A. (2005) *The State of Britain: A Guide to the UK Public Sector*. CIPFA: Public Management and Policy Association report.

Matthews, R. A. and Kauzlarich, D. (2007) 'State crimes and state harms: a tale of two definitional frameworks', *Crime Law and Social Change*, 48 (1–2): 43–55.

Maybray-King, H. (1967) *State Crimes*. London: Dent.

McCulloch, J. and Pickering, S. (2005) 'Suppressing the financing of terrorism: proliferating state crime, eroding censure and extending neo-colonialism', *British Journal of Criminology*, 45 (April): 470–86.

McGraw, K. M. (1990) 'Avoiding blame: an experimental investigation of political excuses and justifications', *British Journal of Political Science*, 20(1): 119–32.

McKenzie, R. and Silver, A. (1968) *Angels in Marble: Working Class Conservatives in Urban England*. London: Heinemann Educational.

Michalowski, R. (2010) 'In search of "state and crime" in state crime studies', in W. J. Chambliss, R. Michalowski and R. C. Kramer (eds) *State Crime in a Global Age*. Cullompton: Willan Publishing.

Michalowksi, R. J. and Kramer, R. C. (eds) (2006) *State-Corporate Crime*. New Brunswick: Rutgers University Press.

Miers, D. R. and Page, A. C. (1990) *Legislation*. London: Sweet and Maxwell.

Miller, D. (1994) *Don't Mention the War*. London: Pluto.

Miller, D. (1996) *Export or Die: Britain's Defence Trade with Iran and Iraq*. London: Cassell.

Miller, D. (1994) and Curtis, L. (1984) *Ireland and the Propaganda War*. London: Pluto.

Miller, T. C. (2007) *Blood Money*. New York: Bay Back Books.

Moloney, E. (2002) *A Secret History of the IRA*. Harmondsworth: Penguin.

Morris, A. J. A. (1984) *The Scaremongers*. London: Routledge and Kegan Paul.

Nagel, T. (1978) 'Ruthlessness in public life', in S. Hampshire (ed.) *Public and Private Morality*. Cambridge: Cambridge University Press.

National Audit Office (1993) *Pergau Hydro-Electric Project*. London: HMSO.

Nelken, D. (2007) 'White collar and corporate crime', in M. Maguire, R. Morgan and R. Reiner (eds) *The Oxford Handbook of Criminology*. Oxford: Oxford University Press.

Neubacher, F. (2006) 'How can it happen that horrendous state crimes are perpetrated?', *Journal of International Criminal Justice*, 4(4): 787–99.

Oborne, P. (2005) *The Rise of Political Lying*. London: Free Press.

O'Brien, J. (2000) *The Arms Trial*. Dublin: Gill and Macmillan.

O'Brien, J. (2005) *Killing Finucane*. Dublin: Gill and Macmillan.

O'Brion, L. (1971) *The Prime Informer*. London: Sidgwick and Jackson.

Office of Public Sector Information (2006) *Statutory Instrument Practice: A manual for those concerned with the preparation of statutory instruments and the parliamentary procedures relating to them*, 4th edn. London: HMSO.

Oliver, D. (1996) 'Comment: The Scott Report', *Public Law* (Autumn).

O'Malley, E. (2007) 'Setting choices, controlling outcomes: the operation of prime ministerial influence and the UK's decision to invade Iraq', *British Journal of Politics and International Relations*, 9 (1): 1–19.

O'Shaughnessy, H. (1984) *Grenada: Revolution, Invasion and Aftermath*. London: Sphere Books.

Parrish, J. M. (2007) *Paradoxes of Political Ethics: From Dirty Hands to the Invisible Hand*. Cambridge: Cambridge University Press.

Paxman, J. (1991) *Friends in High Places*. Harmondsworth: Penguin.

Pemberton, S. (2007) 'Social harm future(s): exploring the potential of the social harm approach', *Crime, Law and Social Change*, 48 (1–2): 27–41.

Phythian, M. (1996) '"Batting for Britain": British arms sales in the Thatcher years', *Crime, Law and Social Change*, 26 (3): 271–99.

Phythian, M. (2000) *The Politics of British Arms Sales since 1964*. Manchester: Manchester University Press.

Phythian, M. and Little, W. (1993) 'Administering Britain's arms trade', *Public Administration*, 71 (3): 259–78.

Police Ombudsman (2010) *Public Statement by the Police Ombudsman under section 62 of the Police (Northern Ireland) Act 1998 relating to the RUC Investigation of the Alleged Involvement of the late Father James Chesney in the Bombing of Claudy on 31 July 1972*. Belfast: Police Ombudsman for Northern Ireland.

Ponting, C. (1985) *The Right to Know*. London: Sphere.

Ponting, C. (1989) *Breach of Promise*. London: Hamish Hamilton.

Porter, B. (1989) *Plots and Paranoia*. London: Unwin Hyman.

Prestowitz, C. (2004) *Rogue Nation*. New York: Basic Books.

Public Administration Committee (2005) *First Report: Government by Inquiry*. HC51-I. London: The Stationery Office.

Pugh, M. (2002) *The Making of Modern British Politics 1867–1945*, 3rd edn. Oxford: Blackwell.

Punch, M. (1996) *Dirty Business: Exploring Corporate Misconduct*. London: Sage.

Punch, M. (2000) 'Suite violence: why managers murder and corporations kill', *Crime, Law and Social Change*, 33 (3): 243–80.

Ranelagh, J. (1991) *Thatcher's People*. London: Harper Collins.

Rawnsley, A. (2001) *Servants of the People: The Inside Story of New Labour*. London: Penguin.

Raz, J. (1996) *Ethics in the Public Domain*. Oxford: Clarendon Press.

RCGP (2003) *Report of the Inquiry into the Death of Victoria Climbié*. London: RCGP Summary Paper 2003/02.

Read, D. (1987) *Peel and the Victorians*. Oxford: Blackwell.

Report of the Congressional Committees Investigating the Iran/Contra Affair (1987) 100th Congress, 1st Session. Washington, DC: US Congress.

Rhodes, R. A. W. (1988) *Beyond Westminster and Whitehall*. London: Unwin Hyman.

Rhodes, R. A. W. (1995) 'From prime ministerial power to core executive', in R. A. W. Rhodes and P. Dunleavy (eds) *Prime Minister, Cabinet and Core Executive*. Basingstoke: Macmillan.

Rhodes, R. A. W. (1997) *Understanding Governance*. Buckingham: Open University Press.

Richardson, J. J. and Jordan, A. G. (1979) *Governing Under Pressure*. Oxford: Martin Robertson.

Ridley, F. F. (ed.) (1984) *Policies and Politics in Western Europe*. Beckenham: Croom Helm.

Risen, J. (2007) *State of War*. London: Pocket Books.

Robertson, K. G. (1982) *Public Secrets*. London: Macmillan.

Robinson, P. H. (1997) *Structure and Function in Criminal Law*. Oxford: Clarendon Press.

Rolston, B. (2005) 'An effective mask for terror': democracy, death squads and Northern Ireland', *Crime, Law and Social Change*, 44 (2): 181–203.

Rolston, B. and Scraton, P. (2005) 'In the full glare of English politics: Ireland, inquiries and the British state', *British Journal of Criminology*, 45 (4): 547–64.

Rosen, P. (2000) *The Canadian Security Intelligence Service. Parliamentary Information and Research Service*. Ottawa: Library of Parliament.

Rosenthal, M. (1986) *The Character Factory*. London: Collins.

Ross, J. I. (2000a) 'Controlling state crime: toward an integrated structural model', in J. I. Ross (ed.) *Controlling State Crime*. New Brunswick: Transaction Publishers.

Ross, J. I. (2000b) *Varieties of State Crime and its Control*. Monsey, NY: Criminal Justice Press.

Ross, J. I. (2003) *The Dynamics of Political Crime*. London: Sage.

Rowlingson, K., Whyley, C., Newburn, T. and Berthoud, R. (1997) *Social Security Fraud: The Role of Penalties*. London: The Stationery Office.

Rush, M. (ed.) (1990) *Parliament and Pressure Politics*. Oxford: Oxford University Press.

Sachs, P. M. (1976) *An Irish Machine*. Yale: Yale University Press.

Sampson, A. (1962) *Anatomy of Britain*. London: Hodder and Stoughton.

Sanders, D. (1990) *Losing an Empire, Finding a Role*. Basingstoke: Palgrave Macmillan.

Sands, P. (2005) *Lawless World*. London: Allen Lane.

Sands, P. (2009) *Torture Team: Uncovering War Crimes in the Land of the Free*. London: Penguin.

Scott, J. (1991) *Who Rules Britain?* Cambridge: Polity Press.

Scott, R. (1996) *Report of the Inquiry into the Export of Defence Equipment and Dual-Use Equipment Goods to Iraq and Related Prosecutions*. London: HMSO.

Scott Lucas, W. (1991) *Divided We Stand: Britain, the US and the Suez Crisis*. London: Hodder and Stoughton.

Scott Lucas, W. (2000) 'The missing link? Patrick Dean, chairman of the Joint Intelligence Committee', in S. Kelly and A. Gorst (eds) *Whitehall and the Suez Crisis*. London: Frank Cass.

Sedgemore, B. (1980) *Secret Constitution*. London: Hodder and Stoughton.

Self, P. and Storing, H. J. (1971) *The State and the Farmer*. London: George Allen and Unwin.

Sharkansky, I. (2000) 'A state action may be nasty but is not likely to be a crime', in J. I. Ross (ed.) *Controlling State Crime*. New Brunswick: Transaction Publishers.

Short, C. (2004) *An Honourable Deception? New Labour, Iraq and the Misuse of Power*. London: Free Press.

Shugarman, D. P. (2000) 'Introduction: the controversy over dirty hands', in P. Rynard and D. P. Shugarman (eds) *Cruelty and Deception*. Peterborough, ON: Broadview Press/Pluto Press.

Simms, B. (2002) *Unfinest Hour: Britain and the Destruction of Bosnia*. London: Penguin.

Skelcher, C. (1998) *The Appointed State*. Buckingham: Open University Press.

Slapper, G. and Tombs, S. (1999) *Corporate Crime*. London: Addison Wesley Longman.

Smith, G. (1990) *Reagan and Thatcher*. London: Bodley Head.

Smith, J. (1985) *Clouds of Deceit: The Deadly Legacy of Britain's Bomb Tests*. London: Faber & Faber.

Smith, L. B. (1986) *Treason in Tudor England*. London: Jonathan Cape.

Snook, H. (2007) *Crossing the Threshold*. London: Centre for Policy Studies.

Stalker, J. (1988) *Stalker*. London: Penguin.

Stanhope, J. (1962) *The Cato Street Conspiracy*. London: Jonathan Cape.

Stevens, J. (2003) *Stevens Inquiry: Overview and Recommendations*.

Stott, T. (1995) '"Snouts in the trough": the politics of quangos', in F. F. Ridley and D. Wilson (eds) *The Quango Debate*. Oxford: Oxford University Press.

Strange, S. (1996) *The Retreat of the State*. Cambridge: Cambridge University Press.

Sullivan, H. and Skelcher, C. (2002) *Working Across Boundaries: Collaboration in Public Services*. Basingstoke: Palgrave Macmillan.

Sunday Times Insight (1986) *Rainbow Warrior*. London: Arrow Books.

Sutherland, E. H. (1983) *White Collar Crime: The Uncut Version*. New Haven, CT: Yale University Press.

Sutherland, G. (ed.) (1972) *Studies in the Growth of Nineteenth Century Government*. London: Routledge and Kegan Paul.

Sweeney, J. (1993) *Trading With the Enemy*. London: Pan.

Tal, D. (2001) *The 1956 War: Collusion and Rivalry in the Middle East.* Tel Aviv: Cummings Centre for Russian and East European Studies.

Tant, A. P. (1993) *British Government: The Triumph of Elitism.* Aldershot: Dartmouth.

Taylor, A. J. P. (1976) *Essays in English History.* London: Hamish Hamilton.

Taylor, P. (1980) *Beating the Terrorists?* Harmondsworth: Penguin.

Taylor, P. (1987) *Stalker.* London: Faber & Faber.

Theakston, K. and Fry, G. K. (1989) 'Britain's administrative elite: permanent secretaries 1900–1986', *Public Administration*, 67 (2): 129–47.

Thompson, D. (1984) *The Chartists: Popular Politics in the Industrial Revolution.* Aldershot: Wildwood House.

Thornberry, P. (2005) 'The legal case for invading Iraq', in A. Danchev and J. Macmillan (eds) *The Iraq War and Democratic Politics.* London: Routledge.

Thorpe, D. R. (1989) *Selwyn Lloyd.* London: Jonathan Cape.

Tiri and TIDS (2006) *Integrity in Reconstruction.* London: Tiri.

Tower Commission (1987) *Tower Commission Report.* London: Bantam.

Treasury and Civil Service Committee (1984) *Eighth Report*, HC302. London: HMSO.

Treasury Solicitors/Government Legal Service (2006) *The Judge Over Your Shoulder.* London: Treasury Solicitors/Government Legal Service.

Urban, G. (1996) *Diplomacy and Disillusion at the Court of Margaret Thatcher.* London: I.B. Tauris.

Urry, J. and Wakeford, J. (1973) *Power in Britain: Sociological Readings.* London: Heinemann Educational.

US Senate Select Committee on Intelligence (2004) *Report on the US Intelligence Community's Prewar Intelligence Assessments on Iraq.* Washington, DC: US Senate.

US Senate Select Committee on Intelligence (2008) *Report on Whether Public Statements Regarding Iraq by US Government Officials were Substantiated by Intelligence Information.* Washington, DC: US Senate.

Verdirame, G. (2004) 'International law and the use of force against Iraq', in P. Cornish (ed.) *The Conflict in Iraq.* London: Palgrave Macmillan.

Walmsley, R. (1969) *Peterloo: The Case Re-opened.* Manchester: Manchester University Press.

Walsh, D. (1986) *The Party.* Dublin: Gill and Macmillan.

Walzer, M. (1973) 'Political action: the problem of dirty hands', *Philosophy and Public Affairs*, 2 (2): 160–80.

Weir, S. and Hall, W. (eds) (1994) *Ego Trip: Extra-governmental Organisations in the UK and Their Accountability.* London: Charter 88 Trust.

Whyte, D. (2003) 'Lethal regulations: state-corporate crime and the United Kingdom government's new mercenaries', *Journal of Law and Society*, 30(4): 575–600.

Wilkinson, S. (2009) 'Fifty years of revolution: UK foreign policy and Cuba's place in the world', paper for the Latin American Studies Association.

Williams, B. (1978) 'Politics and moral character', in S. Hampshire (ed.) *Public and Private Morality*. Cambridge: Cambridge University Press.

Wilson, H. (1971) *The Labour Government 1964–1970: A Personal Record*. London: Weidenfeld and Nicolson.

Winchester, S. (1985) *Outposts*. London: Spectre.

Windlesham, Lord and Rampton, R. (1989) *The Windlesham/Rampton Report on Death on the Rock*. London: Faber & Faber.

Winetrobe, B. (1997) 'Inquiries after Scott: the return of the tribunal inquiry', *Public Law*, Spring: 18–31.

Wood, E. M. (2006) 'Democracy as ideology of empire', in C. Mooers (ed.) *The New Imperialists*. Oxford: One World Publications.

Woodhouse, D. (1995) 'Matrix Churchill and judicial inquiries', *Parliamentary Affairs*, 48: 24–39.

Wraith, R. and Lamb, G. (1971) *Public Inquiries as an Instrument of Government*. London: Allen and Unwin.

Wright, M. (1969) *Treasury Control of the Civil Service 1854–1874*. Oxford: Clarendon Press.

Wroe, A. (1992) *Lives, Lies, and the Iran-Contra Affair*. London: I.B. Tauris

Young, J. W. (2000) 'Conclusion', in S. Kelly and A. Gorst (eds) *Whitehall and the Suez Crisis*. London: Frank Cass.

Youngs, T. and Oakes, M. (1999) *Iraq: 'Desert Fox' and Policy Developments*, House of Commons Research Paper 99/13. London: International Affairs and Defence Section.

Yarnold, B. M. (2000) 'A new role for the International Court of Justice', in J. I. Ross (ed.) *Controlling State Crime*. New Brunswick: Transaction Publishers.

Zunes, S. (2003) *Foreign Policy in Focus*. Global Policy Forum. www.globalpolicy.org.

Index